THE HUSSAR GENERAL

General Gebhard Leberecht von Blücher
The Hussar General

THE HUSSAR GENERAL

The Life of Blücher, Man of Waterloo

Roger Parkinson

WORDSWORTH EDITIONS

To Dr Friedrich Bechtle
for his friendship and kindness

First published in Great Britain in 1975
by Purnell Book Services Ltd

Copyright © Roger Parkinson 1975

This edition published 2001
by Wordsworth Editions Limited
Cumberland House, Crib Street, Ware,
Hertfordshire SG12 9ET

ISBN 1 84022 253 0

Wordsworth Editions Limited 2001

Wordsworth® is a registered trade mark of
Wordsworth Editions Limited

Printed and bound in Great Britain
by Mackays of Chatham plc, Chatham, Kent.

CONTENTS

LIST OF MAPS

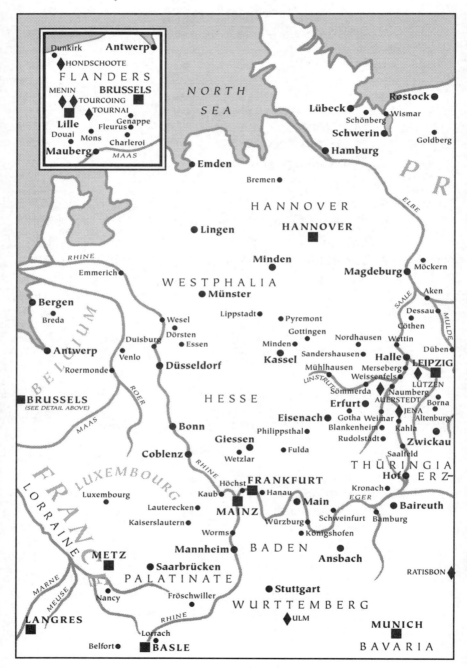

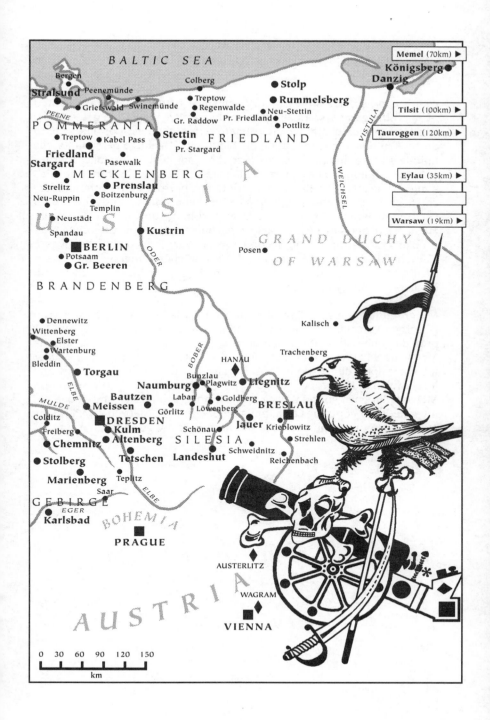

BALTIC SEA

Memel (70km) ▶
Königsberg
Danzig

Tilsit (100km) ▶

Tauroggen (120km) ▶

Eylau (35km) ▶

Warsaw (19km) ▶

Bergen
Stralsund Peenemünde Colberg
Griefswald Swinemünde
PEENE Treptow
POMMERANIA Regenwalde Neu-Stettin
Gr. Raddow Pr. Friedland
Treptow Kabel Pass Stettin Pottlitz
Friedland Pr. Stargard FRIEDLAND
Stargard Pasewalk
MECKLENBERG
Strelitz Prenslau
Neu-Ruppin Boitzenburg
Templin
Neustädt
Spandau Kustrin
BERLIN Posen
Potsaam
Gr. Beeren

Stolp
Rummelsberg

VISTULA

WEICHSEL

ODER

GRAND DUCHY
OF WARSAW

BRANDENBERG

Dennewitz
Wittenberg
Elster
Wartenburg
Bleddin Torgau
ELBE
MULDE
Coldlitz
Freiberg
Chemnitz
Stolberg
Marienberg Teplitz
GEBIRGE
EGER BOHEMIA
Karlsbad

Kalisch

BOBER
HANAU
Bunzlau
Naumburg Plagwitz Liegnitz
Bautzen Laban Goldberg
Meissen Görlitz Löwenberg BRESLAU
DRESDEN Schönau Jauer Krieblowitz
Kulm Strehlen
Altenberg SILESIA
Tetschen Landeshut Schweidnitz
Reichenbach
Saar ELBE

Trachenberg

PRAGUE

AUSTERLITZ

WAGRAM

VIENNA

AUSTRIA

0 30 60 90 120 150
km

PREFACE

THIS BOOK FULFILLS AN AMBITION. Ever since I first became acquainted with the great historical figure of Blücher I've wanted to get to know this tremendous character on intimate terms: the best possible way to do so would be through writing his biography. His huge personality, his unique stature, his bravery, his incredible survival – all make a writer extremely humble. Then there is his place in history, his importance as a military leader, as a Prussian patriot, as a partner in the commander-chief of staff relationship, first with Scharnhorst and then with Gneisenau, which played such a large part in the downfall of Napoleon. Such a partnership bears a close resemblance to the Churchill-Alan Brooke association in the Second World War; indeed, Blücher was a Churchillian figure. Added to all this was Blücher's intervention to save Wellington at Waterloo. And yet there has never been a full-length English biography of Blücher.

My grateful thanks go first of all to Count Alec von Blücher and Frau Dorothea von Blücher for their kindness and encouragement, and for providing me with material about their illustrious ancestor. I also thank Mr Michael Parkinson for his technical assistance and Dr Frank Walker for his helpful suggestions. Mrs Christa Carne, Mrs J. M. Ireland and Mrs Melanie Kirkwood provided invaluable translation work. John McLaughlin gave sound advice and support, as always. And above all, my wife Betty continues to astonish me with her ability to do all things at the same time, and I continue to marvel at my good fortune.

CHAPTER
I

Salad Days

EACH EVENING in times of peace Sebastian von Belling, commander of the Prussian Death's Head Hussars, sank to his knees before his couch and raised his loud voice to the Almighty. 'Thou seest, dear Heavenly Father, the sad plight of thy servant Belling. Grant him soon a nice little war that he may better his condition and continue to praise thy name. Amen.'

The bizarre prayer could well have been echoed by the teenage cavalryman whom Belling captured and adopted as his *protégé*, and who rose to lead the Prussians and their allies against Napoleon Bonaparte. Gebhard Leberecht von Blücher found his 'nice little war' and became a legend in his lifetime: rumbustious, unruly, sometimes an alcoholic, sometimes – like war – a trifle mad; yet no other commander clashed in so many conflicts with Napoleon, and no other single commander played such a large part in the downfall of the French Emperor. Nine times they met in battle, compared with the one occasion upon which Wellington directly opposed the infamous French leader – and without Blücher's timely arrival on the bloody field of Waterloo, Wellington might well have suffered defeat. Yet outside his own country Blücher has been grossly neglected. Almost a century after the Field-Marshal's death his great-great-grandson was asked a typical question by a prominent British officer: 'Perhaps you can tell us the name of the German Johnnie who arrived late at Waterloo?'

Blücher lived through unprecedented turmoil, when great nations were being born armed with terrifying new might. In Blücher's childhood the Germanic area comprised over 300 independent states, with Prussia the most dominant; by the time

1

of his death this amorphous mass had been reduced to less than 40 states and modern Germany had begun to emerge. Blücher, at the head of the Prussian army, was the first to experience the pulsing power of the developing Germanic nation which would later become synonymous with rampant militarism.

He led an army of thousands into conflict, and yet commanded with such a personal touch that this multitude called him Father, and he referred to his troops as his 'beloved children'; he enjoyed few benefits of literacy and – according to his critics – could barely understand a map; and yet, in his seventies, he could match Napoleon's manoeuvring in the gigantic campaigns of 1813 and 1814, when war had taken such a vast and appalling new form, and when Wellington and his British army remained occupied in the relative side-show of the Peninsular War. Everything about Blücher, his hulking size, his bellowing voice, his astonishing mixture of cruelty and humanity, his exorbitant habits and behaviour, emerged far larger than life.

*   *   *

At the time of Blücher's birth, 16th December 1742, Prussia remained fragmented into duchies and semi-independent districts. The country abounded with many families enjoying the surviving prestige of lower nobility, identified by the prefix 'von' to their surnames. Such was the condition of Infantry Captain von Blücher, who had served in the army of Hesse-Cassel, and who settled with his wife, nine sons and one daughter at Gross-Renzow, near Rostock in the duchy of Mecklenburg.

Rostock, with its thriving fish-markets, situated on the river Warnow and looking northwards over the Baltic to Sweden, provided a stimulating environment for Gebhard Leberecht von Blücher, next youngest of the nine sons. The bustle suited him, although he failed to take advantage of the excellent education available at the Rostock State School: study either proved beyond him or bored him and his lack of book learning always remained evident. His spelling was often atrocious and he gave grammar rough handling; he found difficulty in employing the dative case, mixing 'I' and 'me', and he tended to split long German words into his own construction. Yet his lack of learning would never be a hindrance in a career as an army officer, and Blücher's educational defects were by no means uncommon. Another Prussian general, with whom Blücher would be closely associated, experienced the same literary trouble and complained of 'those damned *mirs* and *michs*'; this Prussian commander, Hans von Yorck, also declared: 'In writing it did not matter so much, for you just made a dash which anyone could interpret as he chose, but in speaking you were obliged to say one or the other.'(1) Blücher himself made up for his scholarly lack in other ways – his written grammar may have been weak, but his spoken word enjoyed the strength of complete naturalness and earthiness. Colonel Karl von Müffling, later to serve under Blücher, described his commander's method of learning from life rather than from libraries:

> Despite a sharp, penetrating intellect, Blücher had received no systematic education; only in contact with other people, finding himself on good terms with everyone, acting firmly and with great tact, his inexhaustible cheerfulness and his modest, good-natured behaviour won him friends wherever he went. He never despised knowledge, nor did he over-estimate it. He talked frankly about the neglect of his upbringing, but he also knew very well what he could achieve without this education.(2)

Blücher's father wished him to be a farmer, and at the age of fourteen Gebhard went with an older brother, Ulrich, to live with his married sister and her husband, von Krackwitz, on the nearby island of Rügen, where Gebhard would be taught estate management. Another reason for his despatch to this Swedish island of Rügen may have been his father's wish to keep him away from army influence: all the other sons had entered army service and perhaps Captain von Blücher considered this sufficient. Yet the year of Gebhard's and Ulrich's departure, 1756, saw disturbing events in Prussia: in May the Austrian, French, Russian, Swedish and Saxon leaders joined in a coalition to cripple or destroy Prussia's authority, growing to threatening proportions under the iron rule of a small, scruffy man much addicted to Spanish snuff, who played the flute and quoted French verse for pleasure, but whose work was war – Frederick the Great.

Prussia revolved around the great 'Fritz'. He held together the fragmented nation with its scattered population of four and a half million. In many ways he represented the characteristics of the people. So too did Blücher. Considered by many other Europeans, including Goethe, as barbaric, the Prussians exhibited an uncouth vigour which jarred upon the susceptibilities of the Saxon, the Frenchman, or the Englishman. Through their veins flowed thick Slavonic blood; their sturdy bodies endured the harsh, wet climate of northern Germany, blasted by winds from the Baltic. Masterful, frugal, lacking social graces but always attuned for war, they could be welded by Frederick the Great into a steely instrument for his ambition. He himself had suffered a stern upbringing at the hands of his tyrannical father, Frederick William I.

> Under Frederick the First, [he wrote] Berlin had been the Athens of the North. Under Frederick William the First it became its Sparta. The military character of the government affected both customs and fashions. Society took a military turn. No one used more than three ells of cloth for a coat. The age of gallantry passed away.(3)

Frederick the Great further developed the hard, no-nonsense, masculine Prussian character. Now, in 1756, the great European powers turned upon his nation, aiming to squash this embryo of modern Germany.

But in August Frederick struck first to start the Seven Years' War, with thick columns of Prussian troops moving south over the border into neighbouring Saxony and Austria. By June 1757 more Austrians had moved against the outnumbered Prussian army and the war moved north, with French, Austrians and Russians advancing towards the Prussian capital of Berlin from the south and west, and with a Swedish force of 16,000 men crossing the Baltic to invade north Prussia – via the island of Rügen. War had come to Gebhard von Blücher and he found himself unable to resist the temptation. The island swarmed with troops. Gebhard, aged fifteen, and his brother Ulrich approached the Captain of a squadron of the Swedish Mörner Hussar regiment and offered their services. The attempt to enlist almost met with failure; the squadron captain knew the brother-in-law of the two boys and sent them back home. Von Krackwitz, himself an ex-cavalry Captain, joined with his wife in pleading with Gebhard and Ulrich not to enter the army, but the Blücher brothers refused to listen: Gebhard insisted he would enter sooner or later, 'and the sooner he entered the service, the less time would be lost'.(4)

Back they went across the fields to the tents and pickets of the Swedish hussars.

All the Blücher brothers were now soldiers, but in a variety of armies on either side of the war, Prussian, Russian, Danish and Swedish. They characterized the fickle allegiance common to the time. All had been attracted by the profession, regardless of which army they joined, rather than to the cause; in direct contrast to the situation which would emerge in the Napoleonic upheaval, when men became motivated through intense patriotism and when wars were waged by whole nations, not vague states. Now it made no difference to the nine Blücher brothers that they might find themselves in opposing infantry lines or cavalry charges.

European events gave Gebhard the finest possible introduction to his army career. The Swedish army, including the Mörner Hussars, moved south into North Prussia in summer 1758, reaching Neu-Ruppin by September and almost to Berlin by mid-winter. But allied setbacks in the south meant the withdrawal of the Swedish army in the north, and Blücher and his comrades fell behind the Peene and then to the island of Rügen again. With the start of the next campaigning season in spring 1759, the Swedes returned over the narrow strip of sea separating Rügen from the mainland. Once more they advanced into Prussia, although still staying outside the main area of fighting. Frederick suffered heavy defeats at Minden and Kunersdorf in August, but the allies proved unable to summon sufficient strength to bring about his downfall.

Marches and skirmishes hardened young Cadet von Blücher; he even suffered his first wound, shot in the foot at a small-scale clash in September, near Pasewalk. But the campaign ended inconclusively, for all the energy expended, and Blücher's hussar regiment moved into winter quarters near Griefswold in November. The allies compiled their plans for the following year: Frederick, by turning upon one, would leave the door to Berlin open for the others. Meanwhile, Russian and Swedish forces would ravage the North Prussian area of Pomerania. Once again the armies took to the roads as the spring breezes dried the mud and allowed the carts and horses to move forward; Gebhard started his third campaigning season – and his last for the Swedes.

To the south Frederick repeated his brilliant manoeuvring, and by August the allied plans had been disorganized. Also by August, the Swedish and Russian forces in North Prussia had moved towards Friedland, south-east of Rostock and a third of the way to Berlin. Blücher therefore still fought in his native duchy of Mecklenburg. The Swedes approached Prussian forces at Kabelpass, near Friedland; on the 29th the two sides clashed. Gebhard, still a Cadet, had been sent by his commanding officer with a ten-man detachment to occupy an advanced post, with orders to fall back if menaced. A scout reported to Cadet von Blücher that movement had been seen amongst the trees opposite his post. Gebhard rode forward to investigate with a group of hussars. He trotted cautiously towards the wood and then a whole enemy cavalry squadron burst into the open and rushed at full gallop towards him. Blücher's mount shuddered, staggered and fell, shot by a Prussian bullet. The young Cadet barely had time to roll to his feet before shouting Prussians surrounded him. One enemy hussar, Sergeant Gottfried Landeck, grabbed the 'damn'd little tenderfoot', and Blücher's service with the Swedes was finished.

At nightfall he stood before the commanding officer of the regiment into whose hands he had fallen: Colonel Wilhelm Sebastian von Belling, himself only about twenty-five years old, and rapidly achieving recognition for his dashing handling of his Black or Death's Head Hussars, also named the Belling Hussars as a compliment to his command. Belling, hawk-nosed and hatchet-jawed, interviewed his prisoner: Blücher gave his name and the two men, captive and captor, discovered themselves to be distantly related – Gebhard's father proved to be Belling's wife's cousin. This connection persuaded the Prussian colonel to keep Blücher behind when the other captive officers were despatched back to Stettin, and soon afterwards the young prisoner received even further preference. Belling was always seeking suitable new recruits for his cherished regiment. Gebhard seemed excellent material – aged eighteen, well-built, broad-shouldered, lively and cheerful despite his present predicament. Belling proceeded to persuade his captive to switch allegiance; the day following his fall into Prussian hands, Gebhard was shown a sword, a fur-lined cloak and the splendid uniform of a subaltern in the Belling Hussars – all newly stripped from the body of a Prussian who had been killed by Gebhard's Swedish comrades. Despite the glamour of a glittering uniform and the promise of promotion, Gebhard hesitated, declaring he remained bound by his oath of allegiance to Adolphus Frederick, King of Sweden. Belling applied pressure: he had despatched a request to Frederick the Great, seeking Blücher's promotion to the subaltern rank of Cornet – without mentioning that Blücher had been captured from the Swedes. Within a month, on 20th September 1760, Frederick had given his routine consent to the appointment, which Belling hastened to show to Blücher, who finally acquiesced. Officially he still remained in the Swedish service, and indeed may never have secured his actual release: his father was still attempting to accomplish this for him the following year.

Now, in 1760, all Frederick's resourcefulness and all the stamina of his soldiers would be needed. Frederick the Great marched to war again with his uniform soiled and greasy, his face emaciated, his bones weary; he rode at the head of a ragged, exhausted army; men stumbled barefoot to battle. The conflict had become one of endurance. Blücher had by no means come over to the side which would be certain of victory. Pressure on the Prussians accumulated in late September and early October, and Belling's hussars joined with other Prussian forces in attempting to block the invasion route to Berlin. Blücher was always on the move; no opportunity arose for a determined defence, and the hussars were hustled from one village to another. Behind this Prussian force Austrian and Russian raiders entered Berlin in the first week of October, burning buildings and creating general panic. Ladies and gentlemen in Berlin society climbed hurriedly into their elegant carioles and carriages; government officials burnt documents and plans prior to flight. Frederick the Great rushed from Silesia, south-east of Berlin, with his main army making night and day forced marches along the main roads, and news of the Prussian approach caused the raiders to evacuate the city on the 12th. The main Austrian army, 64,000 strong, began concentrating for battle with Frederick near Torgau in Saxony. Reports filtered through to Blücher and his comrades that a costly and indecisive battle had been fought at Torgau on 3rd November. The weather worsened, rivers rose to flood the roads, the fields became too swampy for the cavalry, and the campaign ended for the year with both sides exhausted.

Gebhard's experiences covered both the exhilaration that he

would always feel in campaigning life and the inevitable hardships. He had met one of his elder brothers also serving with the Prussians, Berthold; another brother, Burchard, had been killed. Gebhard himself emerged unscathed from the skirmishing and sniping in which he had participated during the past two months. He had yet to become involved in large-scale battle, but he had shown no fear under fire and had apparently justified the faith placed in him by his colonel. Soon after joining the Prussians he had become Belling's *aide-de-camp* and then his adjutant, and the two men were firm friends. Blücher always claimed Belling had the greatest influence on his military training. Belling in turn commented: 'My young adjutant will one day become the ornament of the Prussian army, if his natural qualities and talents are blended with a well-digested ground-work of military tactics.'(5) Above all, Gebhard found the life of the hussar, and the tactics the hussars were called upon to undertake, ideally suited to his background and his temperament; Blücher, even when leader of a vast army in later life, would always retain his hussar spirit.

Originally the hussars were only intended for patrols and raids, but later instructions, for example in 1744, expanded the role: the hussars were to cover the army's flanks, front and rear, and in the Seven Years' War they were often used as battle cavalry.(6) They therefore rapidly acquired an élite status which continued to grow and which became surrounded by all the cavalry glitter and *élan*. But one feature, stemming from their humble origins, distinguished the hussars from the older and more traditional cavalry regiments such as the cuirassiers and dragoons: in the hussars men of non-noble or minor noble status were allowed into the officer ranks.(7) Men could even be raised from the ranks. Frederick told his hussar commanders in 1779 to see 'that not so many young windbags serve as officers in the regiments, but that now and then capable, long-serving sergeants be recommended for promotion . . .'(8) Blücher fully supported this attitude.

Blücher never lost the characteristics of the typical hussar officer: fiercely independent, hot-headed, impatient of useless regulations, but maintaining a strict adherence to those he considered necessary, always ready to perform the difficult tasks which others shunned, always able to use his own initiative and forever anxious for the battle to begin. Wellington summed him up: 'He was a very fine fellow and whenever there was any question of fighting, always ready and eager – if anything, too eager.'(9) It would have been difficult to see Blücher fitting into the role of the junior infantry officer, with the prevailing infantry tactics insisting upon rigid control, inflexible lines and a virtual absence of individual judgement; conversely, he would probably have felt almost as much ill-placed in the traditional non-hussar cavalry, with its acute awareness of social distinctions and strict hierarchical system. Blücher remained entirely without snobbery. Belling as an individual friend and tutor, and his hussars as a whole, therefore performed for Blücher an immeasurable service: he later looked upon these years as among the happiest of his life.

Constant manoeuvring and skirmishing continued in the north throughout 1761. Recognition of Blücher's ability came during the year with his promotion to Second Lieutenant in January, and to First Lieutenant in June. But by the end of the year the Prussians were becoming increasingly exhausted, and only the death of Elizabeth of Russia on 5th January 1762, offered hope of salvation. Elizabeth's successor, Peter III, was an admirer of Frederick and immediately began peace negotiations. These led to the Treaty of St Petersburg on 15th May 1762, ending the war between Russia and Prussia; only a week later the Treaty of Hamburg brought peace between Prussia and Sweden. Frederick could now concentrate against the Austrians in Silesia while Ferdinand, Duke of Brunswick, held off the French in Westphalia, and a third force under Prince Henry, Frederick's brother, met Austrians under Marshal Serbelloni in Saxony. Belling's hussars moved southward to join this latter Prussian army in June and operations in July led to Blücher being publicly praised by his battalion commander for his efficiency and bravery.

In August Henry's army moved south through Saxony in an attempt to push the Austrians back into Bohemia, clashing with the enemy at Freiberg at the end of October. Blücher received an injury to one of his feet on the 28th, when a wood splinter pierced his boot, but he probably continued to take part in the main fighting the following day when the Prussians defeated their Austrian opponents; immediately afterwards he left the regiment for a convalescence at Leipzig. This city had been chosen by Frederick for his main headquarters; for the first time young Gebhard mingled with the senior sections of the Prussian army.

Frederick's veterans were now supremely confident. The opposing commanders signed an armistice in November, advantageous to Prussia; Frederick's troops threw themselves into riotous celebrations in Leipzig and the narrow cobbled streets were jammed with milling, drunken men. Blücher immediately joined the hubbub – to such an extent that within days of his arrival in November he was obliged to fight a duel. For the next few years his life would epitomize the gay hussar.

The Treaty of Hubertusburg on 16th February 1763 brought the official end to the Seven Years' War; Belling's hussars moved to garrisons at Stolp, North Prussia. Finding peace-time service tedious, young Blücher soon won notoriety for his wild off-duty behaviour. Whilst on duty he appeared conscientious and sober, and he was known by his men to be humane and fair – he opposed flogging, still a standard punishment, and he forbade non-commissioned officers in his company from carrying sticks for this purpose. But the routine bored him – the daily parade at 11 o'clock in the morning, the sessions of horse management, training and drill, the timetables, orders and counter-orders. According to one contemporary, 'instead of studying he gambled, drank, associated with women and practised practical jokes'. Another fellow-officer agreed: 'He did not know the value of money, only lived for the present, ignoring the future. If he lost money it did not affect his good humour; he could do without anything he was used to except good clothes and good horses.'(10)

Moreover, his wild activities threatened to involve him in even more serious troubles. Duelling was officially forbidden under an exhaustive edict published in 1688 by the Elector Frederick II, which pronounced that 'Almighty God reserved to his Majesty alone the right of vengeance'; this edict declared that all participants in a duel would be punished by death. Frederick William I reproduced this law in 1713 but reduced the scope of punishment: for duels without fatal results he prescribed only imprisonment for eight to ten years, and where a death resulted he made the penalty dependent on the 'lethality' of the wound. Frederick the Great confirmed the edict and condemned duelling in vigorous language: 'This barbarous fashion; this mistaken point of honour that has cost the lives of so many good fellows whom their country might have expected to render it the greatest service.'(11) But Blücher's extreme behaviour inevitably took him to secluded corners where he was called upon to defend his honour – or more likely to allow his offended opponents to defend theirs. His duels were usually fought with swords rather than pistols, and the contest continued until the first man received a wound, however slight, whereupon his chief second would shout 'Cut!' and the duellers would stand back, honour satisfied.

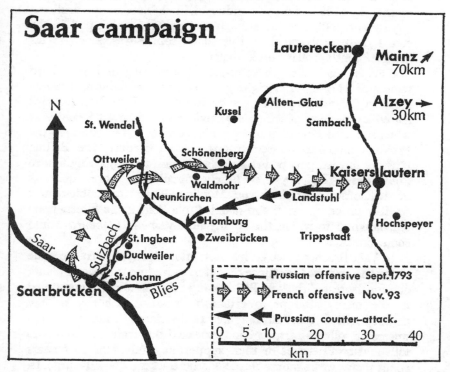

Whether Blücher killed any adversaries in duelling is unknown: such an outcome would have been kept extremely secret. Nor is it certain whether he ever received punishment specifically for this type of activity, although he is believed to have spent a short spell in prison during this period. But in later years he delighted in showing his old duelling scars. He bellowed with laughter when he described his youthful behaviour, including the occasion he received admonishment for some trifling offence from a superior officer, whom Blücher immediately challenged to a duel, only to receive precipitate orders to depart with bags and baggage to

fresh barracks at Neu Stettin.(12) At his new post he found
himself under Major von Podscherly, a strict but fair superior
whom Blücher afterwards praised as an excellent teacher, second
only to Belling.(13) But the wild streak remained. Riding north
through Pomerania to spend leave with his married brothers at
Rostock – his sixty-five-year-old father had died in 1761 and his
mother in 1769 – he even indulged in dubious horse-dealings,
buying and selling stolen animals and perhaps taking part in the
actual thefts. Income from this shady source was added to his
meagre monthly salary of 20 thaler.

Blücher was called to semi-active service again in the hard
winter of 1770–1, after eight years of garrison tedium. Trouble
arose in Poland, disputed over by Russia and Prussia: Frederick
feared a repetition of Russia's behaviour in the Seven Years' War
when she used Poland as an operational base, and in late 1770 the
Prussian monarch massed troops on the border. The Belling
Hussars formed part of Frederick's invasion force, moving first to
Pollitz near Friedland, where Blücher obtained temporary quarters
in the house of Freiherr von Mehling. This local nobleman, a
wealthy property owner and married to a Pole, had a fifteen-year-
old daughter to whom the twenty-nine-year-old Gebhard would
soon return.

In 1771 Blücher received his promotion to Captain. At the same
time orders arrived for his regiment to move into unhappy Poland,
and for the rest of the year Blücher and his comrades were occupied
in the messy attempt to establish Prussian authority on the
invaded nation. Partisans operated in the gloomy countryside and
miserable villages; armed bands sneaked out from the woods to
kill unwary Prussians or their supporters, and Belling's hussars
spent many weary hours in the saddle tracking down insurgents.
Blücher proved himself as tough and unsympathetic as his
colleagues in the ruthless operations. He doubtless shared the
anti-Polish attitude then common in Germany, that the Poles as a
race were shifty and lived in animal-like squalor. 'A thousand
times have I thought: if only a fire would consume them all,'
wrote the normally humane Carl von Clausewitz, 'so that the
purifying flames would change this mound of dirt into clean
ashes.'(14)

Blücher undertook his duties with no evidence of either relish
or remorse. On one occasion he received orders to ride with forty

hussars to track down a guerrilla group near Schneidemühle, and this he accomplished successfully, capturing about thirty partisans; half of the able-bodied ones were carted off to Berlin. He believed in an 'eye for an eye' policy – if any of his men were killed by a sniper's shot or a sudden thrust of the knife, then reprisals should be taken without mercy, cruelty matched with cruelty. He put this policy into practice in early 1772, after a wretched winter spent in the dripping and foul Polish hovels, thick with the odour of wet horses and mildewed leather. One of his sentries had been seized and slowly tortured to death; Blücher believed a local Catholic priest to be responsible both for betraying the hussar position and instigating torture against captured Prussians, and he had the man arrested and shot without bothering to consult higher authority. A serious scandal immediately resulted.

Moreover, Blücher had already suffered a reverse in his relationship with senior officers. Belling had retired and had been succeeded by Colonel von Lossow, who apparently disliked his predecessor and all to do with him, including Blücher. Now the atmosphere between the two men soured still further over the priest incident. Blücher's harsh treatment gave the regiment as a whole an unsavoury reputation, possibly spreading as high as the court in Berlin. Frederick the Great had already ordered a policy of conciliation with the Poles in an attempt to persuade them to support Prussia, not Russia. Blücher's personal position in the regiment which had been his home for over ten years became increasingly unhappy and became intolerable in autumn 1772. Lossow passed Blücher over in promotion, preferring an officer older than Blücher but below him in rank. Blücher suspected his rival had been given preference both through the dislike felt between himself and his commanding officer and also because the other came from a more noble family. On the last day of October the angry Blücher therefore sent a petition direct to Frederick the Great: 'Staff Captain von Blücher of the Belling Hussar regiment asks to be allowed to leave, because First Lieutenant von Jägersfeld has been preferred for the vacancy of the Zülow squadron, and he is convinced of his blameless behaviour; he cannot bear the pain this has caused him.'(15) The request received an unsympathetic response. Frederick, displeased with the undiplomatic behaviour of his hussar regiments in Poland, scribbled in the margin of Blücher's letter: 'Is not a hussar but a gypsy regiment!' The Prussian monarch sent no reply; in spring 1773 the discontented Captain tried again:

> Permit me, with all due submission, to apprize your Majesty how insupportable it is for me to see myself superseded by an officer who has no other essential merit to boast of, than being the son of the Margrave of Swedt. Your Majesty will therefore be graciously pleased to permit me to resign, sooner than expose myself to the most acute sensations during every hour of my life.

This time Frederick reacted with a curt note addressed to Major von Schulenberg, Blücher's friend and immediate superior: 'Captain von Blücher has leave to resign and may go to the devil as soon as he pleases.'(16)

Blücher's career had come to an abrupt end, and in those unhappy weeks of late 1773 he had every reason to believe his departure from the army would be permanent. He had reached the rank of Captain, served in exhilarating, arduous and sometimes unpleasant campaigns, endured dull garrison routine, enjoyed his green salad days of youth, all typical of so many army officers. Now, at the age of thirty and again like so many colleagues, he sought a completely new career as his ex-soldier brothers had done without thought of ever returning to the army.

*   *   *

Farming had been the original occupation preferred by his father for his second youngest son, and Blücher now turned to the land. His transition from soldier to farmer proved easy and seemed complete, largely owing to Freiherr von Mehling, upon whom he had been quartered on his way to Poland in 1770 and whose daughter he now returned to court. Karolina, aged seventeen, responded readily to the ex-hussar and the marriage took place at Pottlitz on 21st June 1773. The newly-weds stayed with Karolina's parents for just over a year while Blücher acquired more knowledge of the career about to commence. By July 1774 the ground-work had been prepared and Blücher and his pretty young wife moved to Stargrad in Pomerania, where Blücher would manage one of his father-in-law's estates, Gerissunde. The venture proved a success; the farm prospered and the Blücher family grew: Karolina eventually bore seven children, three of whom died as babies, and another at the age of two; two boys and one girl survived – Franz, the eldest son, Gebhard, and a daughter named Friederika.

Gone were the wenching, rollicking days; even the bottle and cards were only enjoyed in moderation. Blücher became the typical prosperous farmer: cheerful, hearty, popular, sure of himself and apparently content. After four busy years he stepped out on his own, buying the neighbouring estate of Gross Raddow for 14,500 thalers, which he then enlarged with a grant of almost 10,000 thalers from the government. The farming seasons came and went. But the seeds of soldiering remained, together with Blücher's constant craving for excitement. The year 1777 brought an Austro-Prussian crisis; Frederick mobilized and marched into Bohemia in July 1778.

Already, one month before, Blücher had written to Frederick reciting all his services and begging to be taken back into the army as a Major. No record exists of any answer. The crisis died away. Blücher stayed silent for two and a half years and then tried again, in January 1782. Frederick once more refused to reply; in May Blücher sent another letter and this time Frederick answered: 'Why did you not remain in the service? It's your own fault.'(17) The ex-Captain continued with his farming and other civilian activities: he took office in local government, attempted to learn French in his spare time, joined the Masons in Stargrad, took occasional trips to his brothers in Mecklenburg and returned home with beautiful riding horses. But although he had passed his fortieth birthday Blücher's satisfaction in farming, which had been evident in the years immediately following his marriage, had almost gone. Between January 1782 and November 1785 he pestered Frederick the Great with ten letters, some running to hundreds of words, all written in peeved, badly constructed language. The letter content varied from pomposity to near insolence. To begin with Blücher tried subservience; he sought no financial advantage 'but a most fiery longing to consecrate the best years of his life to His Majesty's service'. The seventh very long letter repeated all the details of Blücher's military career and stressed his longing for renewed opportunity; Frederick merely replied: 'That's nothing.' Blücher turned to threats. He wrote at the beginning of 1785, when civil war had erupted in Holland, that he would quit Prussia to serve the Dutch. Frederick failed to be moved; the bombardment continued. Blücher took strenuous physical exercise as preparation for an eventual return to service, should such a summons arrive; none came.

But Frederick the Great was ageing fast. He had occupied the throne of Prussia for forty-five years; his soldierly spirit had evaporated and he filled his time with literary and musical *soirées* rather than military pursuits; his colossal energy slowed. Blücher's last letter bore the date 16th November 1785. No reply had been received by the following summer when on 17th August Frederick the Great died at Sans-Souci, to be succeeded by his nephew Frederick William II. Blücher's moment had arrived and an excellent opportunity offered itself when the new monarch travelled through Stargrad soon after his accession. The King stayed one night at the town's best inn; Blücher gained an interview and confronted the King with his martial bearing and emotional appeal – and extracted Frederick William's promise of an army appointment. On 23rd March 1787, came the document from the King: Blücher would be a major in his old regiment – now known as the Black Hussars – and his appointment would be backdated eight years, putting him above von Jägersfeld whose appointment had caused Blücher to leave service in 1773.

All he had asked for had been granted, and more; he packed his bags into a horse-drawn dray, selected his four best mounts, and rode from his farm. He had been a farmer for almost fourteen years, he was in his mid-forties and yet his army career had barely begun. Five days before Blücher received his new commission from the King, on 23rd March, his future ally Arthur Wellesley, 18 years old, had been gazetted Ensign in the 73rd Highland Regiment, taking the first step towards the title of Lord Wellington, hero of Waterloo.

CHAPTER
2

Return to Revolution

MAJOR VON BLÜCHER received a warm welcome from his regiment at Rummelsburg. Middle-aged he may have been, but news of his coming revived tales of his antics as a young lieutenant and old comrades still remained: the regiment was now commanded by von Schulenberg, whom Blücher had befriended as a major. Gone were the manners of a sober gentleman farmer. But Blücher had to become accustomed to the changed atmosphere within the Prussian army as a whole. Frederick the Great's lack of interest during his declining years, then his death, had reacted upon the service, aggravated by almost a quarter of a century without serious military activity since the Seven Years' War. The change would become even more noticeable during the eleven-year reign of Frederick William II, a weak and increasingly dissipated monarch, and the results would burst into full appalling prominence in the disasters of 1806. Already, in 1787, the spirit of Frederick the Great's magnificent, apparently invincible army, had started to swirl away. Army life consisted of dreary garrison duty enlivened only by the annual manoeuvres and the occasional emergency.

For two years Blücher had to be content with minimum warlike activity. Winters were spent at the Rummelsburg garrison; spring and summer passed with training and manoeuvres culminating in large-scale autumn exercises at Potsdam. Blücher became intimately involved with all the affairs of his regimental family. His experience of handling men grew, benefiting from the wide variety of nationalities amongst the hussar soldiers – in his first squadron were West and North Prussians, Poles, Hungarians,

Bohemians, Swedes, Italians, Saxons, Mecklenburgers, Danzigers, Ausbachers and others. He knew them all, and their families; despite, or because of, his own lack of education he insisted that army children should be spared academic neglect, and he concerned himself with the establishment of a special garrison school at Rummelsburg. Children liked him and called him 'Papa Blücher'. He displayed a mixture of healthy heartiness and humane concern. Yet he could be a rigid disciplinarian, provided he had made up his own mind that the reasons for the discipline were sound.

But with this benign and sensible character went another facet: his passion for gambling had returned in full strength, together with his colossal appetite for *schnapps* and full-bodied wine. His recoveries after each drinking bout or all-night gambling session were remarkably swift: the following morning he would be out early with the horses, exhibiting superb skill as a rider. He showed a similar dexterity with animals as with men; he disliked indoor riding schools, preferring to give horses and men free rein in the open countryside. In this peaceful way Blücher's army career progressed: he received promotion to lieutenant-colonel in 1788, and the Order of Merit in 1789; in 1790 he became a full colonel. All traces of the farmer had vanished. Blücher sold his land in 1789 and 1790, receiving 24,000 thalers for his Gross Raddow estate and thus making a profit of almost 10,000 thalers in ten years; the Blücher family established their home in Rummelsburg, close to the garrison.

The year 1790 brought fresh activity; the Black Hussars joined other regiments moving northwards along the Polish border. By June Blücher's squadron had reached the mouth of the Weichsel; in autumn 1791 the regiment returned home. Blücher had to face domestic misery: his wife Karolina had died on 17th June, aged thirty-five, never fully recovering from the birth of their last child. Blücher visited her grave in Rummelsburg churchyard then immersed himself even further into regimental life; his drinking spells became more frequent and more severe and now, at fifty, he started to acquire the reputation of being slightly eccentric.

*   *   *

Tremendous international upheavals were erupting. Revolution in France threatened to shake the European monarchical system around which the whole structure of the states revolved. At first many Germans had watched with delight as civil disturbances racked their traditional enemy, France. But winds from France turned chill. *Émigrés* fleeing from France to the German principalities along the Rhineland brought with them tales of atrocities, Royalist humiliation and the possibility of international conflict, and these fugitives demanded Austrian and Prussian intervention. On 27th August 1791 Frederick William joined Leopold II of Austria in the Declaration of Pillnitz: they would help protect the unfortunate Louis of France provided all other European sovereigns agreed. The move merely hardened French feeling against them and gave support to the politician Jacques Pierre Brissot who advocated war.

Conflict crept closer. Vociferous demands for intervention increased in early 1792 and Austro-French relations deteriorated; on 7th February Leopold decided that war was probable and persuaded Frederick William, always easily led, to join in a defensive alliance; on 1st March Leopold died and his son Francis II proved even more bellicose, while in France a Brissotin ministry took power.

War upon Austria was declared by the French Assembly on 20th April. Patriotic enthusiasm brought flocks of untrained French volunteers to the Tricolour, and these raw soldiers were easily brushed aside by the professional Austrians at Lille at the end of the month. Thus encouraged, Frederick William mobilized his Prussian forces and at the start of July an allied army assembled at Coblenz, comprising 30,000 Austrians and 42,000 Prussians. Colonel Gebhard von Blücher hastily penned a passionate plea to the King: 'I pray to God that I will have the opportunity in the coming campaign to prove to your Royal Majesty that I am not unworthy to have this favour bestowed on me.'(1)

Not only Blücher but his whole regiment failed to march to war in this summer of 1792; the Black Hussars remained in barracks while news returned to Prussia of the allied invasion under Karl Wilhelm, Duke of Brunswick. This began on 19th August; at first all apparently went well, then disturbing reports reached Rummelsburg describing disease and demoralization in Brunswick's regiments. Rumours increased until in early October came confirmation that the vaunted Prussian infantry had been shattered by fifty-four French guns at Valmy on 20th September. General Adam Custine swept his French troops after the retreating allies to reach the Rhine; Mainz, considered totally safe, fell to the French and the enemy penetrated into Germany as far as Frankfurt. In the north the French followed the Austrians into Belgium – known then as the Austrian and the United Netherlands. Brussels fell; Antwerp was besieged; the Prussian Fatherland might soon be invaded. And on 21st January 1793 the guillotine hissed down upon the neck of Louis XVI. Prussia and Austria issued an appeal to German patriotism: 'The Fatherland is in danger. The Constitution, religion, property, tranquillity – all are menaced by near ruin. The bloody projects of the French are unveiled.'(2)

Orders reached the Black Hussars in mid-November 1792; the regiment left Rummelsburg at the end of the month. Blücher led his battalion and beside him trotted his fourteen-year-old son, Franz, who would accompany him on campaign. His other son, Gebhard, now aged five, and six-year-old Friederika, would stay with their mother's parents. The regiment moved down the roads of East Prussia towards the capital: the hussars riding in orderly files, behind them servants with strings of bare-backed horses, carts loaded with baggage, tents, mobile forges, spare saddles, canteen equipment, other carts overflowing with fodder for the horses and food for the men, and finally waggonettes transporting the ancillary personnel – blacksmiths, farriers, carpenters, cooks. Summer dust had already been sluiced into a tacky coating on the roads as the autumn rains indicated an end to the campaigning season, and with the advent of winter weather the allied leaders could find time to draw up plans for the following year. The Black Hussars stayed for almost a month in Berlin and Blücher heard these plans. The Dutch forces of the Prince of Orange would link with British troops under York and with Austrians further east under Frederick Josias, Prince of Saxe-Coburg; with Saxe-Coburg's 40,000 Austrians would be Prussian elements including the Black Hussars. The aim would be to sweep the French from Holland and Belgium, while further south the 60,000 Prussians under Brunswick would attempt to drive Custine from Mainz.

Troops milled everywhere in Berlin. 'Discipline was totally relaxed,' wrote an anonymous eye-witness to a friend in London. 'The officers in general were a scandal to their profession. They thought of nothing but feasting, drinking, wenching, gambling, and all the vices which attend debauchery and intrigue.'(3) Blücher joined in with the rest. Frederick William soothed his fears as best he could: the anonymous correspondent added: 'He totally neglected all business in the Cabinet. His sole enjoyment was dallying with an opera dancer who did all she could to make his time pass agreeably.' Frederick William had another five years before dissipation killed him; his army survived another fourteen years before Jena and Auerstedt finally shattered the myth of its efficiency. Meanwhile, the French Revolutionary armies had still to be fully developed into the awesome military machine created by Lazare Carnot, and for the moment Prussia and her allies could muddle painfully through.

Blücher and his regiment left Berlin's brittle society at the end of January 1793. They rode to the Dutch border near Venlo, where the hussars joined the small Prussian corps commanded by Frederick, youngest son of the Duke of Brunswick and aged only twenty-two. In the first days of March the corps moved south along the Maas towards Roermonde, then occupied by the French. Now the Black Hussars experienced their first clash with the enemy in the Revolutionary War, and Blücher witnessed the difficulties stemming from vague leadership and faulty allied co-operation. The plan for the recapture of Roermonde involved a Prussian strike from the north while Austrian units pushed from the south; Blücher received orders on 4th March to advance and discover the exact location of the Austrian forces. He urged his horse forward to reach the low hills overlooking Roermonde itself and he saw that the Austrians had already commenced their assault.

'I could see clearly the attack of the Imperial troops,' he wrote in 1795. A vigorous push by the Prussians from the north could result in severe defeat of the enemy – but a slow Prussian advance might allow the French to escape. 'This I reported to Duke Frederick von Brunswick, with the remark that I thought the enemy would quit Roermonde in the night.' But Blücher's commander disagreed: 'I expect a stiff defence,' he replied. Blücher, always impatient, sent a subordinate officer on a reconnaissance mission towards Roermonde at dawn the following day, 5th March, and he himself left soon after daybreak with his hussar battalion and 100 marksmen; he met the officer galloping back: the enemy had evacuated Roermonde. 'I immediately sent an officer to the Duke with this news. His Excellency came himself and told me he did not believe the report of the subordinate officer.' Blücher

wheeled his horse away in disgust and made straight for the town
– to meet the Austrian commander in the process of entering the
empty streets.(4)

Blücher's personal experience at Roermonde symbolized the
whole character of the allied campaign against the French in
1793. The Prussians, Austrians, British and Hanoverians failed to
gain adequate advantage, despite the benefits which ought to have
been obtained from professional, experienced armies fighting
against raw recruits produced by the French Revolutionary
leaders. The allies were either defeated or robbed of decisive
victory; the battles revealed an amazing will to win on the part of
the new French levies. A powerful mixture of patriotism and
terror was starting to transform armed mobs into soldiers. The
battles of Hondschoote, Menin and Wattignies provided the high-
lights of the 1793 campaign in which Blücher and his regiment
were not directly involved. But Blücher's smaller-scale operations
were no less tense; they indicated that Blücher remained totally
uncharacteristic of the general demoralization which was increasingly infiltrating the Prussian army; they provided first-class
examples in miniature of Blücher's techniques which would be
exhibited on such a massive scale in 1813 and 1814.

His own account of the 1793 to 1795 campaigns, written in the
winter of 1795, describing the skirmishes, ambushes and battles
in which he participated, was modest and stark. But even the
unemotional language failed to cloak the relish with which he
welcomed the prospect of fighting. His future staff officer, Müffling
wrote:

> His imperturbility in dangerous situations, his tenacity in mis-
> fortune, and his courage which grew under difficulties, were based
> on an awareness of his physical strength, which he had often used
> in hand-to-hand fighting during earlier campaigns. In this way he
> had gradually convinced himself that there was no military pre-
> dicament from which one could not ultimately extricate oneself by
> fighting man to man.(5)

Blücher's experiences between 1793 and 1795 underlined this
'man to man' aspect. The almost endless clashes with the enemy
brought extreme personal danger: the hussars, through the nature
of their role, remained the most active in this type of campaign.
Contact with the French consisted of a *mêlée* of rearing horses,

slashing sabres, and close-range pistol fire; the heavy sabres could lop limbs and split heads with a single blow and the aftermath of these short actions revealed horrifying scenes of trampled, mutilated men and horses: the man still astride his horse who had received a diagonal slash across his face, gashing his mouth open so that his jaw hung gaping down over his chest; the headless corpse, still sitting upright in the saddle with hands clutching the reins; the armless hussars, still gripping with their knees. So ordinary and taken for granted were incidents such as these that contemporary participants rarely bothered with details when they wrote journals or memoirs; they simply commented, like Blücher's oft-repeated words in his own accounts, 'we cut them down', or 'we cut them to pieces'. Daily, for month after month, the Black Hussars played their part in this carnage – Blücher had no leave until spring 1794, a year after his arrival at the front. Yet he always pleaded for action. His attitude was revealed from the start, when the Prussians lay opposite the French lines at Breda in mid-March.

'I wanted, as much as possible, to let the young officers get to know their craft,' he wrote. On the 16th March Blücher successfully begged permission to attack the enemy and he trotted out at night with sixty hussars. After a night and a day in the saddle, with his horse stumbling with weariness and his men slouching over the reins, half asleep, he clashed with an outnumbering group of French in a forest. Blücher used the tactic which he always employed when surprised – strike immediately. 'Lieutenant von Schulenberg led the advance guard, when I ordered to attack the enemy right away; he did that with such determination and such good result that several of the enemy were cut down ... From the prisoners I found that the wood was occupied by 400 infantrymen. I could therefore do nothing and marched back.'(6)

Only a few days later he ventured out again, this time with 150 hussars to lay a night ambush for French patrols. None came; Blücher advanced still further towards a French-held village. Muskets crackled from the thatched houses but Blücher pressed on for an attack, until cannon also began to roar from the French position and round-shot thudded into the soil around the line of hussars. Blücher believed the guns presented minimum danger while the men remained spread out, presenting an inadequate target for artillery: the noise and the smoke would be the most frightening feature. 'My hussars wanted to retreat at the first shots, but I was determined to introduce our people right at the beginning to the little dangers of artillery fire when the cavalry is unconfined.' Blücher kept his men under control, although he decided not to press the assault, and when he finally withdrew only two horses had been injured.

Blücher's hussars were learning their practical lessons. But Blücher himself also received valuable tuition from experience when, at the beginning of April, he barely managed to survive his eagerness for battle. The regiment had moved to Antwerp, with Blücher among the first Prussians to enter the relieved city, and then to the vicinity of Lille. Blücher, as always, had pushed to the front to lead a small detachment against the village of Flers, two and a half kilometres from Lille itself.

> Now I suddenly had the French cavalry from the camp of St Magdalene on my neck and I realized I had advanced too far. I wanted to retreat, but enemy infantry tried to block me from the road. I decided to attack before the enemy cavalry could reach me. That had good result. We drove into the infantry and cut them cruelly to pieces; now I was attacked by superior cavalry and we could do nothing but out-ride them.

The French thundered after the retreating Prussians; one enemy officer came on faster than the rest and Blücher, glancing over his shoulder, could see he would be overtaken; as usual, he wanted to strike first; he reined his horse, dragged round the animal's head and spurred his mount towards the galloping Frenchman. 'It was already getting dark when we started fighting. He paid for his bravery with his life and his horse is to this day in my stable.' Blücher would attempt to profit from this experience, not always successfully. 'This action taught me in future not to advance too far without support.'(7)

Blücher and his battalion operated with the allied forces stretching between Lille and Douai. Often the two lines were deployed only a few yards apart and men exchanged greetings and insults. Lord Henry Paget, serving with the Duke of York, described the macabre relationship between the enemies.

> Nothing can be more moderate & *Gentlemanlike* than the present Mode of carrying on the war between us & the French. Our sentries

and theirs never fire on each other & all Officers are allowed to ride about peaceable, tho' within half Gun Shot of their Piquets.

Officers sometimes dined with opposite numbers, continued Paget, but he added: 'It is with the British that they are particularly polite. Other Nations are not so safe with them. . . .'(8) Blücher showed firm respect for the convention concerning captives. On one occasion in early June a French officer prisoner died of his wounds and Blücher ordered him to be buried with military honours; he shouted angrily at the Prussian carpenter who had failed to make an efficient job of the coffin, much to the astonishment of the other prisoners who were watching. Yet once the sabres were pulled from their sheaths, few could match Blücher in determination and even cruelty. His reputation as a fighter gradually grew. Twenty years later the great military reformer Gerhard von Scharnhorst, his chief of staff in early 1813, would comment that Blücher was totally devoid of fear,(9) and this could be hazardous; without fear to tug at his elbow he would plunge into situations where more normal men would hesitate to enter.

Blücher displayed his ruthlessness in July. The commander of the Black Hussars, Count Goltz, suffered a thigh wound on the 4th which finished his regimental career; Blücher assumed acting command of the Black Hussars and immediately declared he intended to seek revenge for Goltz's injury. He successfully sought permission to set a trap for the French. During the night of the 25th he led 200 hussars, a cuirassier squadron and some infantry into enemy territory. The men filed down the dark paths, their sabres blackened to avoid reflecting the moonlight; Blücher had already studied the terrain and now deployed his troops. He split his infantry into two sections, one concealed in a cornfield, the other in brush and scrub, and he gave orders for both to attack a French-held hamlet immediately to their front when they received his signal. Then he positioned his cavalry behind farm-buildings, ordering them to circle the hamlet as soon as the infantry attack began, thus severing the enemy's line of retreat.

The Prussians settled down to await dawn. As light began to filter across the fields a strong French patrol emerged from the houses and started to march towards the Prussian infantry, chattering and laughing as they approached the ambush. But the

H.G.—B

over-anxious Prussian infantrymen fired too soon; the enemy scurried for cover. Blücher immediately bellowed at buglers and drummer to signal the attack: the infantry rose from the corn and brush and began running forward, whilst the cavalry burst from behind the farm-buildings. 'Everything happened exactly as I had ordered,' commented Blücher. He himself drove his horse towards the centre of the fight; his mount stumbled and fell, but Blücher clung to the reins and swung into the saddle again. 'My hussars went into the infantry and cut everything down. . . .'(10)

Similar activities continued throughout the summer, Blücher miraculously avoiding injury save occasional nicks and scratches. Then, at the end of August, his regiment received instructions to move south.(11) French troops under Custine had been driven from Mainz on 22nd July after a stiff seige, so removing this stain on the honour of the Fatherland, although the French only agreed to surrender in return for a pass to safety.(12) The recovery of Mainz allowed the allies to push back the French over the Rhine and almost to the Saar; the Black Hussar battalion under Blücher joined with other regiments moving down from the north into the resulting vacuum.

By mid-Septmeber Blücher had moved into position near Neunkirchen, twenty-four kilometres north-east of French-held Saarbrücken, about 120 kilometres south-west of Mainz and the Rhine. The Black Hussars would form part of the corps commanded by General von Knobelsdorff. Blücher organized his men into forward outposts, where he immediately had a violent argument with the previous post commander, Colonel von Szekuly: Blücher felt obliged to threaten him with a pistol. This altercation over, he billeted his men in a large barn, the wide doors of which would permit easy departure in case of emergency. Instead of the unco-ordinated enemy groups which Blücher had experienced further north, now he had to oppose more continuous and better defended lines.

Within twenty-four hours, on the 28th, Kalkreuth's and Knobelsdorff's corps began a general advance, attempting to reach the Saar river. Blücher led the foremost troops of Knobelsdorff's main column, pushing along the Sulzbach valley towards St Johann. Enemy troops massed for the counter-attack on the road ahead, but Blücher discovered that the French had committed a serious mistake. They had 'positioned themselves in a very con-

centrated dense irregular heap', a vulnerable target for a determined cavalry charge, and giving minimum opportunity for
controlled French musket volleys. Blücher seized his chance; he
charged with seventy men at full gallop into the enemy. His
hussars bludgeoned into the first French files, who fell back on to
troops behind and these in turn were crammed against the men
in the rear. Blücher's small troop carved into the midst causing
fearful casualties, and as the French turned and ran, casting aside
muskets and packs, the Prussians pounded in from behind, cutting
them down along the road to Saarbrücken. Knobelsdorff's regiments took up forward positions and an artillery duel began. For
the next few days both sides tried to disrupt the other through
sudden incursions and sniper and cannon fire.

> Because I rode daily along our chain of advance posts, [wrote
> Blücher] on which occasions I had only my adjutant, Count von
> Goltz, with me, the French *tirailleurs* (skirmishers) always tried to
> shoot us or our horses. Their cheek went too far and I thought it
> necessary to put a limit to them by small attacks, ambushes and
> such-like.(13)

Living conditions were deplorable.

> Knobelsdorff's corps remained in this miserable position in front
> of Saarbrücken for seven weeks [stated Blücher]. The nearness of
> the enemy forbad the erection of tents, the common soldier had
> therefore to lie in earth huts, and because the weather was
> continually foul it caused a lot of sickness.(14)

Nor could Prussian spirits be raised by news of battles elsewhere.
On 6th September York's 13,000 men tangled with 42,000 French
under Jean Nicolas Houchard at Hondschoote just east of Dunkirk:
sheer pressure of numbers forced back the British and Hanoverian
troops and York barely managed to extricate himself, losing his
artillery in the process. Then, on the 13th, Houchard routed the
Prince of Orange at Menin – although, because he failed to
manoeuvre the Austrians completely out of eastern France, he
was dragged to the scaffold by his Paris superiors and guillotined.
Jean Baptiste Jourdan took his place, and spurred by the fate of
his predecessor he drove back the Austrians at Wattignies a month
later. French troops opposing the Prussians at Saarbrücken were

given new confidence; allied troops suffered corresponding dejection as they huddled in their hovels with sheets of rain sweeping over the mist-clad forests. On 17th November a prisoner was brought before Blücher at his camp in the Salzbach valley, and from him Blücher gained the information that the enemy were about to attack in full strength. Next day the offensive began.

Striking fast and hard the French drove north of Saarbrücken to outflank and encircle the allies. Ottweiler, to the rear of the Prussian positions, fell within twenty-four hours, and an enemy thrust towards Neunkirchen threatened to snap the ring shut. Back streamed the Prussian regiments to squeeze through the remaining gap. Blücher now had the task of organizing delaying operations during the withdrawal to the east. The allies managed to escape the enemy trap but continued to retire, waggons wallowing through the puddles and disconsolate infantrymen wading ankle-deep through the quags, muskets slung upside-down to prevent the rain dribbling down the barrels. Blücher's scouts reported that 10,000 enemy were moving forward. He rushed the news to Knobelsdorff and Kalkreuth; in reply came fresh orders, received by Blücher on the 25th, which entailed his most hazardous mission so far. He must 'make for the enemy, who was advancing more and more towards Kaiserslautern [almost halfway between Saarbrücken and Mainz], and carry out a small diversion on the left flank'.(15) Blücher immediately broke camp and led his hussars across the sodden fields towards the French.

Before many miles the small Prussian force encountered a French patrol: the hussars attacked at once, taking eight prisoners. Only two men escaped 'but they were a great nuisance because they let the enemy know of our presence'. The Black Hussars rode closer to the main French advance. Darkness fell and Blücher camped for the night, his men unable to light a fire to cook or dry their clothes through fear of discovery. Before dawn they were on the move again towards Kaiserslautern, far to the east of the Prussian right wing. Then, as the hussars trotted through the meadows beyond the village of Waldmohr, they blundered into a group of French. Blücher reacted first and charged: the enemy scattered into the trees. As the Prussians were reorganizing and allowing their steaming horses to regain breath, 'the enemy came at us from all sides'. Outnumbered, almost surrounded, even Blücher knew he must flee and he shouted to his bugler to sound the retreat. But the leader of the advance guard misinterpreted the call, and taking for granted Blücher's normal tactics he plunged into a desperate, hopeless attack. 'The enemy was astounded,' commented Blücher, and he used their momentary hesitation to urge his horse forward and gallop between the advance guard and the French to turn his men away from the suicidal attack. The Prussians fled to the village of Waldmohr with their pursuers close behind: the hussars flung themselves behind cover, spreading out as they did so, and the far more numerous enemy had to cram forward in a tight bunch in the narrow street. Blücher's men seized full advantage from this enemy concentration. 'After a pitched battle the whole mass of them, who got into each other's way, had to quit the village.'

Blücher had achieved his diversion, but his account continued: 'Because there were ten times as many enemy as us, and I had a retreat of five hours in front of me without any hope of shelter . . . the journey back looked very bleak.' His men were already tired, shaken and sodden, and Blücher moved as slowly as he dared to save strength. The village of Schönenberg was reached safely by the main body of Blücher's force, but the enemy had closed upon the rearguard and began to harry the last retreating Prussians in the village streets. Blücher had made preparations for such pressure, dropping men off as he rode with the first hussars past the houses, and these men clambered up stairways to find firing positions at the windows: as the French ventured forward they received vicious fire from either side. 'The enemy was repelled with bleeding heads, and left some prisoners behind.' Another attack came when the weary hussars were halfway between Schönenberg and Kusel. This time Blücher and his men summoned all remaining effort, turned, wheeled into line and charged – and repulsed the enemy. The French abandoned their pursuit. Almost miraculously Blücher had lost no men, and he returned with sixteen prisoners and forty-eight captured horses. He made camp around Alten-Glau, near Kosel, and completed detailed reports for Knobelsdorff.

Both armies organized themselves for full-scale battle. Forces converged on the Kaiserslautern area: Blücher had orders to harass the enemy from flank and rear as they marched regiments up into line. On the 29th he found himself completely cut off behind the French but managed to slip through to nearby hills.

From there he overlooked the whole battlefield: 'I could even notice the movements of both armies and every cannon shot,' and at dawn on the 30th the French began 'one of the most terrible barrages of cannon firing. . . . I could watch the whole attack from the heights on which I stood.'(16) He could see the impact of round-shot as these iron balls rolled red-hot through the Prussian ranks, and the effect of the canister shots as they spewed hundreds of iron pieces or nails into the opposing infantry.

A messenger cantered up the rise with orders: Blücher must take his battalion down the hillside and through the forest to stab at the enemy's left flank as the French infantry advanced along the valley. The enemy army, commanded by General Louis Lazare Hoche, began to move forward as the cannon bombardment faded, and as Blücher's hussars slithered down the slope. Despite the heavy artillery assault the main Prussian lines stood firm and massed volleys repulsed the French. The enemy were already pulling back as Blücher's men filtered through the fir-trees on the left flank and he could see the enemy infantry columns moving past as he emerged from the wood. No time could be lost – he sent a messenger requesting urgent support from General von Kosboth, then ordered the charge; out into the valley rode his hussars, cantering across the flat towards the French. But there, in front of them, were massed large numbers of French cavalry – six times his own strength, reckoned Blücher – and unlimbered French guns lined the opposite slopes. Blücher's charge glanced against the first French cavalry squadrons: he swerved his out-numbered men into the woods hoping to lure the enemy into a trap. 'I could still foresee that the enemy, as was his wont, would chase me in an irregular mass. I knew I could count on the fleetness of foot of our Polish horses and the cuirassier and hussar regiments which I expected gave me hopes of slaughtering the enemy.'

To allow time for this support to arrive, he made a brief stand in the wood, the horses blundering into the undergrowth as men slashed and parried with their sabres. 'My people fought with the greatest determination, but the forest was too dense, we were outflanked and had to retreat.' Blücher continued: 'My forecast was correct; the enemy pursued us in a wild swarm, but our horses got us out of his grip.' Blücher himself narrowly escaped as he pushed his horse through a small ravine: close behind him came a French officer, who had already raised his cocked pistol when a Prussian hussar screamed a warning. Blücher turned, spurred his horse up the steep slope and other hussars fell upon the Frenchman. Further back fled the Prussians, still maintaining superb control.

Then, as planned, the first reinforcements swept down the rise – a squadron of cuirassiers with others close behind. 'This marvellous squadron threw itself right into the side of the enemy . . . I called to my people "Turn round!" And they, full of trust, obeyed instantly. I threw myself with them at the enemy.' Almost immediately the French fled in disorder, the Prussians cutting down those in the rear. Through the trees they went and out into the open again; the French gained a few yards, splashed across the Lauter river and made for safety. 'Now the enemy started very heavy cannon-fire, which until now he had been unable to use because I had still been in hand-to-hand fight with his cavalry. I retreated out of firing range.' Blücher led his exhausted, triumphant hussars through the forest to the main Prussian lines. 'I can state that I have seldom participated in a more difficult fight than this.'(17) On the whole front Hoche's French army was withdrawing and, after a day of rest, Blücher's hussars joined the pursuit, breaking camp at dawn on 1st December.

Typically, Blücher took the lead. His hussars pushed forward unhindered, finding no enemy save wounded men lying on the baggage-strewn highway. Blücher spared only a moment to scribble a brief message which he handed to a bugler to take to the Prussian headquarters: 'Enemy is not retreating, he is fleeing. I am following him to Homburg.'(18) Then, further down the winding, rutted road, he found an entire enemy column deployed along the edge of a wood with thirty cannons. Blücher halted at a safe distance, his men climbed stiffly from their saddles, and local villagers were questioned over the position and condition of the French. 'From the reports of the peasants,' wrote Blücher, 'their alertness had lessened and the men were extremely tired.' The opportunity lay open for a brilliant victory against numerically superior forces. Blücher felt tempted. But his men were also tired; some had been left on the way with lame horses; the French could rally against him. 'If I had had a pair of battalions I would have had no hesitation . . . but, feeling helpless, I had to desist.'(19)

For two more exhausting days Blücher stayed on the enemy's

heels as they moved back over the river Glau near Homburg. Other Prussian units came up; the front line steadied again as each side settled into more static positions and Blücher's Black Hussars rested thankfully in billets. Respite for the hussars only lasted one day. On 5th December Blücher was summoned to the main Prussian headquarters at Kaiserslautern, where he received fresh instructions: he must advance along the whole enemy line by the river Blies, which flowed before Saarbrücken, and he must discover whether the French intended to launch a fresh offensive towards Mainz; so great was the danger surrounding the mission that Blücher was assured he could take as many infantry, cavalry and guns with him as he deemed necessary. He declined the offer: he preferred to go alone with his trusted hussar battalion.

Next morning, 6th December, the operation began. First, Blücher moved towards Homburg; he intended to cross the Blies above Homburg but found the bridge destroyed and instead decided to detour south. Thick fog hung over the river valley and he made steady, stealthy progress. By nightfall on the 6th his small group had managed to move forty kilometres southwards to Zweibrücken, observing enemy movements and questioning local inhabitants. During the tense hours of darkness an enemy advance patrol clashed with his sentries: all surprise gone, Blücher headed for safety, leading his men along an eighteen kilometre route through the hills to the Prussian lines. He reported to the high command: previous information that the enemy intended to launch another offensive, similar to the last, could be dismissed. 'On the contrary, he was much more frightened of us crossing over towards him and he in no way intended to get another beating at Kaiserslauten.'(20)

Blücher's assessment proved only partially correct. He accurately divined that Hoche had no plans to push forward in the Saarbrücken sector, but the French leader had other intentions of which Blücher could not be aware. Soon after the Black Hussar mission the bulk of the French units began streaming southwards towards Alsace, where they reinforced neighbouring French armies against the Prussians and Austrians in that area. Two French victories, at Fröschwiller on 22nd December and at Geisberg on Boxing Day, forced the allies from the Alsace and Palatinate regions and back to the Rhine; repercussions of this retreat rippled northwards: denied support from their neighbours in the south the allied army before Saarbrücken also withdrew. Blücher's hussars joined with the other regiments in the dreary, demoralizing march eastwards along the road towards Mainz, past the scene of the autumnal triumph at Kaiserslautern.

Winter passed with the French and Prussians occupying rain-soaked positions before Mainz; hardly a day went by without Blücher's battalion being involved in small-scale skirmishes. No opportunity seemed too slight for him to dart into short but nevertheless bloody engagements. His own detailed account of the countless clashes, written eight months after the war had finished for Prussia in April 1796, underlines how vivid each incident remained in his mind. Astonishingly, he continued to survive without serious wounds and he seemed completely tireless. Blücher, in his fifty-second year, could ride and fight longer and harder than the youngest in his battalion; and war activity failed to use up all his incredible energy – he still had strength for his particular brand of non-military pleasures.

> From drilling his squadron, [wrote one contemporary], which was quartered at a distance, he would proceed to a hare hunt or a gay dinner and that same night, perhaps, to a surprise attack on the enemy, or to the laying of an ambush for the next morning. Having temporarily silenced the enemy he would enjoy himself at Frankfurt, gambling or going to the theatre.

Some of the card games he played were illegal; he nevertheless indulged in them 'to a truly immoderate degree'.(21) Gambling, drinking, hunting, fighting – all provided Blücher with his required excitement. His immediate superior General von Rüchel fortunately shared his craving for battle; Blücher noted with approval that Rüchel was 'also a friend of all offensives'; between them they never ceased to 'tease' the French. So, while dis-satisfaction with the inconclusive campaign spread through the army as a whole and men became increasingly anxious to return home, Blücher retained his extreme enthusiasm. One of his squadron commanders, Major Valentini, believed that 'only Prince Hohenlohe, Rüchel and Blücher wanted to continue the war' – Blücher described Hohenlohe, now the army commander, as 'this marvellously brave man' who gave 'everybody an example in cold-bloodedness and determination'.(22)

The two Black Hussar battalions were re-united, and on 20th

March Blücher received official confirmation that he would command the whole regiment; henceforth the unit which he had joined as a cadet thirty-four years before would be known as Blücher's Hussars. He grouped around him young officers whom he could trust completely and to whom he had transmitted some of his own spirit of almost fanatical determination – men like Lieutenant von der Goltz, his adjutant and the son of the previous regimental commander; Major Valentini; and another squadron commander, von Müffling. His battle-hardened hussars enjoyed the distinction reflected from 'Father Blücher'; he, in turn, fostered the feeling that he would always give them maximum support.

A chance to prove this pledge to his men came in April after three of his captured hussars were murdered by French *volontaires* – volunteer soldiers rather than enlisted men. Blücher, who always treated captives with courtesy, wrote: 'I heard about this foul deed from prisoners and cavalry deserters, who themselves had a poor opinion of the *volontaires*. I determined to take revenge.' Within a few days came, in Blücher's words, 'a chance to have them'. One morning a large group of *volontaires* emerged from their camp at nearby Leistadt and opened fire on Prussian hussars in a vineyard. Blücher lay hidden behind a wall with more of his men. The hussars under fire feigned retreat and the enemy became 'even cheekier'. Suddenly, Blücher and his men broke from cover in an awesome charge. The French scattered and fled, but the hussars were in amongst them and within moments none were left alive. 'This example had the desired effect,' commented Blücher.(23)

Large-scale operations were prepared for the allies while Blücher and his hussars continued to operate in the Alzey-Dürkheim area. Baron Karl Leiberich von Mack, Austrian chief of staff, put forward a 'plan of annihilation': the allies would drive into France on all fronts. Lazare Carnot, forty-one-year-old Minister of War in Paris, matched this intention with schemes to clear the invaders from French territory in the north. On 18th May the campaign began with the Battle of Tourcoing in Blücher's previous fighting area near Lille: the French army of the north defeated in detail the badly managed Austro-British-Hanoverian army under Saxe-Coburg. Five days later came the Battle of Tournai, forty kilometres south-east of Tourcoing: both sides retreated with losses of about 3,000 men each, after a fiercely fought contest. News of these battles had still to reach the Mainz area when the Prussians and Austrians began their attempt to thrust from the Rhine to the Saar and into France. General von Möllendorf would lead the Prussian right flank towards Kaiserslautern, while Hohenlohe advanced with the Austrian left flank further south via Dürkheim. Blücher's hussars, strengthened by three infantry battalions and two *Jäger* rifle companies, had one of the most difficult and dangerous tasks. They had to move between the two allied armies to link one with the other: failure could mean a French stab through the centre and the destruction of each. Early on the morning of 23rd May the surge forward began.

CHAPTER
3

Approaching Catastrophe

BLÜCHER'S ORDERS covered page after page of almost illegible writing. They included instructions to harass the enemy around Frankenstein, where roads joined from Kaiserslautern, Neustadt and Dürkheim; afterwards he would clear the enemy from the valley between Frankenstein and Neustadt to permit communications between Hohenlohe and Möllendorf. The countryside varied from pasture-land to forests, disrupted by the Hardt mountains rising west of Neustadt to almost 3,000 ft.; the winding roads provided perfect ambush points. Blücher, advancing towards Frankenstein in the spring sunshine on the morning of 23rd May, found the enemy attempting to make the most of this advantage. But by mid-morning Blücher's leading detachments were fighting in the outlying houses and barns at Frankenstein; within an hour the village had been evacuated, and Blücher's first orders had been accomplished.

He regrouped his men. He could hear artillery from Hohenlohe's main army echoing in the forest-clad hills; Blücher had to push on, towards Neustadt, even though he would be extremely vulnerable to attack from the rear. His men climbed into their saddles again; infantrymen replenished their ammunition pouches from the waggons which had creaked into the village behind them. The road twisted and turned up into the hills. On either side the black woods spread to the edge of the track, and within minutes French muskets flared from the forests and enemy cavalry burst from cover.

'The many enemy infantry and cavalry in front of me defended every step,' wrote Blücher, 'helped by the different obstacles which

Rhine campaign May 1794

FRANKFURT
30km

Mainz

0   10   20
KM

Oppenheim

Kreuznach

Alzey

RHINE

Worms

Kaiserslautern

Dürkheim

Mannheim

Hochspeyer

Frankenstein

Weidental

Trippstadt

Neustadt

Speyer

Edenkoben
Rodt

Kirrweiler

N

Weyer

Fischlingen

Edesheim

Landau

Queich

Lauter

Blücher's advance

had to be cleared away under constant fire. During this work I had to defend myself on all sides.'(1) Gradually the Prussian hussars and infantry climbed higher and the gloomy forest thinned. But ahead lay the village of Weidental, beyond which the road dropped through a dramatic gorge before reaching Neustadt. Weidental would have to be taken, and the gorge forced. Already, as Blücher's troops approached the village, a heavy fusillade clattered from behind barrels, carts and from the open windows. Blücher's infantrymen charged immediately, running, stopping to fire, running again in a dense mass, plunging forward over the last ten yards with long bayonets held stiff before them. The enemy fell back, house by house, then fled along the road to the gorge. Blücher threw out a defensive screen on the high ground beyond Weidental. Cannons were dragged up to this ridge: the axle of one snapped on the rough ground, but the surviving two opened fire on enemy troops appearing from Neustadter ravine. Blücher remained in an extremely perilous position, isolated deep in enemy territory, knowing nothing about the progress of the two flanks of the main army, and within two hours his situation worsened still further. Scouts placed on the road from Frankenstein, along which Blücher had just marched, hurried to the village: French troops were approaching, totalling about two infantry battalions, 1,000 cavalrymen and with at least two cannons. This force, commanded by General Cisée, clearly intended to push through for Neustadt. Blücher, trapped in the middle and with no hope of support from other Prussian units, decided to attempt deception: he hoped to persuade the French commander that Prussian reinforcements were *en route*, behind Cisée. He therefore rode out to meet the French under a flag of truce: he shouted to Cisée that the French should surrender, since they were cut off.

'I hoped this would happen because he couldn't see my strength,' wrote Blücher. 'But the invitation was answered with a general salvo.'(2) Blücher galloped for cover. French troops on the far side of Weidental began to attack, catching Blücher's outnumbered soldiers between two fires. Almost immediately Cisée's infantry began to storm the slope. 'Now the deciding moment had arrived,' commented Blücher in his account. 'I told my brave friend Lieutenant-Colonel von Müffling . . . that we now had no other choice but to go and meet the enemy with fixed bayonets and to use all our remaining strength. His eyes shone with this decision.' Blücher himself ran to join Müffling's battalion.

Solid lines of blue-uniformed French rose from the bushes and advanced from rock to rock, and bullets from their volleys raked the unprotected Prussian ranks. Four officers died within the first few seconds. But the Prussians stayed in line. 'Our brave hussars could not be disheartened,' said Blücher. They stood steady as the enemy line advanced to within thirty yards, then Müffling shouted the command; his men jumped down the slope, cheering, with bayonets stabbing into the French. The enemy, breathless from their climb, gave ground and turned. Prussian bayonets pierced their backs as they blundered and staggered through the undergrowth. Müffling shouted further orders: his men halted, formed line, and their musket volleys continued to cut down the fleeing French. General Cisée, watching from the main road as his attack failed, tried to march his men forward to Neustadter gorge, but Blücher brought his cannons to bear and the frightened French scattered onto the hillside beyond. The Prussians cheered, slapped one another on the shoulder, stuck French hats on their bayonets and waved them high.

Yet Blücher commented: 'My position remained miserable . . . I was in the midst of wooded mountains and exposed on all sides.'(3) Blücher secured himself as best he could and his men settled down for the night, with Blücher sleeping on the ground beside his troops. Welcome news arrived next morning, 24th May. A rider managed to slip past French detachments with a message from Möllendorf: the Field-Marshal had advanced with his Prussians to Hochspeyer, about ten kilometres over the mountains to the west of Blücher's position and south of Dürkheim; he requested Blücher's presence. Leaving his men under the command of Müffling, Blücher made the hazardous journey through the French-held hills; he reached Hochspeyer in the early afternoon and received orders to remain at Weidental. He started back again with two laden ammunition waggons, and arrived late at night. Müffling told him that the enemy had been active throughout the day. But Blücher had already decided on his next move, which clashed with the orders he had just been given. 'Riding back to my position I was thinking that . . . I would make an attack on Neustadt, despite the difficulties of the terrain.' His troops appeared cheerful and confident, and early on the morning of the 25th fresh reports strengthened Blücher's determination: the French had apparently pulled back from the steep valley leading to Neustadt. Blücher immediately went forward. The gorge indeed lay empty; an even more welcome discovery followed – Blücher's advance party met only minimum opposition as they moved cautiously down the silent, misty valley. The French continued to withdraw, and Blücher entered Neustadt during the evening. Within twenty-four hours Hohenlohe made use of this advance by moving to positions four kilometres away. The French now lay behind the Queich, three kilometres in front of Landau. Both sides reorganized during the 26th and 27th.

But the French completed their preparations first. Early on the 28th enemy forces advanced in far superior strength against Blücher's forward position. Blücher saw them coming as he stood on a nearby hill. Enemy units filtered through the village of Edenkoben and continued to march steadily forward, supported by strong artillery bombardments. Hohenlohe cantered up to Blücher, saw the strength of the imminent assault, and readily offered to allow Blücher to pull back.

'With your permission,' replied Blücher, 'I want to attack the enemy right away.'

'This action could cost you many men,' warned the Prince. 'But I hope you may demoralize the enemy. I've nothing against it. God go with you.'

Blücher now began one of his most daring cavalry actions. Only surprise could bring success. With surprise would go momentum: if the enemy were kept off balance, Blücher's meagre number of hussars might throw back the outnumbering enemy, inflicting heavy casualties. No time existed for detailed plans; nor did Blücher need them. He merely ordered four of his squadrons, who lurked out of sight behind a hill, to work round ready to attack the enemy's flank, keeping hidden in the undulating ground until the last moment. Much would depend on this flank attack – and leading the advance guard was Franz, Blücher's son, now aged sixteen and newly promoted to Lieutenant. Meanwhile Blücher would advance straight towards the enemy guns to hold their attention.

Bugles and drums signalled the start; Blücher led his central squadrons out into the open, wheeled them into line and began to trot towards the French mass. Enemy cannon attempted to disrupt the frail line and earth from the shells showered the hussars, but still the controlled trot continued. Disproportionate strength made the attack seem suicidal; the thick French columns appeared about to swallow the tiny cavalry advance, until, at exactly the right moment, Lieutenant Blücher's advance guard of the four flanking squadrons hurtled over the rise, shouting and yelling and waving their sabres; the French desperately hauled guns round to face this new direction, but young Blücher came on through the artillery fire with the main body of the squadrons close behind. His father accelerated his own charge, and the Prussians knifed into the French on the flank and in the centre. One Prussian squadron slaughtered 100 enemy infantrymen within ten minutes. Blücher obtained his momentum; he led hussars to the village of Kirr-weiler, where sabres slashed down the French in the streets and where artillery and ammunition waggons were seized; infantry attempting to stand behind the village were overrun and few survived; another attempted stand in the hills before Fischlingen was also demolished.

Blücher described the victory as complete; nor had he finished. He heard cannon firing over on his right: at first he thought the guns must be his own, but then saw by the colour of the smoke – the French used different powder – that they belonged to the enemy. Blücher hustled together an improvised force of hussars, totalling two squadrons, plus fifty dragoons, and he took this force over the rough ground towards the cannon-smoke at Edesheim. 'When I arrived I saw that the guns were protected by an enemy cavalry regiment. . . . The enemy noticed my intention, and 400 *carabinier* advanced towards me in closed formation to allow their artillery to withdraw.' Blücher attacked immediately. Cavalrymen fought in a tight mass, knee to knee, but Prussian hussars succeeded in carving bloody gaps through the enemy, and others followed into these spaces to force through to the far side. No longer a cohesive whole, the enemy tried to retreat, but the Prussians streaked round behind them. Fearful slaughter continued; French survivors rushed back to Edesheim where, according to Blücher, 'in the narrow gap in the village the great number of fleeing men jammed itself, and there occurred a bloody massacre'.

So the happenings of this day ended [commented a contented Blücher]. We had obtained a decisive victory, using only cavalry, over a whole enemy corps. . . . The battlefield at Kirrweiler, Fischlingen and Edesheim was covered with French dead, whilst our losses were negligible. [He added] After these happenings the enemy kept quiet for a long time. . . . We therefore had no opportunity to fight him.(4)

Fourteen days after his battle Blücher became Major-General. 'My wish was fulfilled,' he declared.

*   *   *

Quiet continued throughout June. Blücher extended his advance posts as far as the river Fischlingen, with his main head-quarters at Edenkoben and with detachments spread in the nearby hamlets and in the hillside vineyards. On 2nd July the French began to probe the Prussians, using massed artillery fire and aiming especially at Edenkoben and Edesheim. Blücher judged the enemy to be planning a major offensive. 'The enemy not only wanted to examine our positions, but also wanted to know how and with what we could defend the positions.' This opinion soon seemed confirmed. 'We heard from reliable sources that the French army had orders from the National Assembly to attack and annihilate us, whatever the cost.' Even before this confirmation, Blücher started his preparations: forward positions were rein-forced, trenches dug, and barricades thrown across each vineyard path. Tension increased during the next week, with the Prussians daily searching for signs of unusual enemy activity. Reports from peasants and patrols were carefully sifted; Blücher constantly scanned the hills with his spy-glass. 'On the 12th I noticed much enemy movement. One could even see troops marching into the mountains. I therefore reckoned the attack would come the next day.'

As dawn broke over the fir-clad hills and vineyards on the 13th several troops of enemy cavalry trotted towards Edesheim, soon followed by infantry columns stirring a pall of dust as they marched across the sun-soaked pastures. Blücher ordered his isolated advance posts to retire to the main defences; the enemy occupied the hamlets of Rodt and Weyer and opened a massive infantry offensive. Volley after volley swept the vineyards, shred-ding the leaves and hammering into the Prussian barricades.

French soldiers rose from cover and advanced in waves through the chestnut trees, but the Prussians threw them back with counter-volleys and bayonets.

Blücher rode along the line, shouting above the musket din: 'Children! Hold on today! Prussian honour is at stake.'

'Yes, Herr General,' replied the troops. 'But just give us the ammunition.'

Blücher wrote in his account: 'Three times I had to give these brave people, who stood steadfast, new ammunition on this day; already many dead sprawled before their ranks.' As each French assault faded, the Prussians peered over their palisades into the sun-dappled woods beyond, waiting for the next. Blücher could only use about half a dozen cannons, all light field pieces, while the enemy brought two dozen into action. The slender Prussian artillery strength lay on the right wing, towards Edenkoben, protected by Blücher's own hussar regiment. Shell after shell screamed towards the Prussian right flank, turning the whole area into an inferno of erupting earth and red-hot metal splinters. Blücher pulled his precious artillery back to safety, but his equally precious hussars had to stay exposed, in order to cover the infantry from cavalry charges. 'I was sorry to see how it suffered under the constant bombardment,' wrote Blücher, 'but was delighted to see how cool they remained: they stood fast, but had lost 60 horses already.' When the Prussian artillery retired the French believed their opponents must be preparing for a general withdrawal, and they therefore pushed forward cavalry from Edesheim towards Edenkoben, with these squadrons protecting horse-drawn guns. Blücher immediately ordered his troops to entice the enemy further on to the level ground by the vineyards. Prussian regiments retreated; French cavalrymen grew bolder.

'Their squadrons followed me in full cry and thought they had won. I now thought the time had come to take revenge . . . I could no longer resist the temptation to attack.' Enemy cannon attempted to negotiate a narrow bridge; Blücher seized upon the confusion. He ordered his buglers to blow the charge and his battered hussars formed line around him; into the enemy squadrons they galloped, and the leading French cavalrymen reeled back. Massed French artillery opened fire, but the hussars rode on through the smoke and hurtling debris. 'Nothing could halt my hussars.' Leading the foremost Prussian squadron was Lieutenant von Kleist, and

Blücher believed the first enemy cannon against which they were charging had just been fired.

'Quickly, Kleist!' he shouted. 'The enemy hasn't time to load.'

Yet Blücher had hardly shouted the words when the cannon roared, belching at point-blank range, and Kleist's troops disappeared in a mass of boiling black smoke. 'I thought I would see few men from this troop again,' wrote Blücher. But the shell failed to explode. His men rushed on to hack down the unfortunate French gun crew and seized their weapon. Another gun fell to the Prussians, then a howitzer, and the chase continued until French infantrymen ran into the vineyards to threaten the Prussian hussars from the flank. 'In this action we took some 80 prisoners and over 100 horses, two eight-pounder cannons and a howitzer: amongst the prisoners was the cavalry commander, General Laboissiert . . . and Colonel Mitrailleur, who commanded the artillery.'(5)

But French infantry columns still maintained their pressure in the vineyards, where the Prussians had defended their positions for almost six sweltering hours. Blücher, sparing no time for rest after his cavalry assault, mounted a fresh horse and rode over to encourage his men. 'There I found the good Lieutenant von Bila, who sat on a stool amidst the rain of bullets and who encouraged his men to carry on firing as they leant on the parapet. . . . I left the defences with an easy mind. . . . Müffling, with the rest of the infantry, also stood fast.'

Then, about 4 p.m., reinforcements sent by Hohenlohe reached the front and changed the situation dramatically. 'I now came to an agreement with this kind and brave prince (Hohenlohe) that it would be best to turn the tables and attack.' Messengers ran down the line; infantrymen grasped handfuls of fresh ammunition and formed behind their parapets. Officers shouted the order and their men clambered over the scarred defences to advance through the vineyards and into the wood. First they walked, then they ran shouting to storm the French. Blücher ordered 150 cavalrymen to sweep towards Edesheim and into the enemy's flank. The charge succeeded and retreat continued, skirmishers attempting to hold off the harrying Prussians; fires gushed in the village of Edesheim to hamper the pursuit, and the French streamed back to safety. Night fell, with flames from the houses lighting the vineyards with a dull red glow. 'So ended this bloody, for us victorious, day,' wrote Blücher. His men flung themselves down in the vineyards, exhausted but elated.

But miserable news reached Hohenlohe and Blücher at nine o'clock. Allied regiments further along the front had suffered defeat and had retreated. Blücher had also to withdraw, despite his victory and the weariness of his men. The dreary march continued through the mountains until the early hours of the following day, 14th July, when Blücher allowed a brief rest. Withdrawal resumed at 5 a.m.; by mid-morning the Prussians reached the outskirts of Neustadt, where Blücher formed his regiments into defensive lines before the French appeared from the hills. The two armies faced one another over the barren terrain, but both French and Prussians were too weary or wary for large-scale action. Instead they 'teased' one another. At one point a group of French officers rode calmly towards Blücher's command position; Blücher lured them on.

I told some officers of my regiment, who were near me, that we would carefully ride back, to give these gentlemen more confidence. . . . This we did. When they were only thirty paces away, we quickly wheeled our horses and spurred them at full gallop at them, which frightened them so much that they quickly fled, and they could see our broad grins when they threw scared looks over their shoulders; ashamed, they lost themselves in the masses.

Blücher conceived another entertainment. He ordered buglers to group themselves together and play a medley of charges and tunes, and the French immediately ceased their sporadic shooting to listen. The music seemed to please the enemy and groups of men and officers walked closer. Blücher ordered his men not to shoot, and the French strolled nearer still. The martial strains of this impromptu brass-band concert drifted over the mountains and the performance continued until evening, when Blücher swept off his hat, bowed in his saddle to the French and trotted away. French officers waved their hats in reply, shouted their thanks and called: 'Goodbye, General – until tomorrow!'(6)

Lack of allied progress in general meant that Blücher had to pull further back during the next few days and news reaching him from elsewhere caused deep depression. Belgium was abandoned completely by the Austrians after Saxe-Coburg's defeat at

Fleurus, and French troops under Jourdan crossed the Roer. French confidence increased and this spirit spread south to the sector around Mainz. Enemy forces were organized into a newly formed Army of the Rhine and Moselle, under the command of General Jean Victor Moreau. Plans were prepared for a major offensive into the Rhineland. Meanwhile Blücher continued to gain satisfaction and recognition from smaller-scale clashes. On 27th August he received the order of the Red Eagle from the King, and immediately celebrated by advancing with 200 hussars and 100 dragoons to tangle with the enemy.(7) But French pressure gradually increased. The allies found themselves steadily pushed into the area immediately before Mainz, although they attempted to keep a salient pointing along the main highway through the mountains towards Kaiserslautern. Fighting became disjointed and piecemeal among the forests and hills; hamlets repeatedly changed hands, and Blücher, always operating in the forward area, frequently came near to capture.

At the start of the third week in September he received orders to block the enemy advance through the wooded mountains south-west of Kaiserslautern. Low clouds hung over the peaks and curtains of rain swung through the valleys, drenching Blücher's men; he hoped the wet would hinder French guns from firing, and the march went steadily forward into the hills, tension mounting. Yet much to Blücher's surprise no contact was made with the French. Then he realized the reason: the French must have left the main road and slipped into the dense woods for better cover. 'I therefore halted, ordered my men to split up into small groups and to search the woods; whoever found the enemy should make a "hullabaloo".' A deadly hide-and-seek operation began. Within minutes an enemy party had been located and surrounded. 'In the wink of an eye 300 infantrymen were either killed or captured. Now it was tit for tat, sometimes here, sometimes there.' These bloody operations ended with a clash against 600 enemy infantrymen; this enemy battalion attempted to take cover in the dripping thickets, but Blücher's men drove the French out into an open meadow, vulnerable to the vicious Prussian cavalry attack. 'The rout of the French was complete. Our men were very bitter and cut everything down. I had to use great force to keep their fury in check, but I could only save 200 Frenchmen, who were captured.' Over 400 enemy lay dead and wounded in the meadow. Blücher's men wiped their sabres and turned for home.(8)

But opposition to the allies remained too great, not only before Mainz but along the whole front. Retreat over the Rhine began in October. Winter 1794–95 proved extremely depressing. Early in the New Year Blücher suffered some weeks of feverish illness, from which he emerged weak and miserable. 'Only the thought of being able to serve the King and his family again makes me wish for recovery,' he wrote, 'otherwise I have so much sorrow that I would be glad to look forward to the end.'(9) His men shivered in deplorable billets, experiencing reaction to the harsh campaign. All troops, on both sides, suffered: further north half the British soldiers were ill and hospitals in Holland often seemed a short cut to the grave. 'I intend to go to England in a few days,' wrote Sir Arthur Wellesley, future Duke of Wellington, 'that is to say, if the French remain quiet.'(10)

The French had no intention of remaining quiet. By the end of January, 1795, the British were streaming back in one of the worst retreats in their military history. Over 6,000 men froze or starved to death in just four days. 'I learnt what one ought not to do,' wrote Wellington later, 'and that is always something.'(11) News of this disaster cast Blücher into even greater gloom. Nothing seemed to lighten his spirits: he suffered all his usual depression which attended inactivity; despite his weakened state after his illness, he sought a return to war. Instead April brought peace. The news reached Blücher, now with his regiment near Münster. Prussia opted out of further conflict by signing the Treaty of Basel with France on 5th April, recognizing French claims to territory on the west bank of the Rhine, and in return French forces withdrew from east of the river. Blücher's career as an active soldier ended, for the moment. He gave himself an honest assessment: 'I did not do great things, but in my area of influence I left nothing undone.'(12)

*   *   *

Both Blücher and the Fatherland had to undergo drastic re-adjustment following the Treaty of Basel. Saxony, Hanover, Hesse-Cassel and Spain also sought peace with France, leaving Austria to struggle with French Republican forces for thirty more months – during which Napoleon Bonaparte burst into prominence with the Italian campaign of 1797. Bonaparte dictated terms to Austria at Campo Formio on 17th October 1797. Prussia retired behind her line of demarcation, abandoning the left bank of the Rhine and holding herself apart from the turbulent course of European affairs. 'We amuse ourselves with displays of the art of the military dancing-master and tailor,' complained Heinrich von Stein, 'and the state ceases to be a military state, and changes into a drilling and writing state'.(13)

A new Prussian monarch mounted the throne in the year of Campo Formio, after Frederick William II died, according to his many critics, of an excess of sensuality. 'Nature, which had once been lavish in his favour, had long been exhausted,' declared a Berlin commentator, 'He fell a dreadful sacrifice to his own excesses.'(14) His son, twenty-seven-year-old Frederick William III, began his reign of forty-three years. Basically good-natured and mild, the new King lacked drive and imagination and proved totally unsuited to lead Prussia through the dangers which would soon beset her. Diplomatically, Frederick William continued the policy of isolation; he stood aloof while Austria, Russia, Britain, Portugal and the Ottoman Empire clashed with France in the War of the Second Coalition from 1798 to 1800. Prussia might have tipped the scales: instead the French Republic survived and the stage had been set for the great Napoleonic upheaval. 'It is disquieting to see us halting and in a state of paralysis,' wrote Stein in 1799, 'when we could restore the tranquillity of Europe upon the old foundations.' Militarily, Frederick William of Prussia allowed the army to decline still further. The new monarch concerned himself more with numbers of buttons on the uniforms than with military developments, while France improved the products of the *levée en masse* and especially the employment of *tirailleurs*, with these skirmishers fighting in a flexible fashion directly opposite to the rigid, archaic, regular Prussian lines.

Prussia passed through an uncertain period full of missed opportunities, and Blücher's experiences after the Treaty of Basel reflected this atmosphere. To start with his affairs seemed to improve. In July, three months after the cessation of hostilities, Blücher married again. Ironically he first met his second wife at a banquet given by her father, Governor of East Friedland, to celebrate the peace. Blücher sat next to the Governor's youngest daughter, twenty-three-year-old Katharina Amalie von Colomb.

Katharina, demure and graceful, immediately felt attracted to this fifty-two-year-old hussar Major-General – rough-hewn, slightly bow-legged, but with a penetrating bold gaze and an overpowering good humour. Katharina was only six years older than Blücher's eldest son, and at first seemed coy, but Blücher never experienced difficulty in persuading young ladies to shed their shyness, and only two months later the couple were married at Münster. The partnership proved happy, although not perhaps to the degree Blücher had felt with Karolina, his first love. His feelings appeared more paternal: some letters to Katharina began *Liebes Kind*, dear child; others started with a pet name, like *Malchen*, a contraction of Amalie, *Liebes Malchen*, or *Liebe Male*, dear wife of my heart. These letters also hinted that Blücher considered his young wife to be over-concerned with domestic matters: she bothered about trivial happenings and complained of loneliness or his lack of letters – although he tried to write about once a fortnight whilst on campaign; she made vexing inquiries about when he would return home. Katharina bore Blücher one child, a son born in 1808 who lived only sixteen weeks. From the start, even his wife's youthfulness failed to satisfy Blücher's incredible energy. Frequently he sat up the night at the card-table, and his riding continued to be exacting – a fall in summer 1795 gave him a limp for the rest of his life, and also in 1795 a gun accident in a hunting expedition sliced away a finger-tip.

Moreover, Blücher's usual troubles returned: peace bred boredom and belligerence. He began his peace-time career dealing with administrative duties at Emden on the North Sea coast, and the tedium soon started to tell on his temper. He lashed out at local civilians who had enriched themselves through war production. 'Emden gained millions in this war,' he complained. 'Inflated by their riches they looked upon the soldiers as the lowest of the low. . . . The rich people of Emden are real beasts.' He longed to return to regimental duties yet complained when a younger general received promotion to provincial Governor. 'We hussars get the dirtiest jobs in war, but do not get distinguished positions in peace.' He tried to move to Stolp, where his regiment was based, but instead received orders to travel to Belgrade. This brought a fresh outburst: 'After the end of a hard campaign it is not permitted for a true servant of the King to stay with his regiment . . .' The Belgrade appointment fell through, and in December 1795

Blücher received the command of troops guarding the frontier area in neutral Westphalia, with his headquarters in Münster.

He spent two years at Münster, struggling to find enough to slake his thirst for action, and struggling to find money on which to live. He continued to grouse about his peace-time duties, especially the paper-work: his laborious letters covered troop movements, recruitment figures, billeting, bills, provisions for men and horses, deserters and their capture, export restrictions on horses, grain, wood for palisades . . . In 1797 he found release from Münster, moving first to Minden where the situation was almost as unappealing. Blücher's area covered a strong Catholic community. He wrote in September: 'When will I be able to escape this land of saints, where people have more money than sense?' Next he went to Emmerich on the border of Holland, arriving in spring 1801; then back to Emden in the summer – when Blücher received promotion to Lieutenant-General – then to Lingen.

Blücher's behaviour during these years revealed the worst of him: peevish and self-centred. Yet in war and peace his character was always more complex than it appeared. In war, Blücher fought in the most ruthless and cruel way possible, yet suddenly displayed humanity to the enemy; he drove his men beyond the limits of endurance, yet never asked them to do more than he himself attempted. He berated his men if they displayed signs of weakness, and goaded them on with sarcasm, yet he also showed a sense of concern and tenderness for his troops, which remained extremely rare in those days. He would never, like Wellington, refer to his soldiers as 'the scum of the earth'. Despite his excessive demands, he always inspired devotion from his 'children' and he felt tremendous affection in return. He would rage at his men for not attacking the enemy with a vigour similar to his own – and the cavalry, his own calling, received his harshest criticism – yet he wept as he rode amongst the dead and wounded after the battle. And even now, in peace-time, his selfish dissatisfaction with his lot suddenly dropped for a moment, as he involved himself with the well-being of his men and their wives and children.

In November 1801, whilst at Lingen, he complained bitterly about the hardships which army families had to undergo. 'It cannot be expected of a young man who has courted and married a young woman to come back to her when she is old. Nine years have passed since the regiment left home . . .' Marriages should therefore be allowed, and the families should be provided for. 'Where should these helpless people go? The commissariat refuses to give them financial help . . . Unless there are some provisions made, there will be many losses of fathers, mothers and children.'(15) Blücher demanded, without success, that the commissariat help with money and better transport for the families.

Summer 1802 brought fresh career opportunities. While Blücher had been playing his unsatisfying peace-time roles, Napoleon Bonaparte cemented his power through his brilliant victory over the Austrians at Marengo in June 1800, and at Hohenlinden in December the same year. On 9th February 1801, the Treaty of Luneville reaffirmed the terms of Campo Formio, and the Treaty of Amiens on 27th March 1802, brought general peace between France and England for the first time in a decade. Military activity died down. Prussia confiscated areas along the Elbe and Rhine, as agreed upon with the French, and amongst these newly acquired districts lay Münster. Blücher received orders to march into the region and occupy it with 3,000 troops; he did so on 3rd August 1802.

He had a difficult task. The population of this bishopric had been robbed of their independence, and the possibility existed of civil war. To begin with Blücher reacted with a firm hand. At the same time he displayed fairness, keeping his troops under tight control, and by September the situation had quietened. Now the way lay open for diplomacy, and on 9th September Freiherr Heinrich von Stein received instructions to partner Blücher as civilian administrator. Prussia's most able statesman therefore combined with Prussia's most distinguished soldier of the Napoleonic period, and the two men became friends. Stein, born near Coblenz in 1757 – the year Blücher joined the Swedish army – would become famous for his ideas for a Germanic nation. Small, unassuming, yet outspoken when he felt it necessary, Stein always seemed solid and utterly dependable, and he proved himself an excellent civil-servant. He was also intensely patriotic, and he warmed to a similar emotion in Blücher. Both would be regarded with increasing suspicion by Napoleon, and as Scharnhorst later wrote: 'I only know two persons who are entirely without fear of man, Minister Stein and General Blücher.'

The two men shared Münster's Royal Palace, and while Stein

attempted to put into practice administrative ideas which later served as a constitutional model for Prussia and Germany, Blücher worked to give the requisite backing of law and order. Blücher's methods won wide approval; within six months the local ecclesiastical authorities successfully petitioned Frederick William to appoint Blücher as governor, on the grounds of his knowledge of local affairs, his honesty, and his ability to keep the peace between soldiers and civilians. Blücher became leader of the Masonic lodge at Münster, immersed himself in his work, and seemed to have ended his over-indulgence in drinking and gambling.

Yet Blücher remained a soldier. He now commanded the forces in Westphalia, East Friedland and Prussian Cleves. Moreover, his position near the German border provided a vantage point from which to observe events elsewhere in Europe, and these increasingly filled him with alarm. The French seemed to be progressing unchecked. As early as 1795 Blücher expressed his concern, but was 'most astonished' to hear 'it meant nothing' to the Berlin politicians. Affairs suddenly deteriorated in 1803. On 16th May hostilities resumed between Britain and France, and French troops ventured over the demarcation line to seize the British possession of Hanover. Blücher rushed to Berlin, only to find the Prussian monarch intended to take no action. 'All the misfortunes of Germany,' wrote Blücher later, 'and of the Prussian monarchy, are traceable to this event.' Gratian Heinrich von Haugwitz, Foreign Minister and President of the Cabinet, declared the official policy: 'The King is determined once for all to show to all Europe in the most open manner that he will positively have no war unless he is himself directly attacked.'(16)

Yet occupation of Hanover allowed the presence of Napoleon's forces between the Prussian territories of Brandenburg and Westphalia, presenting Blücher with a potential enemy to his rear. Frederick William remained silent despite the insult thrown by France at Prussia in 1804 when Sir George Rumbold, English *chargé*, was abducted by French troops. 'Several persons vote in favour of war,' wrote Frederick William to Haugwitz, '*but I do not. I think there are means of settling this matter without proceeding to such extremities.*'(17) Frederick William continued to devote more time to ceremonial military affairs than to war training. 'I don't understand why the most beautiful troops shouldn't also be the best,' he maintained. Blücher, attending manoeuvres at

Potsdam in autumn 1804, complained to the King about the state of his hussars – his 'step-children' – but received no satisfaction and remained isolated at Münster. 'It is unbearable not to have my regiment with me,' he wrote in December 1803. 'If I have to serve the King any longer he will have to give me a Governorship near my regiment. . . . Otherwise I will return to the plough. Country life has more attraction for me now than service.'(18)

In March 1804 Bonaparte ordered the arrest of the young Duke of Enghein, *émigré* prince of the French royal Bourbon-Condé line, who was living quietly in German Baden. French cavalry moved into Austrian territory to effect the arrest, and Enghein was dragged to Vincennes and executed as a British agent. 'It is beginning to look very warlike,' wrote Blücher. Frederick William refused to alter his position, despite pressure from Czar Alexander of Russia and the Austrian Emperor. Blücher had established contact with French officers at Hanover, including Jean Baptiste Bernadotte. Conversations with these officers and the evidence of events elsewhere convinced Blücher that Prussia would soon be involved in conflict, whether Frederick William sought such participation or not. Finally it seemed as if even Frederick William must take action. In early October 1805, French troops marched through the Ansbach region of Prussia on their way from Hanover to the Danube, constituting a direct challenge to Prussian sovereignty. Frederick William brought Haugwitz from newly-begun retirement and despatched him with a threat for Napoleon: if the French Emperor refused a treaty with Prussia similar to the document signed by France and Austria at Luneville in 1801, Prussia would enter the British-Austrian-Russian-Swedish coalition against him. At the same time – at last – Frederick William mobilized his army.

Blücher's regiment rode into Münster in mid-October. Impatiently he awaited orders to advance. 'For four weeks I have spent almost all the time with one foot in the stirrup,' he wrote. 'The French should be told that in the north there are still some Germans who can tame them.'(19) Instructions eventually arrived to deploy towards the Ems. But Frederick William had delayed too long. Napoleon seized the initiative against the Austrians in Southern Germany, slashing enemy communications and forcing General Karl Leiberich von Mack to capitulate at Ulm on 20th October. Russian forces suffered crushing defeat on the field of Austerlitz on 2nd December. Two days later Emperor Francis of

Austria agreed to an unconditional surrender, and Czar Alexander's shattered forces retreated to Russia. The coalition had collapsed. Prussian forces remained idle, except for brief bloody clashes between French detachments and Blücher's hussars at Essen.

Despite the general gloom Blücher seemed happier than at any time since 1794. He had rejoined his regiment. Christmas passed in headquarters at Bayreuth, re-living old battles, looking forward to fresh fights. But prospects for the latter dwindled. Haugwitz signed a humiliating Franco-Prussian alliance at Schönbrunn in December, allowing Napoleon to make sweeping territorial changes in southern Germany; Prussia would receive Hanover, but should she attempt to seize this former British territory, England would inevitably open hostilities against her – exactly what Napoleon wished. News of the proposed treaty was received with horror in Berlin, and politicians refused to ratify the document until alterations were made. Haugwitz returned to Napoleon. But meanwhile Frederick William unwisely demobilized his army, and in mid-February 1806, Blücher returned disappointed to Münster. Daily his frustration grew, and the situation worsened still further. Napoleon refused to discuss matters with Haugwitz, and instead increased his demands. Prussia stood without allies and with her army placed again on a peace-time footing, partly for financial reasons. Neither Haugwitz nor the Berlin politicians could offer any resistance. The Treaty of Paris was signed on 15th February, comprising all Napoleon's previous demands, and the document was ratified in Berlin on 3rd March.

Bonaparte proceeded to treat his latest ally with contempt. He hinted to British negotiators in Paris that he would hand Hanover back. Lord Yarmouth allowed this to be leaked to the Prussians. Napoleon also attempted to strengthen his position with Russia, and began talks with the Czar; at the same time he carved up the Austrian Empire by his proposals for a Rhenish Confederation announced on 12th July. In spring Blücher sent forces to Essen, part of his command area. Frederick William ordered these to be withdrawn after Napoleon had sent angry demands for their removal. At the same time increasing rumours reached Blücher of a possible French offensive over the Rhine; he reported to Frederick William that French troops were being reinforced on the Wesel and fortresses were in a state of alert. Westphalia seemed the immediate French target. Blücher's reaction to the humiliation and to the French encroachments led to explosive letters and petitions to Berlin. He made no secret of his opinions, which French agents duly reported back to Napoleon, and unlike many Prussian regiments those under Blücher's command had been well maintained.

We have still got our full strength [Blucher wrote to von Kleist, the King's Adjutant, on 23rd July]. It would be a mistake to think we couldn't stand up to these windbags. Our army is good and full of good heart, and even if some of our lot are dimwits, these could also be found under Frederick the Great. . . . If the war does not start now, in a few years' time it will be impossible for us to measure up to this colossus. I would be happy if it could be me to start the dance.(20)

Two days later he presented a vigorous and influential petition to Frederick William.

France has no honest intentions to anyone [declared Blücher] least of all to Your Majesty, who forms the sole remaining obstacle to her policy of conquest and oppression of Germany. . . . Even if France sometimes makes sweet talk, all her actions against Your Majesty prove the opposite. The invasion of Hanover, the forced march through Ansbach, and the thieving occupation of Essen and Werden just a short time ago, prove to Your Majesty the truth of what I have been saying, which is also revealed by the arrogant tone with which the French ruler addresses you. All faithful subjects of Your Majesty, all true Prussians, and especially the army, have felt and still feel the indignity of these French proceedings; all wish soon, very soon, to avenge with blood the nation's injured honour. [His emotional appeal concluded:] Your Majesty, lead us to honour and victory. Listen Your Majesty only to advice and ideas of tested and strong Generals. . . . Take note Your Majesty, to the thirst for fame and honour . . . this burning wish to live and die.(21)

With this petition went further alarming reports from Blücher's headquarters. His scouts informed him on 25th July that 7,000 French reinforcements had reached Wesel, and a pontoon bridge was to be thrown across the Rhine at this point; 40,000 French were believed camped at Dorsten, twenty-five kilometres further east. On 28th July Blücher told Berlin: 'I am now threatened on all sides.' Forty-eight hours later he reported: 'Six thousand men have moved into Wesel. More are expected.'(22)

At last Frederick William ordered full Prussian mobilization. An ultimatum was presented to Napoleon demanding the withdrawal of French troops from Prussia's frontiers. All officers were ordered to rejoin their regiments. Frederick William prepared to go to war. His manner of doing so was the most disastrous decision of his reign and perhaps of Prussia's entire turbulent history.

CHAPTER
4

Auerstedt Agony

BLÜCHER'S PETITION helped persuade the reluctant monarch to wage war, yet Frederick William neglected an essential element in his General's advice. Prussian forces were mobilized and Napoleon was therefore warned of Prussia's intention – but Frederick William hesitated to attack even though Blücher had written: 'From hour to hour the French Emperor strengthens his prestige, his influence, his usurped power, improves the organization of his army, procures more tributary kings and princes, by means of oppression extorts new resources.'(1) Yet Prussian forces remained on the defensive: Frederick William ordered Blücher not to advance and declared: 'I do not yet believe that there is any intention on the part of the French to undertake hostilities against us.'(2) Blücher, whose area might be the first to be hit if the French advanced, replied he would avoid provoking the enemy but 'if the French attacked we will treat them accordingly. . . . I will remove all restraints.'(3)

Privately, he expressed his concern to Rüchel: Napoleon was being given far too much time to seize the initiative and he cursed those in Berlin who fed Frederick William's natural caution. His orders 'fill my soul with sorrow', and he added: 'God, how far have we come! But still, all is not lost, because we will most probably see the King in our midst. He will then daily, hourly, hear other opinions than those of the wretched defaulters [in Berlin].'(4) Blücher sought to subdue his restless soldiers and to maintain order in Münster, where inns were closed early to restrict rumour-mongering. He communicated with others who also believed delay to be disastrous; among them was young Prince

Louis Ferdinand, cousin of the King. The two men were similar – according to Clausewitz, Louis Ferdinand 'loved danger as he loved life,' and Stein nagged the Prince for his unruly behaviour: 'What makes you, Sir, disregard so many other moral considerations, offend against so many other principles.'(5) Now the young hot-blood joined with the equally volatile Blücher in attempting to precipitate war with France. But not until late September did the Prussian armies begin to manoeuvre for battle. The French were ready. On 5th September Napoleon had written to General Alexander Berthier, commander of the Grand Army: 'Send officers of the engineers to make good reconnaissance at all risks on the outlets of the roads from Hamburg to Berlin.'

Prussia suffered other disadvantages. The army in general had continued to deteriorate. August Gneisenau, later Blücher's chief of staff, declared: 'In times of peace we have neglected much, occupied ourselves with frivolities, flattered the people's love of shows and neglected war.' Another of Blücher's future chiefs of staff, Scharnhorst, advised his son against soldiering. 'As to the Prussian army . . . it will not, it cannot, in the condition in which it is, or into which it will come, do anything great or decisive.'(6) Manoeuvre periods had been progressively reduced; the Prussians still relied upon rigid lines of infantry, rather than flexible formation, and the army suffered from an inward-looking attitude. Attempts had been made to introduce a national militia to fight in conjunction with professional soldiers, which would have broadened the military base. Blücher, in a paper dated 1805, entitled 'Thoughts on the forming of a Prussian National Army' advocated conscription, reduction of years of service, wage increases and better treatment of soldiers. Such suggestions had come to nothing. In 1806 almost half the Prussian army comprised foreign mercenaries, lacking patriotic motives for fighting. Governmental departments remained unconvinced of the need for improvements, and these military and governmental establishments were themselves ill organized, with five main army agencies competing for power. Lower down, too many of the most senior commanders were old, inefficient and in rivalry with each other.

Deficiencies were revealed immediately the Prussian forces began to march. Colonel von Yorck, Blücher's future corps commander, controlled the *Jäger* light infantrymen which were supposedly the most mobile of the Prussian foot-soldiers, yet even

Yorck carted with him trunks, crates, baskets and a bedstead. Blücher, always appreciative of maximum mobility, had sent a memorandum to the King seeking a reduction of the army's baggage train: the memorandum was merely shelved. Instead the Prussian forces lumbered slowly towards Napoleon's experienced army. The Prussians would be outnumbered. The whole available force had still to be called to arms, and regiments were held back in Silesia and Poland, giving a total of about 110,000 rather than the 150,000 which might have been available. Napoleon advanced through Saxony with 160,000.(7) Prussian forces wandered aimlessly. 'The movements of the Prussians continue to be extraordinary,' wrote Napoleon to Berthier at Munich. 'They want to be taught a lesson.' Gradually both sides crept closer.

On 13th September Prussian troops entered Saxony and Napoleon considered this a declaration of war. The Grand Army began to march forward from Munich and by 3rd October the French corps lay at Königshofen, Kronach and Würzburg. The Prussians lay between the enemy and Berlin, divided into three main field corps. The first, about 20,000 strong, was commanded by the Duke of Brunswick; the second, under Frederick Louis, Prince of Hohenlohe, totalled about 60,000; and the third, about 30,000, was led by Rüchel. During September Blücher had moved south reaching Kassel on 5th October, under orders to command Rüchel's rearguard, and he revealed his usual campaign cheerfulness on 9th October: 'Our army is marching on the left to thrash the French.' But Blücher's aggressive optimism lacked foundation. Scharnhorst, now Brunswick's chief of staff, expressed a more suitable opinion on the 7th: 'What we ought to do I know right well. What we *shall* do God only knows.'(8)

Not until 25th September had the Prussian commanders held their first, indecisive, war council, at which Christian von Massenbach, Hohenlohe's chief of staff, proved especially obstructive. At the beginning of October the Prussians shuffled to the north and north-east of the hilly, heavily wooded countryside around the Thüringian Wald; on 3rd October Hohenlohe's forces deployed in the Merseburg, Freiburg and Weissenfels triangle, while the main army under Brunswick lay between Eisenbach and Erfurt, with Rüchel situated near Mühlhausen to Brunswick's north. Blücher was positioned further north below Göttingen. A smaller force under General von Tauentzien faced the French near Hof.

This splintered deployment reflected the lack of unity at the high command, where arguments continued over the most basic question of all: whether to fight an offensive or defensive campaign. Brunswick advocated the former at a council meeting on the 4th, and proposed a stab south. Hohenlohe and Massenbach violently disagreed, proposing a defensive movement eastwards over the Saale. The Prussians remained without clear-cut plans during the next vital days. Napoleon seized the initiative. He crossed the frontier into Saxony on the 8th, and within twenty-four hours Bernadotte's advance troops clashed with Tauentzien's division and drove it back. To support Tauentzien, Hohenlohe ordered a general advance across the Saale, then cancelled it; the French continued to surge forward. Next day, 10th October, events continued to go wrong for the Prussians, and the latest upset would almost immediately affect Blücher.

French skirmishers engaged Prussian troops manning outposts near Hohenlohe's advance guard at Rudolstadt, commanded by Prince Louis Ferdinand. This fiery young Prince, so similar in temperament to Blücher, had been ordered not to tangle with the enemy until the arrival of the main force. But like Blücher on some occasions he rushed into attack. 'The ardent character of Prince Louis,' commented a contemporary, 'for want of a proper channel, had taken an unhappy course. And the bottle became one of his favourite enjoyments. In this he appears to have indulged himself to such an extent that his senses began to suffer.'(9) Prince Louis Ferdinand threw his forces against the enemy, only to find himself cut off and outnumbered. The Prince was hacked down, stripped and his bloody uniform carried away in triumph; most of his men suffered a similar fate and the shocked survivors staggered back to spread panic and consternation amongst Hohenlohe's inexperienced regiments. Hohenlohe fell back to Kahla and attempted to bolster his shattered vanguard against the advancing French. Selected for this difficult and dangerous task was Blücher, who immediately rushed south with reinforcements, reaching the area south of Blankenhain during 11th October. Frederick William and Bruns-wick decided to collect the whole army together at Weimar, fearing their communications would be disrupted; Hohenlohe fell back still further to Jena. But Napoleon hurried his forward regiments in an outflanking movement towards Naumburg, between the army and Berlin.

Events dictated action for the Prussians, rather than the high command being able to follow an overall plan. These events now led to another change of role for Blücher. Frederick William hastily summoned a panicky war council on 13th October; this resulted in the most disastrous decision of all – retreat back to the Elbe. The route would be based on Auerstedt, Freiberg and Merseburg. A messenger reached Blücher, still acting as Hohenlohe's vanguard, during the afternoon of the 13th: Blücher must

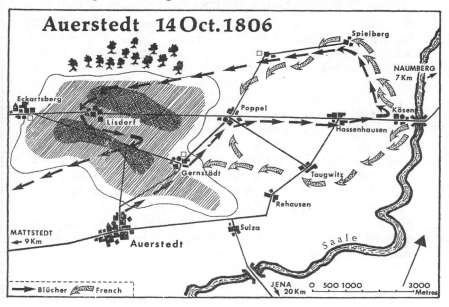

Auerstedt 14 Oct. 1806

Spielberg

NAUMBERG
7 Km

Eckartsberg

Poppel

Kösen

Lisdorf

Hassenhausen

Gernstädt

Taugwitz

Rehausen

MATTSTEDT
← 9 Km

Sulza

Auerstedt

S a a l e

JENA
↓ 20 Km

O   500 1000   3000
|‾‾‾‾‾‾‾‾‾‾‾‾‾‾| Metres

→ Blücher   French

hurry to Auerstedt to receive fresh orders from the King at Brunswick's headquarters. Blücher immediately headed towards the main army. Roads became increasingly clogged with carts, infantry and frightened camp followers; Blücher forced his way onwards, but darkness fell before he reached Auerstedt. All the village streets were jammed with artillery and baggage, men ran here and there in apparent confusion, drums were beating and men shouting. The King had gone to bed. Blücher found sleeping space for himself in a barn. But he learnt from other senior officers of the decision to retreat to the Elbe and the appalling confusion around Auerstedt indicated this movement had already begun. Blücher's force would form the advance guard for the main army.

His regiments would have to move up at maximum speed, overtake Brunswick's retreating army and take the lead again. Blücher hurried an officer back with orders for his regiments 'to try their damnest to get past the marching columns'.

Final, fatal, steps were being taken for battle. While Brunswick's main army retreated through Auerstedt, Hohenlohe attempted to provide a flank further south. He had been ordered by the King to avoid any general engagement with the enemy which might snarl up the overall retreat to the Elbe; by the evening of the 13th, Hohenlohe's army lay amongst the villages north of the forest of Jena, fifteen kilometres east of Weimar. With Hohenlohe was Rüchel's force. Enemy movements were reported in the area, but Hohenlohe believed that the main French force was hurrying along the road to Dresden, away to the east. He neglected to move forward during the night of the 13th to occupy in strength the Landgrafenberg, a plateau overlooking Jena. Yet Napoleon was aware of his enemy's intentions. 'At last the veil is torn,' he wrote to Marshal Joachim Murat. 'The enemy begins to retreat.' He planned to lead his main army northwards over the Saale in the Jena region, while further to the north-east the 1st and 3rd Corps under Louis Nicolas Davout would cross the Saale in the Auerstedt area, between Kösen and Naumberg, strengthened by most of the French cavalry. Napoleon only erred on one point: he believed the Prussian force at Jena to comprise Brunswick's main army, not Hohenlohe's flanking force.

Blücher emerged from his barn at Auerstedt long before light on 14th October. A chilly mist spread over the surrounding countryside, and moisture dripped from the buildings like rain; steam from the horses rose in a fog into the cold dawn air; muskets stacked by the infantry bivouacs were rimy and clammy to the touch. Blücher anxiously waited for the first of his twenty-eight hussar and dragoon squadrons to arrive at Auerstedt, but messengers brought gloomy news. These squadrons had reached a position south of the village at 2 a.m. but they then found themselves cut off by the chaos around the houses. Blücher also heard that the King had already ridden out from Auerstedt along the retreat route. Blücher galloped after and found the monarch soon after dawn, only to receive further bad news. French cavalry were believed to have crossed the Saale at Kösen. 'They have to be pushed back,' declared the King. Blücher hurried further forward along the crowded road, found Brunswick, and learnt that even more French units were on the Prussian bank.

Brunswick ordered him to take cavalrymen from Schmettau's division, and Blücher advanced at a canter with a cuirassier squadron and four squadrons of dragoons. All depended on this slim force: behind Blücher the bulk of the main Prussian army lay blocked and bewildered on the road back to Auerstedt. Blücher had to weaken his strength still further at Poppel, where he left two dragoons squadrons guarding a bridge over a small stream. On he went, to meet Scharnhorst, Brunswick's chief of staff, outside the village of Hassenhausen about three kilometres from Kösen. Scharnhorst was unable to provide firm information: the mist still swirled thick, cloaking enemy movement, but a thin line of Prussian infantry scouts had already clashed with Davout's leading units. Unknown to Blücher and Scharnhorst, by 8 a.m. Davout's three divisions were deploying on the plain before Hassenhausen and more French were bustling across the Saale. Blücher crept forward in the murk.

'I myself advanced with about 20 men to examine the enemy's position,' he wrote later. 'Almost immediately heavy artillery fire hit my left flank.' But Blücher pressed on, peering ahead as guns seared the mist with yellow flame and grape-shot raked his handful of cavalrymen. 'I now noticed a black line on my left, which in the fog I took for a hedge. When I tried to find a way through to get to the enemy, and had got to within 50 paces from the hedge, I found it to be a whole line of infantry.' Blücher's cavalrymen jerked back their mounts and disappeared into the mist again, musket balls humming about them; the Prussian general despatched urgent pleas for reinforcements. An uneasy silence fell. The fog still lay heavy, and whilst waiting for help Blücher felt his way round the enemy's right flank to place himself in an excellent position for a sudden, decisive attack.

But the fog brought confusion to the Prussian high command; arguments over the next step caused delay, during which Blücher remained isolated despite his repeated requests for reinforcements.

I held the enemy cavalry so much in check that they dare not advance from behind their infantry. As soon as I got help my plan was to circle to the left of the enemy battery which annoyed me very much, and take it. This was possible because the battery was no longer covered by cavalry. Then I wanted to attack the enemy infantry at the back and flank with most of my cavalry.

Success could have altered the entire result of the day's battle; in Blücher's words: 'A good outcome of this action was in no doubt.'(10)

But as the mist lifted to reveal Davout's leading divisions, too few reinforcements reached Blücher: three squadrons when he had sought at least ten, and no sign could be seen of Schmettau's infantry and artillery intended to back Blücher's cavalry assault. Yet he still stuck to his plan. 'The advantages which I could see were too good to miss. I gave the squadrons the signal to attack.' He led his cavalry forward, shouting his men on; the squadrons smashed into the first French infantry line and broke through despite murderous grape-shot. The enemy proved too numerous; Blücher withdrew, re-formed, and charged again. Three times he battered forward; three times the Prussians were repulsed. Blücher's adjutants lay injured, their horses slaughtered, and dead Prussian cavalrymen sprawled before the French positions, while wounded hussars and horses struggled to clamber to their feet again. Still no fresh reinforcements reached Blücher; the enemy on the other hand ran into tight squares, perfect defence against mounted attacks, and Blücher lacked artillery to pound these formations.

His improvised force lacked the loyalty of his own hussars, and grew increasingly hesitant to advance into the deadly cross-fire again. Then, as Blücher tried to rally them for a fourth desperate charge, grape-shot struck his squadrons from the rear – the French had dragged round a gun to a nearby hill. 'I had nothing but bad luck,' complained Blücher afterwards. Worse followed. His horse suddenly reared, screeched and fell, horribly wounded by grape-shot. Blücher flung himself clear, climbed to his feet – and saw his surviving cavalrymen fleeing for safety. He grabbed a riderless horse and galloped back to the village of Spielberg, attempting to halt his ashen-faced men. 'I snatched the standard and stood with it on the bridge in the village facing the fleeing men. But it was useless. They streamed past me right and left . . .' Blücher chased his panicked cavalry as far as a wood near Eckartsberg and rounded them up with violent oaths and curses. Nearby stood the King, bewildered by the chaos of battle and as inexperienced as most of his men; Blücher reported 'with bleeding heart' that 'the cavalry has not done its duty'. He offered to make another attempt, to which the confused, hesitant Frederick William merely replied that Blücher must do what he thought best.

But another charge would have been suicidal. The time was now about 9 a.m.; Davout's second division under Friant had come up to join the first under Gudin, and both concentrated around Hassenhausen and Spielberg. Schmettau's men at last received the order to attack Hassenhausen but the French threw them back. Brunswick summoned reinforcements but these, under Count von Wartensleben, were delayed by baggage waggons strewn across the road. One disaster followed another. Scharnhorst and Brunswick had failed to establish a close working relationship, essential between chief of staff and commander, and the two men avoided one another. Now Brunswick suddenly fell screaming, shot through both eyes. His blood-spattered body was carried off; he died on 10th November. At this critical moment Scharnhorst was fighting at another part of the field, and Frederick William neither named a successor nor took direct command himself: the Prussians remained virtually leaderless and confusion intensified. By noon Morand's division began to strike south of Hassenhausen towards Rehausen: the French threatened to encircle Prussian lines on the main road around Taugwitz and Poppel.

Blücher had been frantically trying to scrape together cavalry squadrons in the hills between Lisdorf and Poppel, and he now attempted to beat off Morand's encircling movement from the south. His squadrons were scared, disorganized and improvised, but Blücher's attack could still have played a decisive part – if he had been supported. Blücher described this operation.

> The French cavalry advanced and formed below the hills where our reserves stood, towards the left wing. They were in range of our guns, but these didn't fire. I therefore gave the order to fire. . . . The French cavalry behaved very gallantly: they moved from one place to another, and every time they moved men and horses were left lying where they had stood, but they gave no ground.

Then came another infuriating disappointment for Blücher. 'At the moment I wanted to attack . . . Lieutenant von Unruh brought a command from the King to do nothing else – "because it would not help".'(11)

Blücher had to watch helpless as Morand's regiments broke through unchecked and curved towards Poppel; Friant's regiments continued their encirclement from the other flank. The centre of the fighting shifted to Poppel. French forces swarmed through the orchards and over the walls to take the village; Prussian units fought their way in again, only to be thrown back once more. Enemy wings continued to thrust through the fields and lanes on either side of the main road. Lisdorf fell to Friant's Frenchmen; Gudin's main force, striking direct along the highway, advanced over Prussian dead at Taugwitz. Prussian reserves under General Frederick von Kalkreuth stood at the next defensive point, Gernstädt, and Blücher joined with Kalkreuth in pleading with the King for a counter-attack. Frederick William refused. He believed Hohenlohe's and Rüchel's flanking forces at Jena to be still intact; he now decided to pull out and join them.

Retreat began at about five o'clock on this wet autumnal afternoon. 'I rode back in a foul temper,' remembered Blücher. Moreover, by heading south-west to link with Hohenlohe, Frederick William moved further from Berlin – and closer to Napoleon. As Frederick William's defeated forces marched back to Mattstedt *en route* for Jena, the soldiers saw camp fires twinkling on the dark skyline. Spirits surged: the fires were believed to indicate Hohenlohe's lines. But men began to emerge from the darkness, bleeding, staggering with exhaustion and shock, stinking of powder and filth. They brought terrible news. Those camp fires belonged to the French. Hohenlohe's army had ceased to exist as a coherent fighting force. Napoleon had won a decisive victory at Jena while Davout engaged the main Prussian army at Auerstedt. Sweeping from the Landgrafenberg plateau, Napoleon's forces had made use of the fog to batter back the unprepared Prussian defences. Skirmishers riddled the rigid Prussian lines; more *tirailleurs* and artillery bombardments shattered Rüchel's delayed attempt to provide support, and by four o'clock the battle was over. On this day, 14th October 1806, each of Prussia's three main armies – under Brunswick, Hohenlohe and Rüchel – had been dispersed. Total Prussian losses in killed and wounded reached about 20,000, with over 15,000 more taken prisoner. Twenty generals had been lost. The French suffered 11,000 killed and wounded, the majority at Auerstedt.

Full hell and humiliation had still far to run for the Prussians.

News of the disasters spread like fire. 'It is a strange, terrible idea to abandon oneself, helpless and unresisting, to a foreign power,' wrote Henry Steffens, then a professor at nearby Halle. 'The subjugation of the country, the ruin of all that was sacred and dear to us, filled us with horrible imaginations.'(12) Retreat continued throughout the night of the 14th and threatened to degenerate into headlong rout as the decimated units blundered into one another on the pitch-black roads. First the Prussians fled towards Weimar. 'Those were horrors!' wrote Gneisenau. 'Rather death a thousand times than live through it again. . . . Never did an army sink into such disruption.'(13) Blücher, accompanied only by one junior officer, rode into a French-held village by mistake: the other officer was seized, but Blücher hacked his way to safety. Then, amidst the milling men further along the road to Weimar, he managed to reach the bedraggled, benumbed King of Prussia.

'We're in a bad position,' moaned Frederick William to Blücher. 'It may be we will have to fight our way through.'

'We often saw fires which we recognized as enemy bivouacs,' wrote Blücher, 'which we tried to slip past. . . . I sometimes rode in front, and sometimes with the King. . . . The whole journey was indescribably difficult because we constantly had to stop to find out where and amongst what troops we were.' Retreat continued northwards on the 15th; at dawn next day Blücher forded the Unstrut near Sömmerda. Frederick William hurried north-west for Sondershausen, taking with him fifty hussars hand-picked by Blücher – who warned this bodyguard: 'Whichever of you retreats first from a clash, I will cut to pieces with my own hands.'

Blücher stayed twenty-four hours in Sömmerda to provide a rearguard; on the same day, 16th October, the French Emperor entered Halle, the first Prussian town he had taken. He intended to stay three days in Halle, leaving the direction of the pursuit to Murat, Soult, Ney and Bernadotte. He would leave for Berlin on the 19th, and meanwhile issued his 22nd bulletin: Prussian armies had vanished like autumn mist before the rising sun, he declared. Napoleon's boast seemed correct. Frederick William scuttled for sanctuary in the north-west, abdicating all vestige of control over his men. Defence was offered only by those troops who rallied to the firm leadership of a few remaining generals. And chief amongst the latter was Blücher.

Blücher left Sömmerda at daybreak on the 17th with the fragile

Prussian rearguard. By noon he reached Greussen, sixteen kilometres to the north, where he joined forces with Kalkreuth. French regiments were filing down the hills behind him. Back fled the Prussians to Sondershausen, twenty kilometres further up the road, reached by Blücher in the early hours of the 18th. After two hours of rest he followed the remainder of the retreating forces to Nordhausen and covered these twenty-three kilometres before noon. Late in the afternoon French mobile guns put down such a heavy bombardment that he made one of the most heartbreaking decisions for a cavalry commander: Blücher felt obliged to save his cavalry by withdrawing through the infantry, leaving the latter to their fate. Circumstances improved at Nordhausen, where Blücher found Scharnhorst, who had managed to extricate valuable artillery. The two men now entered a partnership as general and chief of staff, which would be resumed in 1813 and which was to become amongst the most famous in military history.

Gerhard von Scharnhorst, born near Hanover in 1755, appeared at first glance to be extremely dissimilar to Blücher. 'He seemed,' wrote his *protégé* Clausewitz, 'to the people of the outside world, and even to the intelligent part of it, a dull *savant* and pedant, while military men took him for an irresolute, unpractical, unsoldierly book writer.'(14) Sensitive and shy, Scharnhorst seemed more a scholar than soldier, a theorist rather than a practician. Educated, calm and unassuming – all these characteristics formed a complete contrast to Blücher. But Blücher found Scharnhorst had a confidence which matched his own – and he discovered that his chief of staff could always find solid evidence to back up his optimism, unlike the emotional General who played upon his hunches. Scharnhorst, like his successor Gneisenau, could prepare the detailed plans; Blücher, the brilliant leader of men, could carry out these plans.

From the start, this partnership would be forged by the terrifying fire of retreat. Blücher and Scharnhorst withdrew through the foothills of the Harz mountains, then northwards towards Blücher's native Mecklenburg. Day and night the retreat continued, constantly harried by the enemy, with minimum food and rest. On 24th October they slipped across the Elbe at Sandau, having travelled 260 kilometres in seven days and preserving intact their tiny force of half a grenadier battalion and 500 mounted men. On the same day Berlin fell to the French. But during the evening

Blücher and Scharnhorst established contact with Hohenlohe at Neustadt; Hohenlohe, with about 12,000 troops, ordered Blücher to command the rearguard and to remain at Neustadt to cover the withdrawal. For forty-eight hours Blücher fought off French probes, making a difficult overnight march for Ruppin on the 26th. His rearguard continued a non-stop retreat for a further thirty-six hours, towards Boitzenburg. Blücher's officers struggled to keep the cavalrymen awake in their saddles: the unco-ordinated movements of a sleeping rider tired the weary mount even more.

Hohenlohe was struck by fresh and final disaster, from which Blücher was spared through luck and his own aggressiveness. Hohenlohe by-passed Boitzenburg, believing it to be held by the French, and instead made for Prenzlau. He advised Blücher to make a similar detour, but Blücher preferred to press on. 'I told Scharnhorst: even if the enemy is already in Boitzenburg he can't have a whole army there.'(15) Within hours Hohenlohe had surrendered to encircling French units on the road between Prenzlau and Stettin. Blücher hurried westwards. His dwindling contingent became the sole remaining force capable of offering unified resistance; he himself suffered from stabbing headaches, throbbing limbs, inflamed eyes. He lacked officers; he daily risked being surrounded and annihilated, but he refused to admit defeat. He hoped 'to take the French from the Oder and to remove them from the heart of the Prussian monarchy, to gain time for our fortresses to be strengthened, and to let the rest of our Prussians join the Russian army'.(16) 'These damned fugitives hold back nearly half my army,' complained Napoleon.(17) Elsewhere Prussia's will to resist evaporated. One fortress after another fell more or less meekly to the French: Erfurt, Spandau, Küstrin, Stettin. 'It may still be possible under certain conditions to save the monarchy,' wrote Gneisenau, 'but the shame of the army annihilated through misfortunes due to its own fault can never be wiped away.'(18) Blücher remained the exception: all patriotic Prussian eyes were turned upon him as he struggled westwards with his force of 22,000, weakly armed, desperately short of ammunition, pursued by overwhelming numbers of French.

On the last day of October Blücher reached a position just beyond Strelitz. Next morning his rearguard, commanded by Yorck, held off determined attacks from Bernadotte's forward units while Blücher led his regiments down the road towards Schwerin. Yorck suffered a slight wound in the engagement and lost precious men, but the attack allowed vital time for Blücher to escape. Further French harassment took place during the next three days, and Bernadotte demanded Blücher's surrender. The Prussian General refused, and on 4th November ordered a movement north towards Gadesbusch and Lübeck. The latter, with its high walls and encircled by the river Tarve, offered a good defensive position, and such a plan seemed to offer the last, despairing hope. 'In this critical position,' explained Blücher, 'I decided to march towards Lübeck. . . . When the troops were safe from hunger and had rested a while they would be able to fight, even if the possibility of a victory remained remote.' He still hoped to 'put my fate to a decisive battle'.(19)

Only a man with Blücher's calibre of leadership could have kept his weary troops together. Their feet dragged over the chalky road; rain turned the road surface into thick paste, and this spread up the legs of the men, whitening them to their thighs. The hussars rode alongside, their horses also splattered white. Riders slouched in their saddles, their thighs raw, their hands split and bleeding as they held the reins. But late on 5th November Blücher's soldiers stumbled to Lübeck at last. They were denied the rest they so badly needed. Throughout the night of the 5th Blücher deployed units by torchlight; men slumped exhausted on the cobbles, only to be roused at dawn by attacks from French light cavalry. Firing increased during the morning and the Prussians found themselves outnumbered three men to one. After three hours of bitter hand-to-hand fighting at the city gates some Prussian officers ordered their men to retire, believing that Blücher intended to continue the retreat. French troops pushed into the city. This news reached Blücher at his headquarters; he ran downstairs, grabbed the first horse and hurried to the centre of the fighting, striking men – Prussians and French – from his path with the flat of his sword as he struggled to reach the breach. Scharnhorst and other officers were pinned down in a house and fell into captivity; Yorck suffered a serious shoulder-wound and his men started to flee as he collapsed on the cobbles.

'*Jägers!*' bellowed Blücher, 'would you leave your commander bleeding here?' Back came Yorck's men to drag him to temporary safety. But by 4 p.m. the French had entered Lübeck in full force.

Blücher battled his way from the city with 9,000 men and frantically tried to organize last-ditch defences.

Another night passed with skirmishing and sudden flurries of fighting, and increasing numbers of French massed in the surrounding fields. Even Blücher, red-eyed, unshaven, realized the end had come. 'All was for nothing, and I had to bow to my fate.' Bernadotte sent another demand for surrender, and this time Blücher agreed – with one proviso. He despatched his son Franz to the French with his draft of the capitulation terms. These began: 'As a capitulation has been offered me by the Prince of Ponte-Corvo (Bernadotte), and having accepted it for want of every kind of ammunition . . .' Blücher thus maintained that only shortage of ammunition persuaded him to admit defeat, and he insisted this reason should be publicly stated. Bernadotte refused. Blücher replied: 'By God, I'll capitulate on no other conditions whatever, let what will come of it.'(20) The French gave way. Later Blücher believed he should have continued to fight. But now, on the dreary afternoon of 7th November, with his uniform torn and filthy, his hands trembling with tiredness, Blücher mounted his horse and rode slowly to the French and to captivity.

*   *   *

'In his opinion courage produced a military reputation,' wrote Müffling of Blücher, 'and it seemed to him impossible that a brave man could lose such a reputation. He was never troubled by the slightest apprehension that a retreat or a lost battle could take away his own.'(21) Blücher's fame soared throughout Germany and Europe. As Scharnhorst wrote: 'On the whole no one mattered . . . but Blücher, myself and Colonel Yorck.'(22) Nevertheless Blücher bore permanent scars from the shock of autumn 1806; his natural aggression was now combined with a fierce hatred of the French, the violators of his country. Such a hatred had been absent in the 1790s when, despite his ruthlessness, the French were merely an enemy to be fought; now the French became an enemy to be exterminated. While others preached peace, he wanted war; his statements frequently referred to 'bloody revenge'. Scharnhorst wrote to his daughter, Julia: 'While Schmidt is sleeping by me in the carriage I have the miserable liberty of giving myself up entirely to the outbreak of grief. . . . Never have I seen a man more unhappy than the finest fellow I ever knew, General Blücher.'(23)

Prussia experienced the terror and disgrace of complete enemy subjugation. Many rich families fled their homes, or submitted to their conquerors; the poor, as always, suffered infinitely worse. Conscripts in the French army, less capable of fending for themselves than the veterans, plundered food, poultry, cattle and vegetables from the meagre peasant patches. They smashed open cupboards and shops, they ripped off doors and roof-thatch for firewood, and they burnt furniture and precious stocks of fodder. Armies slithered across the naked countryside leaving vast black trails of cindered houses and abandoned hamlets. Napoleon Bonaparte strutted in Berlin while Frederick William hid with his court in north-east Prussia, first at Königsberg then at Ortelsburg.

Blücher began his period as a French prisoner. Status of prisoner of war was usually not especially uncomfortable: a practical mutual arrangement existed for the exchange of captives, and whilst in captivity an officer normally spent his time on parole, with his quarters or lodgings provided for him. Blücher benefited from this chivalrous system. Within hours of his capitulation he had started proceedings for Scharnhorst to be exchanged with a French colonel, Gérard. Scharnhorst in turn later arranged for Yorck to be exchanged for a French staff officer. Blücher could expect an early release. But his mental anguish remained severe; he agreed with Gneisenau's comment that 'to the man of honour nothing is left but to envy those who fall in the field of battle'.(24) He travelled to Hamburg with Scharnhorst, who awaited confirmation of his exchange, and Blücher stayed at this city for four tedious months. The French allowed his wife and daughter-in-law to join him, but he was preoccupied with the news of continued fighting in East Prussia, where a strong Russian army under Count Lévin Bennigsen attempted to sustain pockets of Prussian military resistance. At the end of November Napoleon marched east with 80,000 men to thwart this threat. Napoleon also attempted to enlist Prussians in his army, under the command of the Prince of Isenburg. The Prince published a proclamation on 18th November, read by Blücher with complete revulsion: 'Hasten my bold warriors to march under the Glorious Banner of the Great Napoleon! Partake with him in Victory and Immortal Fame!'(25)

In his north-east corner of Prussia, Frederick William tried desperately to sort some order from the political and military imbroglio besetting the stub of his state. Haugwitz, hated for his pro-French tendencies, had retired to his estate in Silesia, suffering from gout; on the 29th November Blücher's former partner at Münster, Stein, was invited by the King to be Minister of State for the Interior. But Stein refused, believing the King's advisers opposed him and that Frederick William's offer lacked sincerity. His suspicions were apparently confirmed by the monarch's peeved reply to his refusal: 'You are to be regarded as a refractory, insolent, obstinate and disobedient official, who, proud of his genius and talents, far from regarding the good of the State, guided purely by caprice, acts from passion and from personal hatred and rancour.'(26)

Frederick William had still to prove himself a capable political ruler; similarly, his military leadership remained inadequate. On 1st December he issued a proclamation from Ortelsburg. 'His Majesty is far from attributing to his gallant army any share of these dreadful calamities and disappointments which have persecuted both himself and his country. . . .' After this sugary start came the bitter pill. 'But there are also others, and to their shame be it spoken, who have been guilty of most atrocious conduct . . . It is of so flagrant a nature that it cannot be passed over in silence, but must, as an example to others, be punished in the most severe and public manner.' Then followed a long list of names of these who would 'be broke' or 'dishonourably dismissed'.(27)

Blücher completed his official report to the King in November, written at Hamburg with Scharnhorst's help. 'With a sad heart,' began Blücher, 'I have to report to Your Majesty the loss, partly dead, partly taken prisoner, of the corps. It was my misfortune to have to command them in a situation where no other fate was possible.' He believed many generals and commanders failed to merit the King's approval, but Blücher championed the ordinary soldiers. 'They have shown themselves worthy of the name "Prussians", through their bravery and steadfastness in suffering all deprivations of food and rest.'(28) Blücher said his farewells to Scharnhorst in early December, and his chief of staff returned to the fight. But Blücher remained closely in touch with outside affairs. 'I am pretty well, in spite of all hardships, all misfortunes, all sorrows,' he wrote to a friend. 'I think the inactivity I live in has more impact on my health than the above mentioned. But nothing can alter my faith in the future and in my courage.'(29) The day after he wrote this letter, 15th December, he celebrated his sixty-fourth birthday; his physical strength had almost returned, the inflammation had receded from his eyes and his joints no longer ached. Blücher was fit for war again.

After desperate rearguard fighting at Pultusk on 26th December, Bennigsen evaded French attempts to corner him and Napoleon went into winter quarters, faced by the bitter cold and by the exhaustion of his own troops. French forces were over-extended. Blücher believed Prussia's military remnants should seize upon this opportunity, and despite his captivity and watching French agents, he plotted insurrection. At birthday celebrations for Queen Louise, the intensely patriotic wife of Frederick William, Blücher even publicly declared that victory was certain. At the same time he scolded an over-bold fellow conspirator, Eisenhart: 'Man, have you the devil in you? You'll be sent to France, and us with you, if you don't keep your mouth shut.'(30)

News deteriorated in the New Year, 1807. First came a spurt of optimism, when Bennigsen attacked in early January and forced the French to withdraw, and the Russians pursued the enemy into east Prussia. But Napoleon reacted with customary vigour; Bennigsen pulled back, this time pursued by Napoleon who caught up with him at Preussisch-Eylau on 8th February. Within Bennigsen's army was a Prussian corps ably led by Scharnhorst. The subsequent battle, fought in a blinding snow-storm, proved bloody but indecisive. Both sides retired once more to winter quarters, and Blücher's spirits ebbed. He played cards for increasingly high stakes; his drink consumption soared; he began to complain of vivid, disturbing and apparently nonsensical dreams. Then, on 16th March, Blücher received better news: he was now first on the list of senior officers to be exchanged. First came a summons from Napoleon himself. The Emperor wished to interview the Prussian general, and Blücher therefore began an eastwards journey to Napoleon's headquarters at Rosenberg. For the first time he experienced the extent of his fame. His coach was surrounded by cheering crowds wherever he stopped, and the French escort bustled him through Berlin to allow no time for demonstrations. Blücher reached Napoleon's quarters at Finkenstein Castle in late March; he then had to wait fourteen days before the historic meeting took place.

Napoleon, in his thirty-eighth year, had almost reached the height of his power: one more victory would make him virtual ruler of Western and Central Europe, with seventy million people under his control. Now, in spring 1807, his days were packed with both civilian and military decisions. His spring offensive against the Russians would begin on 10th June; he had begun tentative probes to lure Frederick William of Prussia into an alliance. Other topics crowded in; on 21st November he had issued a proclamation excluding all British trade from the Continent.

Napoleon had also recently found time to fall in love again, this time with the twenty-year-old Polish patriot Marie Walewska. 'I saw only you,' he wrote to the curly-haired Marie. 'I admired only you. I desire only you.' Napoleon's energy matched Blücher's, and the two men had other common characteristics. 'You should have seen our Emperor, my dear Mama,' wrote a French light infantryman after Jena, 'always in the thick of it, heartening his troops . . . Marshal Bessières and Prince Murat pointed out that he was exposing himself unduly, whereupon he turned to them calmly: "What do you take me for – a bishop?".'(31)

Blücher's staff officers suffered similar apprehension for his safety. Now Blücher and Napoleon met in one of the state rooms at Kirkenstein Castle. Bonaparte thrust out his hand and expressed his pleasure at meeting 'the bravest Prussian General'. Blücher's reply contained similar courtesy: it had always been his greatest wish, he said, to see 'the great Emperor'. The two men eyed each other. Blücher stood nearly three inches taller; Napoleon, despite his strength, gave the impression of delicacy, with his small almost feminine hands and fine-textured skin. Blücher looked bear-like, weather-beaten, with blotchy skin, tangled hair, and his hands were thick, his fingers stubby. Conversation proved difficult; Napoleon apologized for his feeble knowledge of German, and Blücher for his inadequate French. They used their respective smatterings of these two languages, and when they found themselves groping for words they injected Latin or Polish. The multilingual dialogue developed from platitudes to dabble in military matters. Both steered away from sensitive topics; Napoleon threw out one or two probes concerning the political situation, perhaps seeking Blücher's support for a separate Franco-Prussian treaty, but Blücher failed to respond. They parted in courteous fashion. They were next to meet on a spring day six years later on the blood-soaked fields near Lützen, where Blücher would lead a ferocious cavalry charge to come within yards of hacking down or capturing the French Emperor.(32)

*   *   *

'I hope soon to appear again on the stage,' wrote Blücher to Stein, 'and play my part well.' His exchange, with General Claude Perrin Victor, took place on 25th April. Blücher immediately hurried to Bartenstein where he was reunited with Scharnhorst and received an audience with the King. Frederick William met him with an embrace and the decoration of Knight of the Black Eagle, but Blücher's pleading for a post at the most likely area of fighting soon met with disappointment. He had hoped to command the Prussian corps in Bennigsen's army, and instead received orders on 6th May to take 5,000 men by sea to Swedish-Pomerania. His units would reinforce Swedish troops on the island of Rügen. Fate therefore brought him back to the army for which he had first fought, and to the area where he had first become a soldier exactly half a century before. 'Man proposes, God disposes!' he commented to Karl von Hardenberg.

Blücher reached Stralsund on 30th May and reported to Charles XIII of Sweden. He immediately plunged into energetic work to forge a fighting force from his inexperienced, uncoordinated units, gathering round him extremely valuable officers: Frederick von Bülow, responsible for the infantry, Karl von Borstell, in charge of the cavalry, and Major von Schill, a man soon to become famous for his spectacular defiance of Napoleon. Above all Blücher now came into contact with August Gneisenau, who from 29th April until the end of the war succeeded in defending Colberg, further along the coast, despite being outnumbered by 16,000 enemy troops under Mortier. Gneisenau's brilliant operations at this Baltic port brought him wide personal fame, and earned deep respect from Blücher, who planned to send a strong relief force.(33) But grim news arrived from further east. On 14th June the Russians were routed at Friedland. Königsberg was evacuated; on the 19th Napoleon occupied Tilsit, and the Russians sought a truce which Napoleon granted. Reports of this cease-fire reached Blücher in a letter at the beginning of July. 'I didn't believe it right away,' wrote Blücher to Hardenberg on the 5th, 'and sent it [the letter] to the King of Sweden with my remarks.

The King said: "I don't believe it either, and if it should be true the best way to deal with it is with weapons in hand." ' Blücher and the Swedish King agreed to start their offensive on 13th July at two o'clock in the morning. Moreover, Blücher's letter to Hardenberg contained excellent news. Britain had already agreed to pay Frederick William a subsidy of £1 million and to send forces to reinforce the 16,000 Swedes and Prussians under Blücher, and now Blücher declared: 'The English have finally arrived at Rügen and have about 10,000 men.' Blücher had one criticism: 'The damned British with their money make everything so expensive.' Blücher said he would strike over the Peene, link with Gneisenau's garrison at Colberg, and advance against Napoleon. 'I hope we will give Herr Napoleon a few sleepless nights.'(34)

Unknown to Blücher, so excited with his schemes, all was already lost. Twelve days before he wrote this enthusiastic letter to Hardenberg the French and Russian Emperors discussed peace terms on a swaying raft moored in the River Niemen. Frederick . William of Prussia awaited their decision, standing disconsolately on the river bank in the pouring rain. Schill brought the news to Blücher on 7th July, who refused to believe it. On the same day the peace treaty between France and Russia was formally concluded at Tilsit, effectively isolating Prussia. Frederick William sent urgent commands for Blücher to stop all hostile actions which might provoke the full weight of France's victorious army. For a moment Blücher was tempted to disobey the King and to lead his troops in a hopeless operation against the French. 'If I am well,' he wrote to a friend, 'and can agitate myself, they will all keep in step.'(35)

But Hardenberg sent further shattering information. On 9th July Frederick William – described by Napoleon as a 'booby' – also signed a treaty with the French Emperor at Tilsit. The document deprived Prussia of all her territory west of the Elbe, of the Polish provinces she had annexed in 1793, of the southern part of west Prussia acquired in 1772. Thus emasculated, she was obliged to agree to join in common cause with France and Russia, against England; those British troops so recently arrived at Rügen to help Blücher were now to be treated as enemies. On 12th July another convention stipulated that France would evacuate Prussia east of the Elbe, but only on payment of a large and unspecified indemnity. Prussia's downfall and France's triumph seemed complete.

'Your letters cost me hot tears!' wrote Blücher to Hardenberg. 'What will become of us now?' He condemned the peace to hell, yet added: 'My dear friend, I have to tell you I have not yet given up. . . . German bravery only sleeps; the awakening will be terrible!'(36) Blücher would need all his strength to succour this optimism in the next years of misery. His health, physical and especially mental, would hover on collapse through the strain; peace almost drove Blücher insane.

CHAPTER
5

Despair

IMMEDIATELY AFTER the Tilsit treaty Blücher moved his headquarters to Treptow, near the coast and twenty-eight kilometres
from Colberg, where his forces constituted a small Prussian island
surrounded by French occupation soldiers. His mental state had
already started to deteriorate, revealed in a wretched, nihilistic
letter to his friend Professor Spickmann in Münster.

> My heart sobs over the disaster which has fallen on the State and
> upon my master . . . Oh, if I could only once see the whole world
> in flames before I die! I would cherish this spectacle. . . . The world
> deserves nothing better than to be burned: all is so bad and most
> of the people are evil. Only the view from this ball of earth into a
> better hereafter can bring some comfort, and I only live in the hope
> of it. [Blücher's lament continued:] I can see days in front of me,
> when all will be destroyed. . . . Yes, Spickmann, we will see each
> other again, or all our ideas about the future are nothing but
> figments of our imagination. God forbid this should be so! Shall
> the only thought which still gives me pleasure be 'Nothing'?(1)

Others felt the same. At a court dinner in Memel, Queen Louise
of Prussia raged bitterly against Czar Alexander for his treacherous
conduct, then burst into tears and fled the room.(2) Carl von
Clausewitz, a prisoner of war since Auerstedt, wrote just before
he returned home from France: 'My life is a trackless existence. . . .
What can happen to me? A beautiful death, honourable wounds
. . . one of these must be mine.'(3) Humiliations multiplied daily.
Prussian governmental officials were obliged to swear to 'execute

all the orders of the French and neither to correspond nor to have any other intercourse with their enemies'. Attempts were made to stifle all opposition: the newspapers *Preussische Hausfreund* and *Freimüthige* were suppressed and replaced by the French-run *Telegraph*. The figure of Victory was ripped from the Brandenburg Gate and sent to Paris, and an ugly bare stake projecting from the plinth provided a constant reminder to Berliners of their lost glory. The indemnity to be paid to Napoleon for the removal of French troops steadily increased, from 73 million francs to 154 million, then, after 200 million had been handed over or seized, the French still presented a bill for 140,000 francs, and the French troops remained.

Blücher, named General-Governor of Pomerania in mid-August, engaged in bitter arguments over the deployment of the occupation troops in the Treptow area, and so violent did these disagreements become that Napoleon himself intervened, to support his commanders. Blücher complained about the behaviour of the French troops: 'Because the soldier does not get any provisions, he thinks he is entitled to demand and take what he needs.' Serious shortages led to starvation amongst the peasants; disease spread; cattle stood like skeletons in the bare fields.

Only one good could come from this deplorable situation. Now began an important period of Prussian army reform, undertaken primarily by Scharnhorst, Gneisenau, Count von Lottum, von Goetzen, Hermann von Boyen, Carl von Grolman, and Clausewitz. The instrument for reform was the Military Reorganization Commission, established by the King at Memel on 25th July, two weeks after the treaty of Tilsit. Areas covered by the Commission included universal conscription, the admission of the *bourgeoisie* to the officer corps, and the relaxation of the harsh disciplinary system. Blücher supported all three moves. He had long since abhorred the terrible discipline, which specified vicious floggings for minor offences and, for more serious misdemeanours, included forcing the culprit to run the gauntlet of 200 men armed with salted whips, his hands bound, his feet hobbled, a ball of lead in his mouth to prevent him biting off his tongue in his agony. As a young regimental officer, Blücher had forbidden the use of corporal punishment amongst the men he commanded, and he had adhered to this policy. Regarding the second of the two reform areas, throwing open the officer corps to non-nobles, Blücher's hussar training again convinced him of the benefits of wider officer recruitment. His attitude to the other reform subject, universal service, was fully revealed in a letter to Gneisenau when the latter left Colberg, in summer 1807, to join the Military Commission at Memel. 'Greet my friend Scharnhorst,' wrote Blücher, 'and tell him to get a national army. This is not as difficult as is thought. . . . Nobody in the world should be exempt . . .'(4)

Scharnhorst and Gneisenau kept in touch with Blücher at Treptow, seeking his advice. But he took no active part in the deliberations of the Military Reorganization Commission itself; nor would he have suited the committee-type procedure and the endless haggling with the conservatives who opposed the reforms. Blücher showed less interest in the constitutional reform movement which soon began to proceed parallel to the military reorganization, yet the two were closely inter-related. Civilian and military developments had to be combined: fundamental questions such as relaxation of discipline, conscription and the admittance of non-nobility to the officer corps raised basic issues of the status of peasants, the relationship between army and state, and the traditional position of the aristocracy. The obvious civilian equivalent for Scharnhorst was Stein. Blücher, despite his lack of concern with politics, joined early with those who sought Stein's return from obscurity. He wrote to Hardenberg in July 1807: 'I only wish our friend Stein would come back. He is the man who could give great service to the State.' And again in August: 'Stein *has* to come back!' On 4th October Blücher's colleague from the Münster days at last returned to office as Prussia's leading Minister, and although he served little more than a year, his achievements proved profound.

Vast and vigorous movements were therefore gaining momentum, designed to lift Prussia from the shambles of Jena, Auerstedt and Tilsit and to prepare the nation for renewed battle. Reformers fought for their ideas at Memel, then at Königsberg when the King returned to this city in January 1808. But Blücher stayed isolated save for his correspondence. Blücher, always the man of action, remained intensely frustrated and wretched, and his depression dragged him to a lower mental despair than ever before. As early as mid-August 1807, he wrote: 'My health has suffered lately. The continual disagreements have done more to me than all hardships.' For over a year he suffered one setback after another, great and small, military and personal. All buffeted his bruised mind. Frederick William decreed that only regiments who had fought well in the 1806 campaign should be included in the new army, and Blücher's prized hussars were among those ordered to be struck from the rolls. Blücher complained bitterly: the regiment had only been prevented from engaging at Auerstedt by its inability to move through the retreating crush of troops in the main army. Finally the King decided the regiment could survive, but with a new name – the Pomeranian Hussar Regiment – and with blue tunics rather than proud red. Blücher retaliated by making one of his infrequent appearances at court, defiantly wearing the distinctive blood-red coat.

But Blücher's behaviour grew even more eccentric. His vivid dreams spread into daytime delusions. He would sit for hours, slumped in his chair, staring into space with vacant eyes, his trembling hands clutching the arm of his seat. His talk, normally so firm and decisive, slipped into incoherent mumbling. His body, previously so robust and sturdy, became emaciated, his cheeks hollow, his eyes sunken. Blücher's mind cracked: through depression, perhaps through alcohol or schizophrenia. Venereal disease was another possible cause; certainly he suffered ill-health, including an ulcerated urethra.

'He actually believed,' wrote Boyen, 'that he was pregnant with an elephant. . . . Another time he imagined that his servants, bribed by France, had heated the floor of his room very hot so as to cause him to burn his feet. When he was sitting, therefore, he kept his legs raised from the ground, or else he would leap about on tiptoe.' Horrific tales emerged from Treptow. One day Blücher thrust a hammer into a servant's hand and bellowed at him to strike his (Blücher's) head because he had been turned into stone. His household was roused one night by shouts, thuds and splintering furniture: they found Blücher fighting violently with the imaginary figure of an officer he had once dismissed from the service.(5) Blücher struggled to recover but depression constantly dragged him down again. He worried over his son Franz, who also suffered a long illness during these months of 1807 and 1808; he worried about money, shortage of which led to the confiscation of his house in Münster; he suffered further sadness in autumn 1809, when his only child from his second marriage died. Above all, he feared for Prussia.

Reforms were progressing well, but still not fast enough for men like Blücher. On 9th October 1807, five days after taking office, Stein's famous 'Emancipating Edict' was signed, aiming at ending personal serfdom in Prussia and based upon earlier work by Hardenberg. The Edict proved an extremely suitable counterpart to the reforms which Scharnhorst envisaged for the army. On 3rd August 1808, his birthday, Frederick William issued three important decrees based on the Military Reorganization Commission's proposals: one threw open entrance to the previously exclusive officer corps; the second decree abolished corporal punishment, except in the case of soldiers found guilty three times of serious offences; the final decree went some way to introducing universal service: 'In future every subject of the State, without regard to birth, will be obliged to perform military service, under conditions of time and circumstances yet to be determined.' Scharnhorst and his colleagues pressed on, anxious lest France might prevent Prussia carrying out sufficient military improvement. 'Remember my prophecy,' warned Clausewitz to his wife. 'We shall see rising over our heads a black storm, and we will be enveloped in night and mists of sulphur before we expect it.'(6) French agents watched leading Prussian patriots, including Blücher, and in autumn 1808 Napoleon started to move against the Prussian he considered most dangerous of all, Stein.

Tension increased in the second half of 1808 with the outbreak of insurrection in Spain and the start of the Peninsular War, providing an example for the rest of Europe to follow. 'He who ... stakes everything,' wrote the philosopher Johann Fichte, 'and the utmost that man can lose here below, his life, will never cease to resist.' Stein declared: 'Shall we submit or resist? We must ... keep alive in the nation the feeling of discontent with this oppression. ... We must diffuse and give currency to certain ideas about the way of raising and conducting an insurrection.'(7) Blücher fervently agreed. And renewed hope of hostilities against the French, modelled on the Spanish example, revived the General's spirits during the late summer and autumn of 1808. His eyes shone alert again, his mind became alive, he spent his days planning rather than dreaming. He confounded those critics who had thought him finished.

Moreover, Austro-French relations were fast deteriorating; Prussia's neighbour prepared for war against Napoleon and might soon take the field. Scharnhorst completed a mobilization plan: Prussian troops should advance and join Blücher's corps moving from Pomerania while forces from Silesia united with the Austrians. 'At the moment of this advance,' declared the plan, 'a universal insurrection is to break out.'(8) Blücher reacted to the scheme with delight, then with anger when he heard the King's response. Frederick William believed nothing could be accomplished without Russian help.

Czar Alexander arrived at Königsberg on 18th September for a three-day visit. He proved as hesitant as Frederick William. He believed all must be done to bridge the gap between Austria and France, or Napoleon might postpone the settlement of Spain and turn his whole attention in their direction. Within four days evidence was revealed that Napoleon had decided to root out Stein. Captain von Thile, serving on Blücher's staff, had been sent by Blücher with a message for Marshal Soult in Berlin, where the French Marshal showed Thile a news item in the *Telegraph*. This reprinted an indiscreet letter written by Stein to Prince Ludwig Wittgenstein and intercepted by the French. Stein had stressed the feeling of the Prussian people against France and the excellent example afforded by Spain; he had also referred to Blücher, saying: 'General Blücher is very frail. . . . Colonel Bülow is being sent to give him extra help.'(9) Napoleon moved quickly: not only did he demand Stein's dismissal, but he insisted Prussia should sign a new convention, limiting the size of her army to 42,000 men. 'I will be swift like lightning to suppress any outbreak of ill-will among you,' he warned Prussian diplomats in Paris. Stein relinquished his post on 24th November. Soon afterwards Napoleon issued a warrant for his arrest. Stein fled, first to Austria and then Russia.

Despite Stein's precipitate departure, despite the Paris Convention restricting the strength of Prussia's army, hopes still remained that war might soon begin. In the Peninsula, British troops under Sir John Moore crossed the Portuguese frontier into Spain, and Napoleon hurried south to command the French army himself. Austria accelerated her war preparations. In March 1809, a Prussian Ministry of War was officially formed: Scharnhorst became *de facto* Minister. Blücher's health continued to improve, and encouraging letters left his new headquarters at Stargard.

I am indescribably happy here [he wrote to his former adjutant, Goltz, on 4th April 1809]. I have recovered so well from my unfortunate illness that I am far healthier now than I ever was before. I have such an appetite that I am continually upsetting my stomach through over-eating, and although I was down to a skeleton, I have put on so much weight that I am stouter than I was before. Everything else is back to normal. I work in the morning, and then enjoy life with my friends playing cards as of old.

Blücher complained to Goltz of the 'gentlemen in Königsberg' who had gossiped over his mental illness; he added that he had written to the King to say if his services were no longer wanted Frederick William had only to bid him to leave. 'I would earn my living and have no need of anything. But the monarch treated me as before – and I'll show the others.' He fully expected action to be taken against the French.(10)

Five days after this letter Archduke Charles of Austria marched on French-held Ratisbon in Bavaria; another Austrian force moved south-west from Bohemia, and an Austrian army of 50,000 men crossed the Alps to invade Italy. Revolt flared in the Tyrol. Austria sought Prussian help. 'We take up arms to maintain the independence of the Austrian monarchy, but also to regain for Prussia her freedom and national honour. The insolence that threatens us has already humiliated Germany. Our resistance is the last hope.' Clamour for war swept Prussia. 'What a great moment this is!' enthused Clausewitz. Men like General von Kalkreuth and Borstell, who had opposed the military reforms, now openly insisted that Prussia should join Austria's struggle. Prussia rippled with rumours; messengers galloped down the roads bringing news from Vienna, Paris, Lisbon, London, Berlin. Blücher drilled his men at Stargard and ordered his cavalry on the alert.

Frederick William did nothing. The Prussian monarch remained obsessed with the memory of 1806 and with Napoleon's power. And now Bonaparte proceeded to display this strength once again. On 16th April he arrived at Stuttgart; within thirty-six hours he collected more than half of his army west of Ratisbon, crossed the Danube, penetrated the centre of the extended Austrian army and forced the two halves back to Ratisbon and Landeshut. During the next week he outmanoeuvred and out-fought his enemy at Landeshut, Eggmühl, and Ratisbon, inflicting losses of about 30,000 on the Austrians and sending them flying over the border. Napoleon directed his army northwards, aiming for Vienna. Fresh pleas for help reached Frederick William in Königsberg, but he still insisted upon Russian support before he acted. Scores of Prussian officers quit the army in disgust. Scharnhorst wished to leave, but knew that if he did so the King would be even less likely to act. Gneisenau had already left Königsberg for his country house, where he prepared plans for a Free Prussian Legion to fight with the Austrians if Frederick William maintained his refusal.

One young officer in Berlin, with whom Blücher had every sympathy, could stand the situation no longer and made his personal bid for glory and the honour of the Fatherland. Major von Schill rode out with about 100 hussars in support of an insurrection believed to be on the point of erupting in Westphalia. Other officers and men joined him as he advanced through Potsdam and Wittenberg to Dessau. Blücher immediately despatched an urgent letter to the King, pleading with him to support Schill. 'From this one step alone your Majesty can deduce the temper of the nation and of your troops. They want to free themselves from the oppressing yoke.' Blücher warned that the people might rebel against authority and would follow Schill. 'All that can only be prevented if your Majesty will place yourself at the head of your people, to use their present mood and to get the troops into such a state that they can count again on authority. . . . The right moment is here now.'(11)

On 4th May Schill learnt of Austria's setbacks at Ratisbon and that the Westphalian insurrection was now unlikely to break out. But he pressed on, hoping to reach the north coast, capture a port, and hold it until help arrived. He brushed aside French opposition and headed for Stralsund, Blücher's former base by the island of Rügen. Meanwhile further disastrous news arrived from Austria: on 13th May Napoleon had entered Vienna in triumph. Then came far more hopeful reports. The Austrians concentrated on the north bank of the Danube and Napoleon attempted to smash his way over the river; part of the French army crossed, but Napoleon proved unable to reinforce these units and had to withdraw. Latest information encouraged support for Schill, who reached Stralsund on 25th May. But Blücher's plea to Frederick

William received no response: the Prussian King was both furious with Schill's insubordination and in a cold panic lest Napoleon should turn upon Prussia. And by the end of the month Schill's 2,000 patriots were surrounded by 6,000 Danes, Dutch, Holsteiners and French detachments. Bloody hand-to-hand fighting ended with Schill's death; his survivors fled, some of them to Stargard – where they involved Blücher in a quarrel with his King.

Blücher refused to disarm these brave supporters of Schill and rumours reached Königsberg that he had secretly mobilized his men. A severe royal reprimand reached his headquarters, together with an order to hand over control of part of his corps to another general, von Stutterheim. Blücher immediately demanded permission to leave the service and he threatened to join a foreign army. 'I ask Your Majesty to hand me my discharge without pension,' he wrote, 'even if I am poor and have to look for my daily bread in the service of strangers. I would leave the service with the greatest sorrow. . . .'(12) Frederick William sent no reply, and pressures upon the King increased from elsewhere.

Rebellion against the French broke out in Hesse. Scharnhorst, in the closest daily contact with the monarch, urged him to sign an immediate alliance with Austria, and he also presented a plan to supplement the reduced standing army with a trained reserve. But Frederick William repeatedly refused to take any serious step to join Austria or to make use of Schill's patriotic example. Instead he laid down three conditions which must first be met: Russia must not object, Britain must lend proper support, and above all he personally must be convinced that Austria and Prussia would win. Nobody could possibly provide these assurances, especially the last. More and more Prussian officers began to quit Prussian service, and Blücher feared he might also have to make this drastic decision. The King had lost his trust in him, complained Blücher to Gneisenau in July. 'He has told me off, undeservedly, for the first time. . . . God knows with what sorrow I leave a state and an army in which I have lived for fifty years. I am sick to my stomach.'

So Blücher would go abroad, probably to England.

I have refused for a very long time all offers. But I don't want to dream away my time in inactivity, whilst other brave Germans are fighting for their German Fatherland. . . . If I find anyone who speaks shamefully about me, I swear by the high altar that his life will not be safe from my punishment.

He told Gneisenau that he had sent an officer to the court to find the latest news. 'The return of my adjutant . . . will give me my decision: if the King takes no part, if we take no steps to break our fetters, then whoever wants to wear these fetters can. I won't!'(13) Blücher encouraged Gneisenau to open negotiations with England; he sent his son Franz to London. Impatiently he awaited any scrap of evidence from Frederick William's court which might indicate a change of policy.

Instead, in mid-July came news of Napoleon's crushing victory over the Austrians at Wagram on the 5th and 6th. The outcome of the battle shattered Austria's remaining determination to resist the French. Austrian troops had been driven from the Grand Duchy of Warsaw; Russia and Prussia had refused to join the coalition; British landings in Holland and Belgium had been repulsed. Emperor Francis of Austria asked for an armistice on 10th July. Blücher's sacrifice in leaving Prussia and fighting under another banner would be useless. He would have to stay. Yet even after Wagram he continued to urge action. His emotional letter to Gneisenau in July had condemned those who accused him of wanting to lead Prussian troops against the French contrary to the King's wishes – he had declared: 'I even believe they would make the King believe that I wanted to cross the Elbe with the troops, like Schill had done. But a plague on those robbers!' Now, while the Austrian armistice continued, he sought permission from the King for just such an operation.

Most Gracious King, grant the request of a man who has grown grey in your service, who is as honest as he is devoted to you, who is ready to sacrifice himself for you. . . . If Your Royal Majesty will permit me to cross the Elbe with a corps of your troops I will pledge my head to regain possession of our lost provinces. . . .(14)

But on 14th October the Austrians signed the humiliating Treaty of Schönbrunn with the French. The whole of Germany lay at Napoleon's mercy.

The fate in store for us is horrible [Blücher warned Frederick William]. Only a few months ago Your Majesty could have given the proper turn to what is the common cause of all nations. It pains me excessively that you, most Gracious ruler, should have refused the urgent and respectful request that only true, unbounded devotion made me venture to proffer.(15)

The King took this admonishment well; he wrote a courteous letter to Blücher on 1st November, thanking him for all he had done, but regretting he could not provide him with further instructions. Blücher therefore remained at Stargard with his misery.

Gloom spread across Prussia during this wet winter of 1809–10. Gneisenau resigned from the Prussian army, partly as a result of French pressure, although he continued to serve the state as a secret agent. Scharnhorst continued at the War Ministry, striving to proceed with military reforms beneath the brooding French shadow. The court returned to Berlin in December 1809, with the King passing through Stargard and displaying kindness to Blücher. The return to the Prussian capital seemed shrouded with shame. Then, in January 1810, Napoleon tightened the screw by attempting to squeeze more money from the Prussians. Prussia pleaded for time, but on 7th March the Emperor was reported to have warned Princess Thurn, sister of Frederick William's Queen Louise: 'If the King does not pay, he must cede Silesia to me,' and he wrote: 'I shall know how to enforce payment.'

The threat plunged Berlin into political chaos. In July a new ministry came into power, headed by Hardenberg: he agreed to find the money but army funds had to be drastically reduced, and his money-raising methods caused widespread discontent. Moreover, Napoleon made another demand during this turbulent spring of 1810: Scharnhorst must leave the War Ministry, and this valiant reformer left his post in June. But something was saved: the King declared that 'Major-General von Scharnhorst should continue, so far as it could be done secretly, in the same relation to the officials of the War Department as hitherto.'(16)

Scharnhorst and Hardenberg struggled to salvage something from the mess, and Blücher remained in close contact. He sent frequent reports to Berlin of French activity, obtained through his *Kundschafter* – spy – network. In turn French agents kept close watch on this belligerent Prussian war-horse, and Napoleon viewed his former prisoner with intense suspicion. Back in 1809 the

Emperor had angrily asked Prussia's envoy in Paris: 'Who is supposed to be ruling in Prussia? Is it that man in Silesia (Goetzen), or is it Schill, or is it *Bluquaire?*'(17) But Napoleon had other preoccupations during 1810. He endeavoured to fend off further war with both Russia and Austria – and he struggled to sire a son. Both aims were connected. His marriage to childless Josephine was annulled, and Napoleon asked his ambassador in St Petersburg to send him a report on Czar Alexander's sister, Anna. 'Let me know . . . when she can become a mother, for in the present circumstances even a matter of six months counts.' Marriage negotiations broke down and Franco-Russian relations soured as a result. Napoleon turned his attentions upon Marie Louise, eighteen-year-old daughter of Emperor Francis of Austria. This time he met success.

While Napoleon gained a new bride, Frederick William of Prussia lost his fiery Queen Louise, leading voice in the anti-French party. Her death on 19th July increased Prussia's misery. 'I am as if struck by lightning!' despaired Blücher. 'The pride of womanhood has departed from the earth. God in Heaven, it must be that she was too good for us! . . . How is it possible for such a succession of misfortunes to fall on a state!'(18) The loss seemed to epitomize Prussia's sad fate. 'The lonely, joyless life of the King reacted on those around him,' wrote Countess Schwerin, prominent in Berlin's society. 'It grew ever stiller and less brilliant in the Berlin world. The age seemed to have grown more and more evil, more and more sad.' Frederick William lost himself in his grief. 'For a long time,' commented Boyen, 'the King when he came to receive reports wore on his breast the handkerchief with which the Queen had dried her last sweats and kissed it when he thought no one was looking.'(19)

British troops continued their struggle in the Peninsula, but elsewhere nations hovered on the brink of war, attempting to find allies, to strengthen their positions and to discover intentions of potential adversaries. Blücher had an especially unpleasant task. He was obliged to treat the British as enemies, and to stop British vessels carrying out smuggling operations on the Baltic coast. In autumn 1810 Blücher warned these smugglers that he would 'rap their knuckles'; in early 1811 shots were fired at a ship approaching the coast and the vessel sheered off. Disturbing reports meanwhile accumulated of French activities. Relations between Paris and

St Petersburg had continued to deteriorate, with the Russians increasingly concerned over Napoleon's attitude to Poland. 'Even though your armies were to camp on the heights of Montmartre,' stormed Napoleon at the Russian ambassador, 'I should not yield an inch of Warsaw. . . . You're counting on allies? Where are they? You look to me like hares who are shot in the head and gape all around, not knowing where to scurry.'(20)

If war should break out between France and Russia, Prussia would be in the firing-line and would be subjected to renewed French occupation. Yet such a war would offer fresh opportunity for Prussia to rise up against Napoleon. Tension rapidly increased during 1811. Gneisenau drew up a detailed memorandum urging Frederick William to mobilize his army on the first signs of war between France and Russia, and to allow insurrection to be organized. The King merely scribbled in the margins of the document: 'Nobody would come' and 'Good – like poetry!' Gneisenau angrily retorted: 'Religion, prayer, love of one's ruler, love of the Fatherland – these things are nothing else than poetry . . .'(21)

The King refused to act despite French troop movements. In January Blücher's spies informed him of a threatened French occupation of Swinemünde, on the coast north of Stettin, and he sent reinforcements to the port; in April he moved north, establishing his headquarters first in his old base at Treptow and then at Colberg in May. Blücher's energies were devoted to improving defensive works at Colberg and the surrounding roads: 'I relied on my bit of brain but mostly on my eyes,' he wrote. But Blücher had to battle against shortages of money and equipment. 'I am constantly on the move,' he wrote to Boyen. 'My wallet becomes thinner every week.'(22)

Blücher, like Gneisenau, could find no backing from Berlin. Work on the fortifications threatened to founder through shortages of finance, and even his spy system almost collapsed because the agents were denied payment. Blücher delved into his own pocket. 'I can't exist any longer like this,' he complained to Berlin in August. 'Don't I deserve to be given my outstanding pay for the last six months? . . . It is too much to be treated like a pack-animal and not even be given fodder.'(23)

'I am heartily tired of life,' wrote Stein during this summer of 1811, 'and wish it would soon come to an end.'(24) Blücher's former colleague remained disconsolate at Prague; other patriots were also rapidly losing heart. Scharnhorst, who left Berlin on diplomatic missions to various European capitals, often in weird disguise, described these days as a 'stormy, shaky, condition . . . a dark and darkening future, a labyrinthian confusion.'(25) Scharnhorst visited Blücher on 29th July, *en route* for St Petersburg, and he attempted to reassure the demoralized General, who in turn continued to demand support from Berlin and to urge action against the hated French.

> 'I am going to stop my many letters to Berlin,' he finally told Gneisenau, 'because I have received no reply. . . . If the great man intends to destroy us – or at least to make us useless – it would be unwise of him to leave us time to collect our force and put it in the right place. . . . We have to get to work without losing any time.'(26)

Gneisenau himself needed reassurance. Clausewitz, now at the Berlin War School, mapped out a defence plan for Silesia, in which he envisaged Gneisenau leading forces against the French, making 'a Spain out of Silesia'. Gneisenau, disgusted and weary, refused to consider himself for this possible role.(27) Nor did many senior Prussian officers agree with the idea of insurrection. 'With the exception of Blücher, Yorck and Gneisenau,' wrote Boyen, 'the great majority was against guerrilla warfare. . . . The great majority of officers could not equate their tactical training with such a method of warfare.'(28)

In this bumbling, miserable fashion Prussia slid steadily towards her greatest humiliation since Jena and Auerstedt. In October, Scharnhorst obtained Czar Alexander's promise that if Napoleon were to occupy part of Prussia, or strengthened his forces on the Vistula, the main Russian army would advance through the Duchy of Warsaw, and an army corps would be sent to East Prussia. Alexander also authorized his General von Wittgenstein, deployed with three Russian divisions near Tilsit, to move forward if Yorck in West Prussia requested help. Frederick William could now count on some Russian help – but insufficient to save his whole kingdom. Scharnhorst rushed to Vienna, but the Austrians had still to recover from their 1809 ordeal and refused to turn against the French. In Berlin, news arrived of increased pressure from Napoleon: either Prussia must enter his treaty network, the Rhine Confederation, or sign an unconditional alliance with France.

'The storm of 1812 had not yet broke,' commented the Russian poet, Alexander Pushkin. 'Napoleon had yet to put the great people to the test. He was still threatening, still hesitating.' For weeks Frederick William's carriage stood waiting in his palace courtyard, ready for flight to Königsberg. Then, on 11th November, the Prussian King despatched a letter to Blücher which, for all its friendliness, ordered him into temporary retirement: Blücher was too outspoken and hence too dangerous.(29) Blücher journeyed to Stargard and there he heard of Prussia's final degradation.

On 24th February 1812, Frederick William put Prussia's signature to a French alliance. He agreed to supply a corps of 20,000 men for Napoleon's use, which resulted in nearly half the official line army being swallowed up in the 27th Division of Napoleon's Grand Army. The gates of the country were thrown open for French forces to advance against the Russians, and the people of Prussia had to provide oats, hay, liquor and food.

And so we are enemies Sire! [wrote Czar Alexander to his erstwhile ally.] But how can you think, Sire, that even should Russia be subjugated your safety will be assured by France, or that even during the actual continuance of the war Napoleon will ever really look on you as a trusted ally? No Sire! Great were the dangers you would have incurred by joining Russia; but will it not now be the same?

With this grim warning hanging over his bowed head, the King of Prussia departed with his court for Potsdam and French troops occupied Berlin behind him. Blücher moaned to Gneisenau: 'All is lost and honour too.'(30)

Blücher received a royal command to hide himself still further from the scenes of principal activity, and in early spring he travelled south, along roads crammed with French troops and baggage convoys. Frederick William had given Blücher the castle of Schneitnig, situated in an expansive park near Breslau, and here he remained throughout the tortured year of 1812. He sat surrounded by plans, maps, diagrams, his darkened room thick with tobacco smoke, as he studied news of momentous events elsewhere.

*   *   *

Soon after dawn on 24th June the main part of the Grand Army began to sweep into Russian territory across the Niemen. The

1812 campaign had begun. 'From now on,' wrote Heinrich Vossler, a German serving with the French, 'I was to witness, and indeed experience, scenes of every imaginable distress, wretchedness and misery.' The Grand Army advanced beneath a sultry, sullen sky. Napoleon led over 450,000 men into Russia, less than half of them French. The main Russian army under Barclay de Tolly gradually fell back, largely through lack of firm plans than through an actual decision to lure the French deep into enemy territory. Retreat continued after the battle of Smolensk in mid-August. On 29th August the elderly Mikhail Illariorovich Kutuzov took command of the Russian armies and continued the withdrawal, this time coming to the deliberate decision that such a policy would bring victory. To satisfy those who demanded battle, he stood and fought at bloody Borodino on 7th September, suffering nearly 40,000 casualties. The French lost 28,000, plus valuable equipment which Napoleon would never be able to replace.

Borodino marked the beginning of the end for Napoleon and his Grand Army. The Russians withdrew, the French followed, but old fox Kutuzov had lost none of his cunning. During the afternoon of 13th September the Russian commander called a war council, with his army in sight of Moscow. 'You fear a retreat through Moscow,' he is reported to have said, 'but I regard it as far-sighted. It will save the army. Napoleon is like a stormy torrent which we are as yet unable to stop. Moscow will be the sponge that sucks him in.' The French began to enter Moscow later this same day; Napoleon arrived at the Kremlin forty-eight hours later. But Czar Alexander refused to listen to his demands for talks. Napoleon had staked everything upon the seizure of Moscow; this, he believed, would be the method to bring victory, as his seizure of other capitals had been in the past – Vienna in 1805, Berlin in 1806. But another, more ominous example existed. The capture of Madrid in 1808 had increased Spanish resistance rather than the reverse. Russia followed the Spanish example. Napoleon delayed as long as possible, then, on the night of 19th October, the French withdrawal began, out into the wilderness to face the Russians and their appalling winter. Maloyaroslavets, Smolensk, Orsha, each signposted the way to French disaster. On 27th November the disintegrating Grand Army reached the Berezina; Napoleon surpassed himself in fending off the Russians while he led 40,000 men over the icy rivers to the western bank, but 9,000 fit soldiers and 8,000 stragglers were left behind, and half the survivors perished on the next stretch of the retreat to Vilna.

Napoleon left his army on 5th December with urgent business to attend to at home. Europe might rise against him to take advantage of his Russian defeat; a new French army must quickly be created. The Emperor reached Warsaw on the 9th and coined a *cliché*: 'There is only one step from the sublime to the ridiculous.' Three days later he arrived in Posen, then he crossed into Prussia where political cartoonists were busy drawing grisly caricatures to amuse the people: a line of tattered troops trudging through the snow without weapons, with a vulture hovering above. On 14th December the first French survivors crossed the Niemen and staggered towards French units left to guard the river. Count Louis Philippe Ségur provided this harrowing description:

> Instead of the 400,000 companions who had fought so many successful battles with them, who had swept so masterfully into Russia, they saw emerging from the white, ice-bound wilderness only 1,000 infantrymen and troopers under arms, nine cannon, and 20,000 stragglers dressed in rags, with bowed heads, dull eyes, ashen, cadaverous faces and long, ice-stiffen beards. This was the Grand Army.(31)

On the same day, 14th December, Napoleon paused on his journey through Prussia to write to Frederick William. He asked the King to increase the Prussian contingent in the French forces from 20,000 to 30,000. Only two days later, as Napoleon stepped on to the French bank of the Rhine, his citizens and his allies learnt the full extent of his losses when his 29th Bulletin appeared in the Paris *Moniteur*. To patriotic Prussians the announcement opened huge new vistas. 'The strange event was there,' wrote Henry Steffens in Breslau, 'and at last the loud call to rise was shouted through the land. . . .'(32)

A highly important group of men began to converge on Breslau to plot the next Prussian moves: Scharnhorst, Gneisenau, Justus Grüner, the thin, fiery, red-haired president of police in Berlin, then Count Chasot, who had shot a French officer in a duel for having spoken with contempt of the Prussians, and the leading literary figure Moritz Arndt. Later the most anti-French Prussian of all arrived in the city, gruff, slightly stooped and bandy-legged but nonetheless imposing – Lieutenant-General von Blücher.

'My fingers itch to seize the sabre,' Blücher told Scharnhorst. Arndt described his face: 'Here was concentrated the cunning of a hussar, the play of features sometimes extending up into his eyes, and something of a marten listening for its prey.'(33) Steffens met Blücher and his companions and joined in the discussions.

> In the agitated state of the people these arrivals occasioned great astonishment [he wrote]. The police watched their activities suspiciously, though without interference. I was brought into immediate connection for the first time with those men whose position and principles marked them as the hope of Germany. They passed much time in my house. . . . Sometimes we met at a tavern, and remained in close conference till midnight; a small room behind the public saloon was reserved for us.(34)

But the group at Breslau remained helpless, for the moment; all depended upon the actions of General Yorck, commanding the Prussian troops still officially allied to the French, and fighting the Russians about 100 kilometres north-east of Königsberg. The King of Prussia must be pushed into action, and this could only be accomplished by Hans David von Yorck. If he stayed allied to the French, then all might be lost; if he took the drastic step of removing his troops from the French army, he could end the indecision which had paralysed Prussia. Blücher and his comrades had doubts over Yorck's strength of character, yet they remained too far away to influence proceedings.

Other Prussians closer to Yorck shared similar doubts but were determined to push his hand. Amongst these patriots was Carl von Clausewitz. Clausewitz, although serving with the Russians, established contact with Yorck's forces on Boxing Day. It appeared Yorck was seriously considering an agreement, but wished to postpone it, briefly, while he moved nearer to the Prussian frontier. Apart from the fact that he was awaiting the return of an aide whom he had sent to Berlin for instructions, it would appear better if he tried to unite with the French under Marshal Alexander Macdonald before coming to terms with the Russians. Manoeuvring, amounting to a charade, continued for three more days while Blücher and his companions anxiously awaited news in Breslau. Clausewitz repeatedly struggled to convince Yorck that union with the French under Macdonald was impossible: Russian forces under Wittgenstein blocked the way. He rode to Yorck's camp again on the night of the 29th.

'Get out,' bellowed the Prussian commander. 'I've finished with you. . . . I want no more talk, or I shall lose my head.' Clausewitz continued to plead and, at last, Yorck agreed to meet the senior Prussian officer serving with the Russians. A time was fixed for eight o'clock the following morning at nearby Tauroggen, and there Yorck signed the historic convention which declared his army would be neutral in the struggle between Russia and France. If Frederick William rejected the Convention of Tauroggen, it was agreed that the army would refuse to serve against the Russians for a period of two months. The first step in the War of Liberation had been taken.(35)

But now Yorck had to explain himself to Frederick William, and the Prussian monarch had to summon sufficient strength to deny the French and support the Russians – who had begun crossing into his country on 21st December. Yorck grew bolder after he entered Tilsit to rest and refit his army on 1st January 1813. 'I speak here the language of an old and faithful servant,' he wrote to Frederick William on the 3rd. 'Your Royal Majesty's kingdom, though smaller than in the year 1805, is now destined to become the liberator and protector of your people – and of all Germans.'(36) Two days later Yorck decided to disregard his new neutrality and to assist the Russians should their offensive be endangered. He went even further; on the 8th he entered Königsberg and appealed to other Prussian commanders to join his cause. 'Have men sunk so low,' he declared to Bülow, 'that they will not dare break the chains of slavery? . . . Now or never is the time.' He used the same words to Frederick William, still silent in Berlin: 'Now or never is the moment when Your Majesty may tear yourself from the extravagant demands of an ally whose intentions towards Prussia, in the event of his success, were involved in a mystery which justified anxiety.'(37)

Yorck in Königsberg and Blücher in Breslau anxiously waited while Prussia slid into turmoil. Blücher heard reports of near riots as the people became increasingly hostile to the French. Napoleon's officials were scorned and sometimes stoned. The ordinary Prussians knew nothing of the delicate situation between Yorck and his monarch, but everywhere they could see the evidence of Napoleon's terrible defeat in Russia. 'One saw no guns,' wrote a schoolboy, Ludwig Rellstab, 'no cavalry, only suffering men crippled by frightful wounds, men with hands, arms, or feet either missing or else completely destroyed by frostbite.' Farm-carts rumbled and groaned along the frosty roads, each filled with straw upon which lay horribly wounded men. 'The stench from these carts was frightful,' continued Rellstab. 'The festering and maybe gangrenous wounds gave off a really pestilential stench. . . . All who witness such scenes shuddered.' But pity proved rare. Berlin was no longer safe for French troops; street urchins jeered at cavalrymen who had lost their mounts and offered to lead their non-existent horses, and shoe-shines were offered to infantrymen hobbling across the cobbles with bare, mutilated feet. In Berlin, Breslau, Königsberg and towns and villages everywhere, men talked of insurrection against the French and of the liberation of the Fatherland.

But Frederick William had to walk a swinging tightrope. On the one side lay the continuing threat from Napoleon and the nightmare of 1806; on the other lay the overwhelming desire of his people, which the King perhaps shared, to rise and restore German honour. The Grand Army might have been destroyed, but other French troops remained. Around Berlin were 12,000 French soldiers and 70,000 more were garrisoned in Prussian fortresses. Prussian forces in the vicinity of Berlin numbered less than two thousand. A move against the French at this stage seemed dangerously premature and, as Frederick William had commented on 28th December, the day before Tauroggen, a war on the Rhine would be extremely costly: 'Three hundred thousand Frenchmen must be killed before it can be realized.' Events would prove him correct.(38) Meanwhile Frederick William refused to make a public move against Napoleon until he had been assured of effective Russian assistance. On 10th January news reached Königsberg that the King refused to ratify the Convention of Tauroggen and had sent an officer to arrest Yorck – this officer was stopped *en route* by the Russians.

In Breslau, Blücher raged against Frederick William's apparent refusal to 'root out all roguish French trash from German soil, together with Bonaparte and all his appendage'.(39) But Frederick William made no further direct move against the rebels at Königsberg. Yorck apparently realized the King's predicament, and sent his second-in-command, Kleist, to open talks with the Czar in an attempt to secure support for Prussia. Kleist returned to Königsberg on the 11th with flattering messages and promises from Alexander. Two days later Yorck despatched another letter to the King. 'With bleeding heart I burst the bond of obedience and wage war on my own account. The army wants war with France, the people want it, and so does the King, but the King has no free will. The army must make his will free. . . .'(40)

This letter reached Berlin at a moment when suspicious French troop movement around the capital were being reported to the King; on the 19th he felt obliged to issue a public proclamation against the Tauroggen Convention. Outwardly, all hopes seemed gone, and Scharnhorst, Blücher and the others could only express their irate opinions in their Breslau tavern. On 24th January Napoleon wrote confidently to Eugène Beauharnais that he expected Frederick William to supply him with cavalry, of which he was acutely short after the Russian disaster.

But the situation suddenly changed. The proclamation of the 19th marked the deepest black before the dawn, and now Frederick William decided upon opposition to the French. Stein had visited the Russian commander, Kutuzov, on the 16th and had consulted with the Czar two days later. He arrived at Königsberg on the 21st or 22nd, commissioned by Alexander to organize the defence of the area against the French. The Russian leader clearly intended to support Prussia against the common enemy; Frederick William would receive the protection he sought. On 22nd January the King escaped with his entourage for Breslau and preparations for war intensified in early February. Yorck summoned a special session of the East Prussian states on the 4th, and demanded the formation of a militia force, the *Landwehr*, totalling 20,000 men with 10,000 reserves; with the adoption of this plan to put civilians into uniform, as envisaged by the military reformers since 1807, East Prussia became committed to the liberation struggle. In Breslau, Blücher urged that the French should not be allowed to regain breath but should be chased from Germany 'like the holy thunderstorm' – he pleaded for 30,000 troops to perform the task.(41) But diplomatic negotiations with the Russians took time; Frederick William still moved cautiously, although he issued an important general order on the 12th: 'I have been convinced by the justifications and reports delivered to me by Lieutenant-General v. Yorck that he was forced and compelled by circumstances . . . to the capitulation which he concluded with the Russians.'(42)

Blücher with his belligerence, and Scharnhorst with his quiet assurances, attempted to persuade the King to declare publicly his complete defiance of the French. Scharnhorst proved successful; events reached a climax at the end of the month. The Austrian envoy at the Prussian court in Breslau reported on 25th February: 'The day before yesterday, General von Scharnhorst assured me that the King, after a long private struggle, had finally acquiesced to his view.'(43) Next day, 26th February, Frederick William at last signed an offensive and defensive alliance with Czar Alexander at Kalisch. Russia undertook to provide 150,000 men, and Prussia would send a minimum of 80,000 regular troops into the field. The Convention of Tauroggen had been vindicated; the War of Liberation could begin. Blücher's moment had arrived.

CHAPTER 6

For Freedom and Fatherland

SOME DOUBTED BLÜCHER'S suitability for command of the Prussian army. Counted against him were his age, seventy, his outspoken opposition to the monarch during the alliance with France, and his eccentric behaviour during the troubled years of 1807 and 1808, especially the elephant episode. 'If he had a thousand elephants in his belly,' insisted Scharnhorst, 'he must still lead the army,' and immediately pressed for his appointment. Blücher wrote hopefully: 'Up to now nobody has said anything to me, yet I think my selection is decided and I shall await everything calmly.' Scharnhorst once again emerged successful: on 28th February a royal order was handed to Blücher, granting him all he had sought.

I have decided to give you the command of those troops which are the first to go into the field [declared Frederick William]. I order you therefore to mobilize in the quickest way possible. The important charge which you receive herewith will convince you of the trust I have in your expertise of war and in your patriotism, and I am sure that you will rise to this fully.(1)

On 8th March he received further orders from the King: not only was he to command all the Prussian troops assembled in Silesia, but also the army corps of the Russian general Ferdinand von Wintzingerode.

Nevertheless, criticism of Blücher's appointment continued. Boyen, for example, considered him too wild and erratic; some preferred Scharnhorst, and indeed Scharnhorst could probably have acquired the command if he had wished. Even after Blücher's victories there would be those who insisted the credit should go to Scharnhorst, as his chief of staff, and afterwards to Gneisenau, Scharnhorst's successor. Count Louis Langeron, soon to be a corps commander under Blücher, expressed this view:

> His energy was prodigious. . . . His eye for ground was excellent, his heroic courage inspired the troops, but his talent as a general was limited to just such qualities. . . . He had little knowledge of strategy, he could not find where he was on a map, and he was incapable of making a plan of campaign or a troops disposition.(2)

Langeron's remarks were partly motivated by personal dislike – and neither did Blücher consider Langeron to be a capable commander – yet the criticisms had some justification. Blücher remained incapable of subtlety: detailed, drawn-out campaign plans were perhaps beyond him, and complicated troop disposition bored him. But these aspects of his generalship stemmed from his character, which demanded a direct approach with minimum complications to clutter proceedings. He had no time for long-winded schemes. He concerned himself with the broad outlines of strategy and left the accompanying details to others. Blücher's achievements in 1793, 1794 and 1795 underlined his ability to handle tactical situations with supreme confidence; now he would employ the same methods on a strategical scale. These methods involved fast movement, retention of the initiative, a clear grasp of the overall prevailing situation, a complete inability to feel fear, and magnificent control over men. These were the qualities of a great general.

Karl von Müffling, who had served with Blücher in the 1790s and who succeeded Gneisenau as his Quartermaster-General in 1813, gave this sober assessment:

> He trusted the officers of his staff only when he considered them enterprising; but once they had earned this trust he gave it unreservedly. He allowed them to put forward their plans for marches, positions, and battles, he grasped everything quickly, and if he had given them his approval and signed the relevant orders he would accept no outside advice, and no expressions of alarm made the slightest impression on him. [But Müffling continued:] One must admit that his temperament made [him] too lively and too restless.

As soon as the troops had been given their orders, he could hardly wait for them to be executed . . . It was inadvisable to lay before him plans for a battle which might last the whole day and only be decided in the evening: his character required a quicker decision.(3)

The chief criticism to be made against Blücher lay in the fact that he demanded everyone to be as energetic, ruthless, relentless and decisive as himself. Few matched up to him, and he cursed them when they failed.

Blücher relied heavily on his staff, and this, in the new form of warfare now appearing, was a virtue, not a fault as Langeron claimed. Ability to delegate planning responsibility proved essential from 1813 onwards. A single commander could no longer conceive, arrange and execute a campaign. 'The French had burned away the old concept of war, as if with acid,' wrote Clausewitz. 'They unleashed the terrible power of war from its former confines. Now it moved in its naked form, dragging massive force with it.'(4) The French *levée en masse*, the system of universal service proposed by the Prussian reformers, the *Landwehr* – all began the process of creating the Nation in Arms. Colossal armies would be pitched into battle, swollen by conscription. By summer 1813, the allied field force would total over half a million men, with a further 250,000 in garrisons and in reserve. A method of manoeuvring this unwieldy monster had to be evolved. Napoleon tried to keep control in his own hands, and failed.

In Prussia the General Staff emerged: staff officers with common instruction, outlook and experience were spread through the army to serve with respective commanders, providing cohesion and continuity of policy, and in 1813, 1814 and 1815 the members of the Prussian military reform group constituted the most important staff personnel. Scharnhorst and then Gneisenau went to Blücher, Boyen to Bülow, Grolman to Kleist, Rauch to Yorck, Clausewitz to Count Walmoden and then to von Thielmann. The most successful commanders were those who worked well with their chiefs of staff, and none appreciated the services of the staff more than Blücher. The loss of Scharnhorst in June 1813 would cause him tremendous pain; fortunately Gneisenau filled the void. Blücher always paid warm credit to these two exceptional men.

Gneisenau, [he declared] being my chief of staff and very reliable, reports to me on the manoeuvres that are to be executed and the marches that are to be performed. Once convinced that he is right, I drive my troops through hell towards the goal and never stop until the desired end has been accomplished – yes, even though the officers trained in the old school may pout and complain and all but mutiny.

Blücher summed up the partnership in a speech at Oxford after the first year of war, when he received an honorary doctor's degree: 'Well! If I am to be a doctor, you must at least make Gneisenau an apothecary, for we two belong together always.'(5) Neither side of the partnership could have performed without the other, and among the potential candidates for the Prussian command in February 1813, only Blücher possessed the power to lead a huge army into battle inspired with maximum loyalty.

Such leadership was more essential in 1813 than ever before. Not only would the army be large, but the ranks would be filled by relatively untrained and often completely inexperienced troops. Prussia's situation generated unheralded patriotism; Blücher's personality channelled this emotion into military power. He had written to Scharnhorst in January: 'This is the moment for doing what I advised in the year 1809: namely, for calling the whole nation to arms.'(6) On the same day as he signed the Treaty of Kalisch, Frederick William appealed for volunteers for the *Jäger* corps; a week later he issued an edict for the general army call-up, based on measures put forward by the military reformers. 'What an inward transformation of the whole being this crusade for Freedom and Fatherland has effected in everyone!' exclaimed the historian Frederick Förster. 'Our whole existence has been inspired with a sense of dedication.'(7)

Even before Frederick William's compulsory edict, hundreds of men of all types and classes flocked forward to join the colours – students, peasants, schoolboys, bakers, labourers, merchants, and professors like Henry Steffens in Breslau. 'Thousands pouring into the town mixed with the inhabitants in the crowded streets, amidst troops, ammunition waggons, cannons, and loads of arms of every description.' Steffens addressed a university audience to persuade others to follow. 'Tears gushed to my eyes,' he wrote. 'I had no new cause to proclaim – what I said was but the echo of the thoughts and feelings of every hearer.'(8) The poet Ernst Arndt reached the peak of patriotic passion:

The harvest awaits the cutter. The moment has come
For plunging the steel into the enemy's breast:
A path for Freedom! Purify the soil!
The German soil, oh, cleanse it with thy Blood!

Only Russia provided Prussia with an ally at the start of the
Liberation War – Austria failed to summon sufficient courage and
Sweden prevaricated. The Russians had been weakened by the
same terrible winter weather which destroyed Napoleon's Grand
Army; losses during November and December totalled at least
250,000. The Treaty of Kalisch stipulated a Russian army of
150,000 men, yet many of these were weary and ill-equipped, and
newcomers were as untrained as their Prussian colleagues. Moreover, a strong dislike generally existed between the Russians and
Prussians, stemming from traditional emnity, hostilities between
the two countries in 1812, sheer ignorance and prejudice.

Old Blücher was the only one who liked us [wrote Frederick von
Schubert, senior Quartermaster on the Russian staff]. Gneisenau
hated the Russians. . . . Neither the generals nor the officers of each
army had any intercourse. . . . The chief thing was that Prussian
pedantry, their boasting and bragging, and their economical habits
made them anything but comrades for our officers, who were all
bon vivant, who recklessly spent their last *heller* [a low value coin]
on drinking or gambling and who did not understand pedantry or
boasting.(9)

Judging from Schubert's description, Blücher's character seemed
more Russian than Prussian, and his liking for the allies therefore
seemed understandable.

Blücher and his staff struggled with their problems prior to the
opening of the gigantic spring campaign. Napoleon's difficulties
were infinitely greater. 'The Prussians are no nation,' he raged
after hearing of Kalisch. 'They have no national pride. . . . We
have always despised them.' On 4th March French troops
evacuated Berlin, and Napoleon threw himself into preparations
for war. Over 400,000 men had fallen in Russia or proved too
weak or wounded to be of any further fighting use. A thousand
guns were left behind. Especially serious were the cavalry casualties
because they took longer to replace – about 160,000 horses died or
were captured. Now Napoleon had about two months in which to

raise new forces. Already, on his way back from Russia, he ordered fresh levies to be raised; those who had escaped previous levies, through age, infirmities or the nature of their occupation, must be screened again. Training began almost immediately with all available weapons, however antiquated, and officers tried desperately to inculcate spirit into their bewildered raw recruits. 'The Army was composed of young soldiers who had to be taught everything, and of non-commissioned officers who did not know much more,' wrote a French colonel, de Ferenzac.(10)

Prussia officially declared war against France on 13th March. Napoleon received the news on the 16th. 'Better a declared enemy than a doubtful ally,' he exclaimed. Frederick William embodied the *Landwehr* into his army – this militia comprised men between the ages of eighteen and fifty not already serving in the regular army. The *Landwehr* therefore marked an important step towards universal service, and enthusiasm inside Prussia became even more fanatical. Women turned their husbands' blue Sunday suits into uniforms, sent their jewellery and silver plate to the mint, and considered it highly honourable to tear wedding rings from their fingers and wear a simple band instead, inscribed: 'Gold I gave for Iron.' As many as 150,000 rings were exchanged in this fashion; Gneisenau wrote that the sight of 'so much true nobility' moved him to tears. Blücher became daily more impatient for the fight to begin, despite a feverish illness. By 18th March he had recovered sufficiently to travel and journeyed to his Army of Silesia.

The general plan of campaign had been prepared. Three allied armies would move to the river Elbe to block a French advance: in the north General Wittgenstein would advance from Berlin with 44,000 Russians, accompanied by Prussian contingents under Yorck and Bülow; in the centre the overall commander, Kutuzov, would lead the main Russian army; further south Blücher would march from Silesia to Dresden in Saxony. About 280,000 Prussians had been mobilized, amounting to six per cent of the entire population, but insufficient time had been available for instruction and for producing equipment. The *Landwehr* did not become effective until later in the year, and meanwhile the Prussian first line only comprised 68,000 men. Many were still untrained, and other problems confronted Blücher. Saxony, the country he was now about to enter, had still to declare support for Prussia, and might prove aggressive. Such hostility could have disastrous effect, with Blücher facing the French to his front and the Saxons astride his communications.

Blücher relied upon a policy of firmness with his own soldiers and fairness towards the Saxons. On 23rd March, as his leading regiments crossed the border from Silesia, he issued a warning to his men: the Saxons must be treated as 'future fellow-countrymen', and he continued: 'Soldiers of my Army, you know me. You know that I care for you like a father. But you know equally well that I tolerate no breach of discipline, and any such behaviour will be severely judged by me.'(11) These words reflected Blücher's individual literary style, unlike the eloquent proclamation drafted by Gneisenau, his Quartermaster-General, and issued to the Saxons in Blücher's name: 'We Prussians enter your territory stretching out to you a fraternal hand. A terrible judgement has been held in Eastern Europe by the Lord God of Hosts. . . . Guided and directed by the finger of Providence we are marching forth to fight. . . .'(12)

Blücher pressed into Saxony with all possible speed, taking only fourteen days to move the 250 kilometres from his Silesian base to the Elbe at Dresden: *en route* he showered the Saxons with shoes, clothes, food and further proclamations: if the people helped him, then he would give help in return. The Saxons allowed him to set up his headquarters in elegant Dresden, but Blücher sought outright assistance rather than mere acceptance. 'I am swamped with compliments here,' he wrote to his wife Katharina from the Saxon capital on the last day of March, 'but it seems that that is all the Saxons will give voluntarily.'(13) Moreover, Blücher's liberal distribution of presents and proclamations caused irritation in Berlin, where the Prussian and Russian monarchs were engaged in delicate negotiations with the Saxon ruler, Frederick Augustus. Blücher's presumptive appeals for the Saxons to rise against the French threatened to complicate the talks. 'I am not worried,' Blücher wrote to his wife. 'It is the end that counts.'(14)

Blücher had begun to experience the difficulties inherent in a multi-national alliance, and these problems soon multiplied. Kutuzov, old and ailing, was disinclined to take his forces far into Germany. He had always seen his duty as the liberation of his country, not of Europe, and by the time Blücher reached the Elbe the Russian commander had not even started from his base at Kalisch. Yet without Kutuzov's army moving into the centre of the allied front, Blücher's Army of Silesia remained isolated in the south. Reports reaching his headquarters indicated he was outnumbered by the French opposite him. Eugène Beauharnais commanded perhaps 80,000 men, with reinforcements arriving daily, and with small German states such as Bavaria and Württemberg declaring continued allegiance to Napoleon.

Blücher strengthened his defences as best he could. On 5th April his men attacked French positions at Möckern, driving the enemy back over the Elbe, but Blücher was unable to prevent Eugène's regiments linking up with French forces further north. He pushed as far forward over the Elbe as he dared, but a letter to his wife on 12th April, addressed from Colditz, hinted at his anxiety. 'I am still in good health, and that is the main thing since everything else will and *must* turn out all right.'(15) Nor could the allies expect immediate support from Austria. Both sides attempted to woo Emperor Francis and his Chancellor, Clement Wenceslas Metternich, but the latter advocated a far-seeing Austrian role: neither the French nor the allies should gain complete predominance, allowing Austria to emerge from the confusion with even greater authority. Saxony made clear she would be governed by Austria's action, and on 20th April the two countries signed a treaty of 'armed neutrality for the attainment of the healthful goal of peace'.

Two days earlier Blücher received long-awaited reports. Napoleon was moving to join his army. The Emperor left St Cloud on the 15th, reaching Mainz the following afternoon. Battle grew imminent. On 25th April Napoleon rode forward to Erfurt, the assembly area for the main French forces, and on the same day Gneisenau wrote to Hardenberg: 'The enemy are crossing the Saale, still in small detachments; but yet they are to be seen at every fordable point. I believe we are on the eve of great events. . . .'(16) Blücher's army still lay around Colditz, south-east of Leipzig; the Saale flowed across the front, about 70 kilometres to the west. Napoleon planned to advance towards Leipzig, forcing the allies to accept battle or fall behind the Elbe. The Emperor felt confident; he had managed to assemble an army of 226,000 men and 457 guns, including regiments summoned from Spain. But many of these soldiers proved woefully inexperienced. 'The best trained had been issued with muskets a month before,' wrote General Armand Caulaincourt, 'but the majority had been armed only since their march through Mayence, that is, twenty-four hours or a week.'(17) Already, Napoleon began to suffer from cavalry deficiencies which restricted his forward reconnaissance. 'Neither the men nor the horses had been to war,' commented the cavalry commander Colonel de Ferenzac, 'the former were twenty years old, the latter four – we said ourselves that they were chickens mounted on colts.'(18)

Yet allied problems also remained to be solved. Kutuzov at last began his advance from Kalisch, accompanied by King Frederick William and Czar Alexander – whose presence merely complicated proceedings. Then, on 28th April, the sixty-eight-year-old Russian General died. Choice of successor as allied commander-in-chief lay between Blücher, the most experienced and able, and the Russian candidate, Wittgenstein. Russia provided the largest allied army; Frederick William therefore bowed to Alexander's wishes, and Wittgenstein took overall command.

By the last day of April Napoleon's Army of the Main lay in the vicinity of Naumburg, while Eugène's Army of the Elbe was drawn up around Merseburg. To block the French advance, Wittgenstein deployed the main allied army in the area between Zwenkau and Altenburg, south of the Naumburg-Leipzig road and east of the Mülde River. The Prussian troops under Blücher, to the south of the allied line, seemed ready for conflict, in spirit if not in training and experience. 'Never,' wrote Boyen, 'did I see troops which inspired such confidence.' Clausewitz agreed: 'Never was an army animated by a better spirit. Without any sign of pride and wantonness there was a quiet trust in the sanctity of their cause.'

Both sides shuffled for position on 1st May. Bonaparte ordered Eugène to bring his Army of the Elbe forward from Merseburg to Schladebach, and he deployed his own Army of the Main at Lützen, Weissenfels and Naumburg. The Emperor entered the small town of Lützen during the evening. He ordered Ney to stand fast here and also to occupy in strength the nearby villages of Klein-Görschen, Gross-Görschen, Rahna and Kaja, all of which extended south of Lützen. The allies had retained the advantage of superior reconnaissance patrols; and Russian detachments now reported that the French flank at Kaja seemed weakly defended. Ney had neglected to probe the area south-west in the direction of Peggau and Zwenkau, and failed to realize that strong enemy forces were deployed within striking distance. Wittgenstein decided to seize the opportunity. French outposts could be surprised, and the enemy flank overrun, thus striking at the centre of the French army to slice it in half.

Late on 1st May a rider galloped into Blücher's camp on the east bank of the Elster, south of Wittgenstein's force. The attack

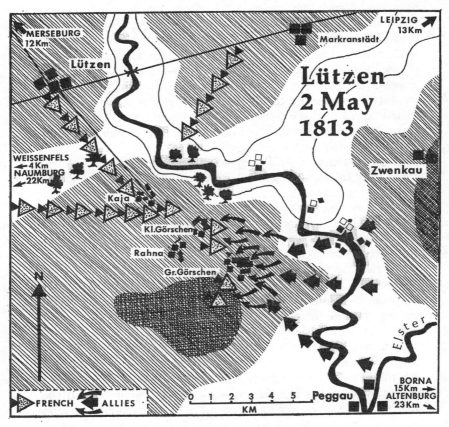

would begin at first light next day, 2nd May. Blücher would open the offensive. To do so his army would have to undertake a night march to Peggau, from where it could advance upon Kaja and the other villages by Lützen. Blücher immediately issued his orders, and soon after midnight the regiments began to creep forward for Blücher's first battle since his surrender to the French seven years before.

At first all went well. Then, just before dawn, Blücher discovered that Wittgenstein's staff had made a serious and potentially disastrous error, ordering Yorck's corps forward in a direction which crossed Blücher's path at the Elster. Confusion increased in the darkness as regiments attempted to sort themselves out, and the mistake led to a delay of about three hours. Blücher's men would be denied much-needed rest before the fighting began. The mistake threw Blücher into a vile temper. The allies lost some of their advantage of surprise, and the 88,000 Prussian and Russian troops on the battlefield would be outnumbered – Napoleon had about 140,000 in the vicinity. Plans nevertheless went on unchanged. Wittgenstein aimed to push forward to the flat fields around Lützen, where the terrain offered a chance for the allied cavalry to use its superiority. But before this level area lay the villages of Gross and Klein Görschen, Kaja and Rahna, from which the French infantry and guns had first to be expelled, and it would be in and around these villages that the full holocaust of battle would rage. By mid-morning Blücher had positioned his troops on the slopes facing Gross Görschen. Napoleon himself was absent from the area. Not expecting an engagement that day, he had ridden with Ney to join General Jacques-Alexandre Lauriston, moving onwards on the road to Leipzig north of the battlefield. While on this road Napoleon heard the booming guns which opened the conflict. He reacted immediately, sending Ney galloping back to his corps, then ordering all troops *en route* for Leipzig to turn south and march upon Kaja. Marmont and Bertrand, west of Lützen, were also commanded to send troops to the area.

Blücher and his staff waited under meagre cover for the allied infantry to take the vital villages. Battle had begun at about 11 o'clock. Waves of infantry advanced across the pastures, up to the low walls around the houses – only to be met with terrible volleys from the French defenders. Repeated assaults failed to prise the enemy from this excellent cover, and French artillery pounded the Prussian positions. Steffens, standing with Blücher's staff and experiencing his first battle, wrote: 'It seemed to me as if the balls came in thick masses on every side – as if I was in a heavy shower of rain without getting wet.' Each salvo caused terrible casualties in the massed Prussian battalions waiting to attack; cannon balls rolled through the ranks, ripping off legs and

feet, and grape-shot cut bloody swaths as the men stood defenceless. Choking smoke swirled everywhere. Blücher, peering through
this fog, could see the lines of infantry struggling forward again
over the shell-scarred slopes. The lines broke at the stone walls;
some Prussians managed to scramble over, only to be massacred
by French bayonets, and the survivors streamed back again. More
enemy cannon balls arched into the smoking sky to crash upon the
Prussians. A member of Blücher's staff gave this description of his
commander:

> Blücher, with the most absolute imperturbability, remained for the
> most part at points of more or less greatest danger, indefatigably
> smoking his pipe. When it was smoked to the end he would hold it
> out behind him and call 'Schmidt!', whereupon his orderly would
> hand him one freshly filled and the old gentleman smoked away at
> his ease. [The eye-witness account continued:] Once ... a grenade
> fell directly in front of us. Everyone shouted, 'Your Excellency, a
> grenade!' 'Well, let the hellish thing alone then!' said Blücher very
> quietly. He stood by until it burst and then, and not until then,
> shifted his position.(19)

Numbed newcomers like Steffens, to whom all seemed incom-
prehensible, marvelled at the behaviour of the veterans. 'Gneisenau
seemed quite joyfully in his element,' wrote the ex-Professor.(20)
Yet each infantry attack left a thicker debris of men around the
walls of the villages; each artillery salvo brought further heaps of
shattered bodies and whinnying, dying horses. Prussian troops
seized one then another battered house at Gross Görschen; the
French threw them from the ruins again. Groups of infantry ran
forward while others retreated from the previous attack; lines were
reformed, smashed, reformed again, each time with fewer men;
groups of riders cantered from one section of the chaos to another;
horse artillery careered across the slopes and over the bodies,
unlimbering to fire, then dashing on again; wounded men tried
to stagger or crawl back to safety, or sat white-faced waiting for
help. Blücher sat on his horse, smoking his pipe. The General
became increasingly eager to attempt a full-scale cavalry charge
in an attempt to dislodge the stubborn French. Steffens was
handed a message for Wittgenstein requesting such a cavalry
attack.

Now began the darker part of my day [wrote Steffens]. I rode forward, and looked about. I had no idea where to find Wittgenstein. . . . I felt a tottering, a swimming, which sprang from my inmost soul, and increased every moment. I was plainly seized with a panic – the cannon fever. I found Wittgenstein notwithstanding, and delivered my message.

Steffens made his way across the battlefield again, his horse picking its delicate way through the bodies, and he returned to Blücher's staff. 'All was in active engagement, every man knowing his duty and working hard in his appointed place.'(21)

But Blücher's patience had almost gone. He witnessed assault after assault as the infantry clawed at the villages; standing idle never suited him. He abruptly reined round his horse and galloped off through the smoke to find Wittgenstein and obtain the order to launch his cavalry; his staff hurried after him. Wittgenstein, startled by his sudden appearance, persuaded Blücher to be patient, and the Prussian commander returned angrily to his post, puffing in a bad-tempered fashion at his pipe again as the infantry marched once more to the slaughter. Napoleon reached the fighting at about 2.30 p.m. and found his 3rd Corps in a desperate condition at the villages. But the men rallied with his appearance, and he rode in the thick of the fight so all could see him. 'This is probably the one day of his whole career,' commented the French Marshal Auguste Marmont, 'on which Napoleon incurred most personal danger on the battlefield.' Opposing lines of infantrymen, their faces blacked by cannon powder and streaked with sweat, remained locked on to the villages. Gross Görschen fell to the Prussians, and the cheers rang thin over the battlefield, reaching Blücher; the French attacked again and drove the Prussians into the raging inferno between the hamlets. 'The whole quadrangle was so thickly sown with dead and wounded,' declared an official account of the battle, 'that it seemed as if several battalions had bivouacked there.'(22)

But now, as the spring afternoon lengthened, Blücher received the order to attack with his cavalry. The troopers lined up amidst the smoke, bugles sounded the advance, and the cavalry thundered into the maelstrom. One charge after another swept down the slope, and seventy-year-old Blücher fought in exactly similar fashion as he had as a hussar twenty years before – he led his men into battle, sabre high and his voice roaring encouragement above the din. All his staff officers did the same, including Scharnhorst on the right wing and Gneisenau on the left.

I was right in the middle of the enemy [wrote another staff officer, Clausewitz]. Since we could not influence the command of the battle, we [the staff] could only fight with sword in hand. [He added:] To play such a direct part in the fight would at any other time have been a distinction for an officer of the general staff. But at Gross Görschen everyone did this or something similar.(23)

Kaja fell under the pounding Prussian cavalry and infantry charges, then Gross Görschen, and the Prussians managed to cling to the rubble. But infantrymen were staggering with exhaustion; cavalrymen could barely lift their heavy sabres and their horses stumbled at each step, fetlocks and flanks sprayed with blood. Charges took place at no more than a weary trot and Prussian casualties continued to soar. Staff officers were amongst the wounded. Clausewitz had been gashed above his right ear and blood streamed down his neck; Scharnhorst was carried wounded to the rear, although his injury was at first not believed serious. Then Blücher narrowly escaped death. He led charge after charge, for two terrible hours, then he joined his cavalry with Yorck's troops for another assault, this time against Klein Görschen and Rahna. French musket balls hissed from the defences; his horse fell. A bullet struck Blücher's back. Seizing another mount he ordered a staff officer to ride to Yorck, instructing him to take command, and then Blücher quit the field, blood saturating his uniform and saddle. He found a surgeon and believed himself dying: so much blood gushed from his back that he feared the bullet had pierced through to his stomach. 'I shall collapse soon,' he muttered to those clustered around him. The surgeon knifed away the sodden uniform. The musket ball had cut along the flesh in a long, raking gash, but had failed to penetrate further. Blücher's movement in the saddle when riding from the fight had worked the bullet to the surface again – and he found it in his boot when he undressed that night. Blücher waited impatiently for a rough bandage to be fastened and for two other bullet snicks to be sponged. Aides helped him back into the saddle, and he hurried to the battle again.

More enemy regiments were rushing to the field and Napoleon gradually gained numerical superiority. Macdonald pressed the right of the allied army at about 5.30 in the evening; Bertrand and Marmont closed on the left. Napoleon continued to display superb tactical control, and ordered a battery of about eighty guns to be dragged into line south-west of Kaja. Yorck attempted a cavalry charge against this artillery, but failed to prevent the concentration, and the French cannon opened fire. Napoleon threw his most powerful infantry force into battle – four columns of the Young Guard supported by the Old Guard and the Guard cavalry. They advanced to their famous cry: *'La Garde au Feu!'* and they swept down the slopes and on to the villages. Rahna, Gross and Klein Görschen were stormed and taken, although with fearful French casualties. Mortier, leading the Young Guard, lay pinned beneath his wounded horse and around him were heaped 1,069 of his prized troops, slaughtered by Prussian muskets. The time was almost seven o'clock. Wittgenstein frantically tried to stem the French advance but his flanks were being pressed in and the centre began to collapse. News reached Wittgenstein that Kleist had been thrown from Leipzig; the French therefore threatened the allied line of retreat. The allies began to fall back further from the villages. Twilight spread across the hideous mess. Both sides suffered exhaustion, but both still held their original positions.

Blücher believed with typical aggressive optimism that victory could still be seized, and he demanded one last cavalry charge. Wittgenstein reluctantly gave permission. Blücher's hussars climbed back into their saddles and wheeled their drooping horses into line. Blücher, despite the throbbing gash in his back, trotted to the front and bellowed his own battle-cry – soon to be as famous as that of Napoleon's Guard: *'Vorwärts!'* The line stabbed into the darkness, down the slope, over the wreckage of battle, on towards the French position near Kaja where Napoleon stood in a square formed by his Guard. Enemy soldiers ran for their lives with Blücher's cavalrymen slashing them down as they fled. But the Guard stood firm. Musket fire quickened, the cavalry horses were blown, the charge milled round the square then faltered.

> Burning villages lit the skyline [wrote one of Napoleon's staff officers], when suddenly on the right flank of the French army a line of cavalry dashed by with a muffled roar, coming right up to the square behind which was the Emperor. I believe that had they advanced quickly two hundred paces further Napoleon and his whole suite would have been taken.(24)

Blücher retreated with his survivors.

Wittgenstein insisted upon withdrawal. Blücher continued to scorn this defeatism. Gneisenau, who replaced the injured Scharnhorst, supported Blücher and both persuaded Wittgenstein that although the army would withdraw, a large proportion of the force would remain on the battlefield overnight. In this way they could march out in daylight, in full defiant view of the enemy. Bustle continued deep into the night. Across the fields glowed burning buildings and French camp fires; the air lay thick with explosive fumes. 'Our troops were marching in slow and perfect order,' wrote Steffens, 'while other detachments were reposing by the bivouac fires, which lit up the trees.'(25) Next day, 3rd May, the allied troops marched back to Peggau and then eastwards to Borna. They left 15,000 men behind, but French losses were higher, reaching 21,000. Blücher considered the battle a victory, despite the withdrawal, and his men agreed. 'The army was in such perfect order,' commented Steffens, 'that many considered the retreat an unnecessary disgrace.' Grumbles reached Blücher's ears, and early on the 4th he addressed assembled troops in the street at Borna as the regiments prepared to move. An officer saw him approaching and shouted the order to present muskets. 'Oh leave the arms alone!' Blücher called. An eye-witness account continued:

> It fell very quiet. Blücher rode up and with a mighty voice gave his address. . . . 'Good morning children! This time everything went very well. The French must have noticed with whom they have to do battle.' Then, taking off his field cap, he continued. . . . 'The King thanks you. There is no powder left, therefore we have to go back behind the Elbe. . . . Whoever now says we are retiring is not worth his name. . . . Good morning children!'(26)

Blücher repeated his message to each division as the troops headed for Meissen. 'I must confess,' wrote Steffens, 'that there was something beside the words which gave such effect to the address, and that much was owing to the appearance and manner of the aged but powerful-looking man.'(27) Napoleon also tried to encourage his exhausted troops as they prepared to move from Lützen. He moved amongst them, shouting: 'The battle of Lützen will be rated higher than the battles of Austerlitz, Jena,

Friedland and the Moskva [Borodino].' But he confided to Caulaincourt: 'My eagles are again victorious, but my star is setting.' Blücher's private words were as enthusiastic as his public message. 'The enemy has lost far more than we have, almost double,' he wrote to his wife on the 4th. 'The French may blow on the wind as much as they like [but] they'll hardly be able to forget the 2nd May.'(28)

Blücher told Katharina that he had been hit three times, but only his back wound remained sore – he would bring her the bullet as a souvenir. Clausewitz also wrote home with details of personal casualties. 'General Blücher is severely bruised. General Scharnhorst was shot in the leg, but it is nothing serious, and he is back. . . . Only two officers from the Guard Fusilier battalion are neither dead nor wounded . . . and many others of our acquaintance all of whom I cannot name. . . .'(29) Officers and men were reorganized as the army withdrew towards the Elbe at Meissen, and as French advance units made half-hearted attempts to harry the Prussian rear. Blücher suffered increasingly from his back. For almost a week after Lützen he stayed in the saddle, and the jolting re-opened the gash; on the 9th the weeping wound obliged him to travel in a carriage, much to his disgust. Scharnhorst also neglected his injury. He had been ordered to ride to Vienna, to try and enlist Austrian aid for the allies. Infection spread from the leg wound, and he sent a depressed letter to Gneisenau from Zittau on the 10th: 'My friend . . . Take my sons into your care.'(30)

Gneisenau displayed his ability as Blücher's acting chief of staff, and promised to be a worthy replacement for Scharnhorst, although the two men differed considerably. Gneisenau had more traits in common with Blücher. Whilst, like Scharnhorst, he was an intellectual, he also showed a strong sense of the dramatic and could be extremely emotional. This sometimes led him to be impetuous and biased, for example with his dislike of the Russians and later of Wellington. But Gneisenau, like Blücher, could inspire intense devotion. 'I never saw such a blend of noble pride and real humility,' wrote Steffens of Gneisenau, 'of confidence and modesty. . . . There was something princely in his look.'(31) The eminent Prussian politician Theodor von Schön declared in his diary: 'Gneisenau is a man for great deeds. He has both vigour and cultivation. A man of heart and head! Of all the military men we have, assuredly the one I would most willingly entrust an army to.'(32)

From the start Blücher and Gneisenau found they shared similar views over the need for an aggressive policy. Wittgenstein promised after Lützen that he intended to fight another battle as soon as possible. Blücher and his acting chief of staff believed this battle should begin immediately: the allied army remained confident whereas Napoleon had suffered heavy losses and his troops would be demoralized. The French supply organization lacked experience, and deficiencies had been revealed – the French took three days after Lützen before beginning a determined advance after the allies. Blücher brought his regiments to Meissen still in perfect order, and the Prussians took up excellent positions on the east bank of the Elster. Then, on about the 10th, Blücher received orders to pull back still further. The line of the Elbe was to be abandoned. 'The chief evil from which we suffer,' wrote Gneisenau angrily to Hardenberg, 'is the leadership of the army. Count Wittgenstein is unequal to it.'(33) The Prussians withdrew and the French followed with Napoleon entering Dresden – it would be the last time the Emperor entered a capital city at the head of his army.

Blücher's plea for a firm offensive at this critical moment seemed justified. About 17,000 French were lost during the pursuit of the Prussians from Lützen, through desertion, weariness and allied counter-attacks. But allied disagreements increased, with Frederick William insisting Berlin must be defended, and with the Russians wishing to move east to Breslau, thus remaining close to Russia and Austria. Wittgenstein, caught in the centre, could only attempt a compromise, and he ordered the army to take up positions at Bautzen, ready for battle – but insisting this battle would only be fought on defensive lines. The allied army therefore remained inactive after reaching Bautzen on the 14th, while the monarchs continued their arguments in a nearby damp, dreary castle.

Blücher's good humour revived slightly with the prospect of renewed conflict. He wrote to his wife on the 15th:

I am feeling much better now . . . so much so that yesterday and today I rode again without any great discomfort. It will be two to three weeks before my wound is properly healed. Otherwise I am well. [He continued:] We are again in view of the enemy and look forward to a second battle. I think it will be harder for Napoleon than the first. We have all recovered very well and are ready to fight. Our brave people are very excited. Don't worry. God is on the side of justice.(34)

Stein visited Blücher's headquarters near Bautzen on the 18th. 'He is in good health,' Stein wrote to his wife. 'His wound is almost healed; he talks of nothing but battles and fighting.'(35) But one day followed another without the allied commander-in-chief taking action, and Napoleon attempted to buy even more time. On 17th May he despatched Caulaincourt to the Czar with an armistice offer. The bid failed; the Czar refused to see the French emissary, and Napoleon prepared for battle.

Preliminary French manoeuvring began on 19th May, with Napoleon ordering three of his corps to march on Bautzen, supported by a fourth. Marshal Ney was also commanded to approach the town, except for two of his divisions which would advance on Berlin. Soon afterwards Napoleon changed his plan: all Ney's troops must concentrate on Bautzen. Meanwhile Napoleon rode along the line opposite the allied army on the 19th to study enemy positions; these spread along the eastern bank of the Spree near Bautzen itself, with Blücher's 32,000 Prussians forming the right, or northern flank, around the village of Kreckwitz. Napoleon returned to his camp behind Bautzen and issued last orders – a frontal attack would be launched the following morning, 20th May. Ney was instructed to strike from the north, from the Berlin road, thus threatening the allied rear, but as this flanking assault would take time to begin, Napoleon planned to make Bautzen a two-day battle.

Dawn on the 20th revealed a perfect May morning. Three hours later the first cannons roared behind Bautzen and muskets suddenly crackled along the Spree. Blücher and his staff were positioned on the heights of Kreckwitz, to the east of the hamlet bearing the same name. The day would be amongst the most frustrating of Blücher's life. The Prussian commander and his acting chief of staff, annoyed already with Wittgenstein's intention to fight a defensive battle, were further incensed by the allied leader's disposition of forces, which they considered too cautious and incapable of achieving victory. The cavalry remained virtually inactive. Blücher and his staff stood helpless while enemy infantry battered a way over the Spree and into the Prussian and Russian positions. The granite-capped Kreckwitz ridge commanded an extensive view of the whole battlefield; Löbau lay to the left, Bautzen to the front, and the Spree flowed on the right, sparkling in the sunlight. Infantry action continued throughout the after-

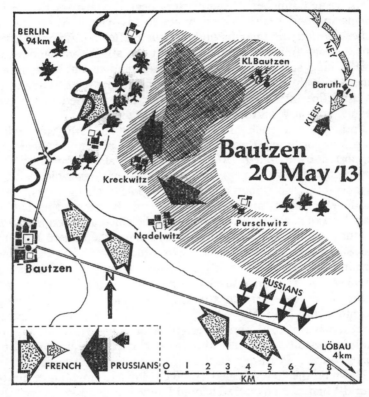

noon, with the fighting fiercest in the direction of Russian-held Löbau and in the Prussian sector between Blücher's headquarters and Bautzen. 'We could hear that the firing was very sharp and heavy,' wrote Steffens. 'Some cannon-balls came amongst us, and scouts were continually coming and going.'(36) But Blücher could do nothing to influence events; he merely sat on his horse or on a rock, pipe in his mouth, or walked impatiently up and down desperate for action. The Russian positions began to crack. 'I saw first one and then another collapse,' commented Steffens, 'and the

contending masses advancing or falling back from either side.'
Darkness fell with the French successfully lodged in small pockets
on the east bank of the Spree. A sullen silence replaced the
echoing cannon. Blücher sat with his back against the rocks,
wrapped in his ankle-length cloak; below glittered French bivouac
fires and flames flickered from eighteen hamlets and villages,
burning from the battle.

Napoleon sat in the bishop's palace at Bautzen, consulting his
maps. His plan envisaged the allies being pinned down by frontal
attacks and artillery bombardment while Ney worked his way
round the flank, and then the allies would either be trapped, or
obliged to undertake precipitate withdrawal back against the
Bohemian mountains. Napoleon then reckoned Austria would
refuse to enter the alliance against him and the Prussians and
Russians would have to accept a dictated peace. So, at four o'clock
in the morning of 21st May, the French were summoned to their
battle positions. Blücher's staff could hear the distant bugle calls
for the infantry to stand to their weapons and for the artillerymen
to prime their guns. Just before six o'clock these guns flashed and
boomed in the valley below, along an eight-mile front. Infantry
advanced under cover of this bombardment, filtering over the
Spree and into the hills. It seemed a repetition of the previous day
– but Ney steadily moved towards the villages of Wirschen and
Baruth behind Blücher's position, and in front the French infantry
and guns steadily pressed back the allied defences. 'The enemy's
cannonade was directed towards the central hill where we were
posted,' said Steffens. 'It came nearer every minute.'

Lines of infantrymen left the valley bottoms and began to file
up the slopes; an especially heavy bombardment was brought
down to the left of Blücher's position as the French tried to blast
a gap for Mortier's troops to seize Kreckwitz. In front Bertrand's
men ran shouting and cheering at the Prussian lines; the defenders
shot and bayoneted them back down the hillside. But then an
over-excited messenger brought Blücher the news that Ney would
'soon be in your rear'; the Prussian commander roared with
laughter at the vulgar ambiguity of the phrase. 'I am extra-
ordinarily pleased,' he replied. 'The fellow will soon be in the best
position for me to give him the honour which can only be issued
from my behind.' He believed Ney's extended advance could be
lopped – if Wittgenstein consented to an immediate counter-

attack. Messengers left Blücher's command post to urge Wittgenstein into action, but one after another these riders returned with
unsatisfactory replies.

Blücher stormed with anger at each report of Ney's encircling
movement, of the inadequate attempts to deal with this threat, of
the punishment being suffered by his men before Bautzen. His
self-control snapped. Steffens witnessed the scene.

> I shall never forget Blücher's rage when he called furiously for his
> horse, intending to lead on a charge of cavalry. [Steffens continued:]
> The Generals, however, surrounded him with entreaties to abstain
> from so desperate a measure, which would risk everything by
> sacrificing his own life. They restrained the veteran with the
> utmost difficulty.(37)

By four o'clock in the afternoon only Kleist's troops held the thin
screen standing between Ney and the rear of the Prussian
positions. Wittgenstein ordered withdrawal. The allies moved from
the defences which they had held with such loss for two days.

Yet Napoleon had been denied decisive victory, and once again
French casualties were higher than those of the allies – about
22,500 against 11,000. Napoleon is reported to have exclaimed:
'What, no results? No trophies? No prisoners? And such butchery?
These beasts have learned something.'

The allies withdrew in good order, falling back on Silesia to
maintain contact with Austria, and Napoleon took twenty-four
hours to organize his army for the pursuit. Vigorous allied counter-
attacks shattered his advance guard at Reichenbach on the 22nd
and at Haynau on the 26th. During the ten days after Bautzen the
French lost nearly 20,000 men – almost as many as in the battle
itself – and although more perished through sickness and desertion
than through allied action, the casualty figures showed that
Prussian resistance had far from finished. And on the same day as
Haynau, allied prospects promised further improvement when the
Russian General Barclay de Tolly replaced the unsatisfactory
Wittgenstein as supreme field commander. Opportunity existed
for firm leadership, but Barclay, who had lost his command of the
Russian army to Kutuzov at the opening of the 1812 campaign,
soon proved as dilatory as Wittgenstein. He had already told the
Czar that army reorganization would be impossible whilst active
operations continued; in view of the situation and the lack of

ammunition, he urged withdrawal to Poland. Frederick William was horrified by this abandonment of Berlin. Disagreement in the allied headquarters intensified in the last days of May. 'We are burdened with heavy chains,' complained Gneisenau, 'and have little hope that things will improve, because there is no one to seize and combine the elements of victory.' Gneisenau believed Barclay to be 'absolutely lacking in ideas'.(38)

Napoleon threatened to outmanoeuvre his enemy during this chaotic period. Leading French units crossed the Katzbach on the 27th and two days later Davout and Vandamme reoccupied Hamburg. Nicolas Oudinot had been ordered to march on Berlin. The allies were pressed south to Schweidnitz. Napoleon pushed forward again, took Breslau on 1st June, and seemed likely to increase his initiative. Yet Napoleon's army also needed time to draw breath; his supply system still proved totally inadequate and his men were half-starved and barefoot, his ammunition had almost been expended, his cavalry force remained weak. Above all, Napoleon sought time in which to approach the Austrians. At the end of May he therefore increased his efforts for an armistice and this time he met with success: the monarchs agreed to a truce on 1st June. Five days later the armistice was extended until 20th July and later to 16th August.

Blücher and Gneisenau expressed their disgust with this cessation of hostilities. They moved into quarters at Strehlen and fretted for further fighting, although the relative inactivity allowed Blücher's wound to heal. In fact the armistice brought considerable advantages to the allies, and Napoleon later admitted that the truce turned out to be one of his gravest mistakes. He failed in his attempt to win over the Austrians after a disastrous meeting with Metternich at Dresden on 26th June. The Austrian Minister put forward the price to be paid for allegiance with Napoleon: Austria must be given northern Italy, Russia must obtain Poland and Prussia must regain the left bank of the Elbe. Napoleon railed against the Austrian Emperor, his father-in-law.

Meanwhile the Prussians could benefit from experience gained so far in the 1813 campaign, and Blücher hurried forward improvements. Clausewitz, bitterly hostile to the armistice, nevertheless wrote a paper on the advantages to be gained, and this document was issued to the troops at the instigation of Blücher's chief of staff. 'He, who carelessly lets the truce flow past . . . cannot go forward with courage and confidence, with cool judgement and a clear view of the future . . .'(39) The weeks of truce were crammed with training, replenishment of military supplies, intensified war production; the *Landwehr* and volunteer *Jäger* detachments were strengthened – because of the *Landwehr* the Prussians could now send an army of 162,000 into the field. The whole country seethed with military activity.

In the midst of these preparations came a moment of especial sadness for Blücher. News reached his camp that Scharnhorst had died at Prague on 28th June because of his neglected wound. The outcome of his illness had been expected but the loss, both personal and professional, still meant a bitter blow. During his chief of staff's last days Blücher had commented: 'Better to lose another battle than to lose Scharnhorst,' and he repeated the words after receiving the report of Scharnhorst's death: 'A lost battle would not have been a greater loss to us.' Blücher relied increasingly upon Gneisenau. 'If he goes,' wrote Blücher to his wife, 'I will follow, dead or alive.'(40)

Events once more moved towards war. On 27th June the Reichenbach Treaty was signed in strict secrecy by Austria, Russia and Prussia; the treaty, prepared by Metternich, contained Austria's pledge to declare war on France if Napoleon continued to disagree with the impossible proposals put forward at the Dresden meeting. Encouragement reached the allies from far-away Spain: on 19th July news arrived of Wellington's victory at Vitoria, fought on 21st June. 'Wellington's brilliant victory fills us with joy,' wrote Stein. 'Long live the Marquis of Wellington!'(41) Blücher commented: 'We have to get the French in the same way. We can do it, if we use all our strength.'(42) He warned his staff to be ready. 'My friend,' he wrote to Gneisenau, away on leave, 'come soon to me. As our friend is dead it seems vital we go hand in hand together.' Blücher and Gneisenau grumbled at being excluded from the allied planning for war, and Blücher falsely feared he would be considered too old for renewed conflict. 'They shan't get me to retire,' he exclaimed.

At the end of June Blücher wrote to a friend in Pomerania: 'With God's help we shall start again in four weeks' time.' On 23rd July he received his orders: he would command the Army of Silesia again, but with more men than before: his initial strength totalled 200,000 troops. Austria presented as an ultimatum to Napoleon the terms already put forward by Metternich; the terms remained completely unacceptable. The armistice ended on 10th August and within twenty-four hours Austria declared war. 'At last we know where we are,' said the French Emperor, of whom Blücher now remarked: 'He's only a stupid fellow.' Vast armies immediately began to march, clogging the roads of Prussia, Poland, Austria, France and the Rhine kingdoms with massed columns of men, squadron after squadron of clattering cavalry, creaking, rumbling lines of guns, and thousands of waggons. The largest campaign in the history of war had begun.

Carnage at the Katzbach

COLOSSAL ARMIES HAD been created. The allies totalled over 520,000 men, with another 260,000 in reserve and garrison duty. Napoleon managed to assemble 442,000, in addition to 126,000 in the second line and in fortresses on the Elbe, in Poland and in Prussia. The allies had grounds for optimism, but Blücher's spirits suddenly sank in August, immediately before the start of hostilities. On the 9th he answered a summons to the royal headquarters at Reichenbach, where he heard detailed plans prepared for the conduct of operations, and these brought such an outburst of disgust from Blücher that for a moment it seemed Prussia would have to find a new commander. He demanded an interview with Barclay de Tolly, at which he threatened to resign.

Planning suffered from royal interference, and from an undue stress on the need for mutual allied support. Three armies would take the field: Blücher's Army of Silesia, the Army of Bohemia, and the Army of the North. In command of the Bohemian army, mainly comprising Austrian troops, was Prince Karl zu Schwarzenberg, who had led the Austrian contingent in Napoleon's forces during the 1812 campaign. An even more recent convert from the French Emperor commanded the Army of the North: Bernadotte, to whom Blücher had surrendered at Lübeck in 1806, and who had come over to the allies during the summer with the title of Crown Prince of Sweden. Blücher had no objection to working alongside Napoleon's previous colleagues, although he suspected their abilities. Schwarzenberg, who took over as commander-in-chief from Barclay on 17th August, proved cautious and overmethodical, although he showed himself adept at dealing with monarchs. Bernadotte was also cautious, and this former French Marshal had exerted strong influence over the war plans to which Blücher took intense exception. Blücher's whole character rebelled against defensive war; and the campaign would be conducted on extremely defensive lines. Bernadotte explained his policy in a letter dated 6th August: 'I shall tire him out by manoeuvring. Our numbers are almost equal. We must keep what we have. One remains the stronger if one spare's one's troops. Let us hold on!'(1)

The war plan therefore stipulated that Bernadotte would advance cautiously by the Middle Elbe towards Leipzig, while Blücher moved forward for Torpau where Napoleon's positions in Saxony could be threatened, but both Bernadotte and Blücher would avoid battle. Instead, the plans envisaged Bohemia as the centre of operations. Schwarzenberg's Austrians would be given priority, and if Napoleon attacked this main Bohemian army both Bernadotte and Blücher would have to hurry to Schwarzenberg's aid. The objective would be to wear Napoleon down.

To underline the importance of Schwarzenberg's Army of Bohemia, upon which Napoleon was expected to launch his principal thrust, Blücher was told to despatch 120,000 men from his 200,000-strong force, to bolster the allied commander-in-chief. Other reinforcements soon raised Blücher's Army of Silesia to 105,000, but the newcomers were less well trained. The most he could obtain from his heated meeting with Barclay de Tolly on 7th August was reluctant approval for his plea to be allowed to attack a French force inferior in number, but only if an extremely favourable opportunity should be revealed. In return for this slight concession Blücher withdrew his request to resign. 'We have done all in our power,' he wrote to a friend, 'but the Russian Guards and the heavy cavalry are kept in a glass case while our people sacrifice themselves.'(2)

But at least Blücher felt satisfied with the atmosphere at his own headquarters. He had an excellent staff under Gneisenau; Müffling was his Quartermaster-General, and Goltz, another veteran of the Rhine campaign, remained his principal Adjutant. A member of his staff described the 'joyfulness of the spirit and the trust in victory' which prevailed. 'Everyone was convinced that he was doing his best in the service of the ablest and most trustworthy man.'(3) Blücher felt less easy over his corps com-

manders; one, General Fabian Gottlieb von Sacken, seemed solid
and dependable, but doubts existed over the other two senior
officers, Yorck and General Louis-Alexandre Langeron. As
Clausewitz had commented about Yorck at the time of Tauroggen,
he was 'gloomy, choleric and reserved, and a bad subordinate',
although he could also display outstanding bravery. As for
Langeron, Blücher later commented that he was 'not one of the
people as I need and like them to be'. The coming campaign would
be intensely exhausting; Blücher would need to dredge every last
drop of strength from his men, and from his commanders.

One evening in early August Gneisenau rose to his feet to
present a toast. 'Gentlemen, we shall taste this year's grapes on
the Rhine. Do not mistake me, I mean the last grapes which, in
November, will yet be hanging on the vines.'(4) On 14th August
Blücher's army started to move towards the French. 'Today I
continue the advance with the army to the Katzbach,' wrote
Blücher to Hardenberg on the 16th, 'and tomorrow, should the
enemy beat a retreat, shall be after him quickly enough.'(5)
Twenty-four hours earlier, his forty-fifth birthday, Napoleon had
left Dresden to join his army deployed along the Elbe. The allies
still expected him to advance against the Army of Bohemia, but
Bonaparte had noticed the withdrawal of strength from Blücher's
Army of Silesia to support Schwarzenberg further north, and
altered his plans – the first French thrust would be made against
Blücher. Skirmishing soon started between French units and
Blücher's Prussian and Russian regiments. On the 19th these
engagements intensified along the Katzbach river. 'I am well,'
wrote Blücher to his wife, 'and writing this surrounded by the
dead and the living.'(6)

On 21st December Napoleon reached his army and commanded
an attack. Prussian and Russian forward regiments lay close
enough to the enemy over the River Bober to hear the cheers
which greeted the Emperor's arrival, and Blücher obeyed his
instructions to retreat when threatened. Depressed and angry, he
nevertheless tried to overcome his own feelings in a proclamation
to the troops, issued as they marched towards Goldberg: 'The
enemy wants to compel us to a decisive battle. But our advantage
demands that we avoid such a battle. Therefore we will retreat,
and probably hurt him very much because he will lose time.'(7)

All Blücher's powers of leadership were now required. He had to manoeuvre the enemy into a position whereby the Silesian army could turn and strike to its advantage. But his men had to be driven harder than ever before and their eagerness for battle had to be curbed. Withdrawal resulted in exhaustion; men collapsed by the roadside; supplies could not be organized properly during the rapid changes of direction; regiments threatened to split apart, and their commanders raged at the apparent appalling waste. Withdrawal continued for seven wearying days, while the enemy constantly snapped at the Prussian and Russian heels. Napoleon complained that each time he attempted to attack in strength, the enemy slipped away again. Blücher rode backwards and forwards along his tired columns, urging the men on.

Langeron commented on the 23rd: 'Clapping his hands, he shouted continuously, "Oh how marvellous!" . . . I had to waken him from his admiration and make him realize that if he stayed for another five minutes near the front line he would repeat his admiration to the nearby enemy.'(8) Langeron soon began to grumble when his troops began to lose cohesion under the continued strain. Strongest opposition to Blücher came from Yorck; by 24th August he could stand the situation no longer and rode to Blücher's headquarters, now at Jauer. Yorck had already pleaded for a rest day for his suffering troops and his request had been refused. Now he burst into the room where Blücher and Gneisenau dined with their staff.

'You're destroying the troops!' he shouted. 'You are marching them to no purpose!'

Blücher summoned him into an adjoining room, where Gneisenau repeated the plans and described Yorck's objections as unreasonable. Blücher sat silent, while Gneisenau claimed Yorck's behaviour bordered on the insubordinate – Gneisenau, in fact, was technically lower in rank than the corps commander. Blücher's chief of staff flung open the door for Yorck and asked: 'Has His Excellency any further order?' Yorck ignored Gneisenau, bowed coldly to Blücher, and left.(9)

But Blücher's constant manoeuvring between the Katzbach and Bober relieved pressure from Schwarzenberg further north. The Austrian commander advanced first to Leipzig, then changed direction towards Dresden. Napoleon immediately hurried north, leaving Macdonald in command of the troops opposite the Prussians and Russians in the Katzbach area. 'Almost everybody says that the French Emperor is with his army,' Blücher wrote to the King, 'but I am not very sure about this. It is possible that the Emperor has left part of an army corps behind to deceive me.' By the morning of the 25th intelligence reports revealed that Blücher's chance had come, even though his assessment remained inaccurate.

The page has turned [he wrote to his wife from Jauer]. For three days Napoleon provoked me to battle with his entire forces, but I refused, thus thwarting his plans. Yesterday evening he retreated. I shall follow him at once. . . . I am well, and very happy that I have led the great man by the nose. He will be very angry that he could not force me to fight.(10)

Within twenty-four hours Blücher obtained one of the greatest victories of his career. French forces in the Katzbach region were about equal in number to Blücher's Silesian army. Troops on both sides were exhausted and both suffered from shortages of ammunition and supplies. But a vital difference existed in the spirit of the respective commanders. Blücher's record of the Rhine campaign in the 1790s showed him at his best in sudden, aggressive action, and such an opportunity now opened. Macdonald's record displayed an inability to react with sufficient vigour; he also had a reputation for being unlucky.

'He is good,' commented Napoleon. 'He is brave. But he has no luck.'

Fate continued to work against him on 26th August. Blücher had withdrawn south over the Katzbach on 22nd August, establishing his headquarters at Jauer while the French still lay north of the river. Late on the 25th, as incessant rain sluiced his soldiers, Blücher prepared orders to attack over the river the following day; the crossing would be attempted around the junction of the Katzbach with the smaller river, the Neisse. Blücher therefore deployed Langeron's corps to the west of the Neisse near the village of Seichau, while the two corps under Yorck and Sacken moved over higher terrain to the east. The advance began during the morning of the 26th, men marching forwards with their great-coats and knapsacks rendered sodden and shapeless by the continuing downpour. Almost immediately Yorck's forward sections rushed back dramatic reports: the French had also started to advance, unaware of Blücher's offensive. The Katzbach had been crossed; French columns formed on the south bank just to the east of the junction with the Neisse, and now pushed southwards along the edge of the rain-swept plateau, across which Sacken and Yorck were advancing.

Blücher and Gneisenau snapped out orders: messengers galloped through the rain, and the Prussians and Russians ran to take

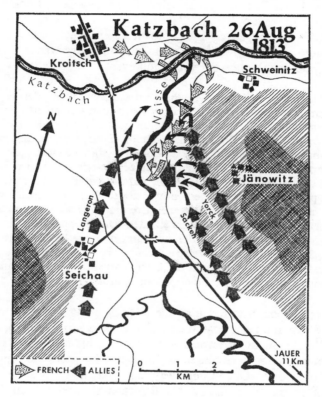

fresh dispositions. The allies enjoyed the advantage of higher ground. Sacken ordered artillery into line, and his men struggled through the mud to pull the twelve-pounders into position; Yorck carefully organized his men into attacking formations. Above them the thunder rumbled from the inky-black sky. The French had by now advanced over 3,000 metres from the Katzbach on a line parallel with the Neisse. To one side dropped the steep bank of the Neisse, and the river swirled swollen and swift. To their other side climbed the plateau. The French marched in columns, with troops hunching their shoulders against the rain and with drums covered to prevent the wet ruining the skins. Up on the plateau Blücher rode amongst his men.

'My brave lads, this day decides!' he shouted. 'Prove to your King and to your country that your courage is equal to your loyalty. Prove it, I say, at the point of your bayonets. Look yonder – there's the enemy!'

Solid lines began to move down the slope; cheers sank to murmurs and then to silence. One contemporary writer gave this description of the horrors which followed.

> Cool, steady, and compact, the [Prussian] battalion advanced to storm three batteries protected by two squares of infantry in the enemy centre. The cannon-balls plunged into their ranks, mowing down whole files. The Prussian column, silent as death, moved on unshaken. A galling fire of grape-shot now thinned their ranks . . . shouts of 'Forwards! Forwards!' stifled the cries of the wounded and the dying. Whole sections fell, and the dauntless survivors did but press on the more vehemently to use the bayonet. Closing with the enemy, a dreadful pause of irresolute suspense seemed to intervene, when, as the officers shouted 'Down upon them! Down upon them!' a furious murderous charge with the bayonet ensued. . . . Scarcely ten minutes elapsed before the enemy's phalanx was transformed into a pyramid of ghastly corpses. The other square, shuddering at the fate of their advance, broke.(11)

Yorck's men battered into the French along the bank of the Neisse, battalion after battalion striking the enemy's reeling flank, and Yorck fought as ferociously as any of his soldiers. 'He is a venomous fellow,' commented Blücher. 'He does nothing but make objections. Once under way, however, he bites harder than any of them.' Sacken and his Russians showed similar brutal energy, with the regiments surging around the enemy flank to send the French scurrying towards the river. One after another the French units fell back to the bank of the Neisse, abandoning artillery, and their cavalry charges bogged down in the mud. The crammed area between the Neisse and Katzbach became a raging gehenna: the bank fell abruptly into the river and deep water prevented a French escape save over one or two treacherous fords. Prussian and Russian infantrymen forced in from the front with swords, bayonets and musket-butts, and enemy in the rear plunged into the flood: as many French drowned as fell to the allied weapons. 'It was exactly like a battle of antiquity,' wrote Gneisenau to Clausewitz. 'Towards the end of the day there was a time when the firing ceased entirely until more cannon could be dragged up over the drenched ground. Only the cries of the combatants filled the air, while the decision was left to the bared weapons.'(12) By evening almost 15,000 enemy lay dead and wounded; Blücher's losses were less than a quarter of this number, and more French would fall during the ruthless pursuit.

'This is the day I've long wished for,' wrote Blücher to his wife when he established his camp at Kroitsch, north of the Katzbach. 'We have the enemy completely beat. . . . I follow the enemy with all my cavalry. It rained all day so that I couldn't find a dry spot for myself. I am well, also my staff.' He ended his letter 'in haste, I'm tired and exhausted.'(13) Blücher reported to the King: 'Perhaps victory has never been bought with so little loss of blood.' But now came pursuit and renewed chance of inflicting heavy enemy casualties – if the allies could drag themselves forward with sufficient speed. Blücher pushed forward during the next six days, despite the utter weariness of his army. Unity between Blücher's commanders split again under the strain. As Blücher flung his forces down the water-logged roads towards Löwenberg on the Bober, his generals complained bitterly that their men were dropping with exhaustion and hunger.

Yorck raged at Gneisenau: 'I've won victory for you, but where are the provisions? The poor soldiers are near starving.'(14)

Blücher remained unmoved; he refused to spare himself and he expected others to act in similar fashion. 'We are pursuing the enemy,' he told his wife on the day after Katzbach, 'and I shall allow myself the promise of advantages.' He berated Yorck for his tardiness.

'It is not enough to be victorious,' he shouted. 'One has to know how to use the victory. If we don't follow the enemy body and soul, he naturally gets up again, and we have to achieve through a new battle what we would have got out of this one.'

He accused the cavalry of being over-careful. 'One shouldn't bother about the lamentations of the cavalry,' he told a staff officer. 'If one can achieve . . . the annihilation of the whole enemy army, the state can surely afford to lose a few hundred horses.'(15) And daily evidence revealed even greater agony being suffered by the enemy. Total French losses during the retreat westwards almost reached the number of men cut down in the battle, and the manner of their dying proved equally horrible. Gneisenau told Clausewitz: 'The roads between the Katzbach and the Bober are evidence of the terror that fell upon the enemy. Corpses that have been run over are still sticking everywhere in the mud.'(16) Blücher's health was weakened by the strain, but he rode on despite his fever and despite his seventy years; he believed only his 'iron will' brought victory. 'After the battle everyone wanted to be in peace, but I ordered that all possible strength must be dragged from horses and men to pursue the enemy relentlessly. The pursuit justified my decision.'

Blücher's customary modesty returned by the time his army reached the Bober at the end of the month, when he issued a generous proclamation to his troops.

> To your bravery . . . to your exertions and steadfastness, to your patient endurance of hardships and want I owe the good fortune. . . . We have struggled with cold, wet and privation, and some of you have been insufficiently clad; yet without a murmur you exerted yourselves to pursue your defeated enemy. I thank you . . .

The proclamation bore the stamp of Gneisenau's eloquent drafting, but the peroration resembled the prayer uttered by Belling, Blücher's first military tutor: 'Let us sing praises to the Lord God of Hosts by whose aid you have overcome the enemy, and let us publicly, in Divine Service, thank Him for the Glorious Victory. . . . And then, once again, up and at your enemy!'(17) Blücher enclosed this document in a letter ot his wife, dated 1st September, from Löwenberg. He added: 'Tomorrow morning the bridges across the Queiss, which the enemy destroyed, will be re-built. Then I shall follow them. . . . Yesterday I was very ill, but today I am better.'(18)

Pursuit must continue into Saxony. Depressing reports had reached Blücher's headquarters: Schwarzenberg had cast aside his chance of victory at Dresden. Napoleon reached the Saxon capital late on 25th August, while the allies still dawdled, and battle began on the 26th, continuing throughout the 27th. Napoleon gained victory. The allies retreated on the afternoon of the 27th, leaving 25,000 men behind, half of them prisoners. Roads eastwards across the Elbe were blocked by Vandamme, while Murat covered the route west towards Freiburg. The greater proportion of the allied army therefore retreated south along the narrow road towards the mountains of the Erzgebirge, and these units suffered from confusion, demoralization and increasing exhaustion. The fate of the main army threatened to rob Blücher of the effects of his victory; he could only urge his men on from the Bober, to relieve pressure on Schwarzenberg.

Then, on about 2nd September, infinitely better news reached Blücher as he approached Görlitz. First came confirmation of a brilliant victory won by Bülow over Oudinot on the approach road to Berlin. The battle had only been fought after a violent argument between Bülow and Bernadotte, with the latter preferring to abandon the Prussian capital. 'What is Berlin?' declared Bernadotte. 'It is a town, that's all.' Bülow rode forward on 21st August to overwhelm Oudinot's forces in the bogs of Grossbeeren, fifteen kilometres to the south of the capital. The French fell back on Wittenberg, losing 3,000 men. Even happier reports arrived at Blücher's camp – Schwarzenberg's Army of Bohemia had managed to recover to win victory at Kulm on 30th August. While the bulk of the army had retreated through the Erzgebirge, Kleist's corps and a force under Eugen von Württemberg had headed towards Kulm, about thirty kilometres south-east of Dresden. Reinforcements rushed to the reeling Austrians, and on the 30th they turned upon Vandamme. Within hours the French suffered a devastating attack from their rear as Kleist's troops swarmed upon them. Vandamme himself was captured and his corps of almost 40,000 was virtually destroyed as a fighting force. Allied progress in general seemed suddenly excellent. 'Our Grand Army in Bohemia has won a victory and all goes well,' wrote Blücher to Katharina from Görlitz on 4th September. 'I have not been well for two days, but am better now. . . . I am still pursuing the enemy. In two days I expect to be near Dresden.'(19)

But Napoleon remained determined to cling to his Dresden and Leipzig bases. Fresh forces were pushed against Blücher on the 4th and 5th September, and Blücher immediately manoeuvred out of reach. By 6th September he had sneaked forward to Löbau. 'Napoleon is very angry that we have finished his army,' he told his wife. 'Now he takes his main army and marches against me, and for two days did his utmost to make me fight. He is twice as strong as I am. All his manoeuvres availed him nothing; I always step aside.'(20) On the same day, 6th September, the French received yet another painful setback, this time at Dennewitz about fifty-five kilometres south-west of Berlin. Ney, who had replaced Oudinot, was surprised by Bülow and lost 9,000 men killed or wounded, plus another 15,000 taken prisoner. Shortly before a conscript division under Gérard lost 3,000 killed or wounded at Hagelberg, with Bülow again responsible for the victory.

'Through these events fear crept into Napoleon's heart,' wrote Marshal St Cyr. Within two weeks his subordinate generals – four of them Marshals – had lost five battles, at the Katzbach, Grossbeeren, Kulm, Dennwitz and Hagelberg. About 70,000 French troops had been slaughtered or taken prisoner, 298 guns had been lost, and corresponding allied totals were 38,000 and 26 respectively. Grand Army soldiers and officers suffered weariness and disillusionment. Captain Coignet, serving at Napoleon's headquarters, heard many officers 'blaspheming' against the Emperor, saying he would bring them to ruin. 'I was petrified to hear such remarks,' wrote Coignet, 'and said to myself "we are done for". '(21)

Yet the allies showed even greater lack of cohesion, despite recent successes. Bernadotte, Schwarzenberg, Czar Alexander, Frederick William, Blücher – all quarrelled with each other and with subordinates. Frederick William was still anxious over Berlin and pleaded for action in this area, pleas which Bülow answered with brilliance and bravery. Yet Bülow found himself continually hampered by Bernadotte's attitude. Soon Blücher would experience similar hesitation by the Crown Prince. But Bernadotte and Schwarzenberg, allied commander-in-chief, remained in agreement over the general strategy to be pursued. This was described by General Joseph Radetzky, Schwarzenberg's chief of staff, as avoiding 'any unequal struggle and so to exhaust the enemy, fall upon his weakened parts with superior strength, and to defeat him in detail'.

In principle, such a strategy seemed sound; in practice it proved extremely difficult to achieve, and especially when Schwarzenberg was subjected to so many different pressures from the various rulers and national interests. Blücher appreciated Schwarzenberg's problems, despite his own disagreement with the allied commander; later he proposed a toast to 'the commander-in-chief who

had three monarchs at his headquarters and still managed to win!'
One of the monarchs, Emperor Francis of Austria, had an easy
relationship with Schwarzenberg, but the other two gave him
constant anxiety. 'The Czar is good but weak,' wrote Schwarzenberg, 'but the King (of Prussia) is a rough, coarse, unfeeling fellow
who is to me as loathsome as the poor, brave Prussians are
pleasant.'

Yet close allied co-operation was now even more essential. None
of the victories over the French had been decisive defeats for
Napoleon; the Emperor remained at large. The allied armies must
combine for the decisive battle, but not too soon. A premature
junction could allow Napoleon the opportunity to strike, and
whereas Blücher might welcome such a chance of an early meeting
with Napoleon, Bernadotte and Schwarzenberg still insisted upon
a more cautious approach. The strategy of manoeuvre necessitated
the allies remaining in contact, although separated, and achieving
this was likely to be increasingly difficult as winter weather
rendered communications uncertain. Inter-allied understanding
offered the only solution, but in early September this appeared
further away than ever. Knesebeck, general *aide-de-camp* to
Frederick William, described the confusion at the allied headquarters.

> To say what we shall do here is very difficult, because we never
> finish with councils of war. Schwarzenberg is a man of sense, but
> he has not got the confidence of the monarchs or belief in himself.
> Hence the everlasting arguments. The Russian generals will not
> obey orders. The Emperor sometimes issues his own orders. As a
> result, one order follows upon another, and nobody knows who is
> cook and who is butler.(22)

Blücher, still in the vicinity of Löbau, experienced his own
problems. Yorck grumbled again, and Blücher considered
Langeron unsatisfactory. His reliance upon Gneisenau steadily
increased, and Blücher refused to listen to complaints from any
other officer. 'I do not hold war councils,' he declared. He told
Kneseback: 'Gneisenau, Müffling and my Goltz are those with
whom I agree, but I have a devil of a job with the other "safety-
first" officers.'(23) His feverish spells still troubled him, his limbs
ached in wet weather, and his eyes became easily inflamed, but he
always presented a cheerful front to his troops. According to

Wenzel Krimer, a surgeon in the Silesian Army: 'Blücher's usual greeting was "Good morning children!", even in the evening. To this the soldiers would respond with "Hurrah! Father Blücher!" '(24)

Now, in mid-September 1813, manoeuvring began again. 'Today I march to Bautzen,' he wrote to his wife on the 15th, 'and in a few days shall be before Dresden, or I shall cross the Elbe between Torgau and Dresden.' Blücher had just received a letter from Katharina dated the 6th. 'You're depressed and unhappy and that worries me. Away with these low spirits, everything will be all right.' His letter concluded: 'Be happy, everything will turn out fine. Napoleon is in the soup.'(25)

'The chessboard is very confused,' admitted Napoleon to Marshal Marmont. A situation bordering on stalemate prevailed; rather than attempting bold measures, Napoleon was obliged to restrict his activities and to wait for allied mistakes. His communications were harassed, his troops weary and newcomers untrained, his hospitals were crammed and supplies still short. Both sides therefore waited for a favourable opening. Blücher ordered his army forward to tempt the French from Dresden, and once again his troops moved over the battlefield of Bautzen, stepping over the rusting remains of the conflict in May. Blücher camped his army some way from Bautzen to avoid an undue burden on the local civilians; Steffens found the town 'almost as tranquil as in times of peace'.(26)

Despite their tranquil surroundings Blücher and Gneisenau were once again engaged in heated correspondence with the main allied headquarters. Schwarzenberg urged Blücher to march to join his army; the Silesian commander and his chief of staff continued to insist upon advancing towards the Elbe and Dresden from the east. They saw no point in easing their pressure upon Napoleon. Their opinions were strengthened when Napoleon began to pull back forces from the Silesian Army front, owing partly to Blücher's threat, partly to a premature report that Bernadotte had crossed the Elbe in the north at Rosslau, and partly to defeat inflicted on French troops on the Gärda by Russo-German regiments under Walmoden. Clausewitz, who had taken part in this last battle, wrote on 20th September: 'This war must be made to move like a Catherine wheel, violently spinning through an impulse from within.'(27)

Confusion still existed at Schwarzenberg's headquarters, and Blücher wrote to Katharina from Bautzen on the 20th: 'I am still before Dresden. . . . The rain has made the advance difficult and delayed us.' His letter contained personal bad news. Blücher had received information that his eldest son Franz, serving with the main army, had been wounded and captured. 'It is a sword wound in the head, not dangerous; the Russian Czar at once sent a messenger to the enemy to inquire. Napoleon wished to see Franz and did so: he talked with him quite nicely and sent him a Doctor. . . . He is probably in Dresden.'(28)

The skies cleared in the third week of September and the roads dried; and Blücher's patience snapped. 'Since the others will not do so,' wrote Gneisenau on the 26th, 'we shall open the play and shall assume the chief role.'(29) Blücher and Gneisenau believed defensive manoeuvring had proved successful, but the benefits could only be obtained by a switch to the attack. As Clausewitz wrote in *On War*: 'A swift and vigorous assumption of the offensive – the flashing sword of vengeance – is the most brilliant point in the defensive.'(30) Blücher now drew this flashing sword and ordered the advance. He would sweep across the Elbe; if the other allied armies followed his lead, then an iron ring could be forged around the French. And the move Blücher intended to make would be amongst the most brilliant and decisive of the whole war.

Gneisenau presented Blücher with detailed plans. A direct advance towards Dresden might encounter overwhelming opposition. But a march to the north-west would bring the Army of Silesia closer to Bernadotte's Army of the North, and such a stab above Dresden would threaten to drive between Napoleon's bases at Dresden and Leipzig; moreover, Berlin would be covered. Blücher therefore sent an officer to locate the best crossing place over the Elbe, with the site to be such that an army of 50,000 men could hold at bay an enemy of three times that strength. This officer, Major von Rühle, reported back at the end of September: he believed the most suitable crossing point lay at Elster, between Torgau and Wittenberg, with Wartenburg selected as a possible battlefield on the French west bank. The river curved at this point, so protecting either flank, although Rühle's cursory inspection failed to reveal the swampy, broken nature of the ground. Elster and Wartenburg were therefore marked on Blücher's map. As September ended the march began. Maximum speed had to be maintained to obtain surprise, and Blücher urged his men forward in customary relentless fashion, sparing no one and least of all himself.

Blücher, although he might readily overlook indiscipline among brave soldiers [wrote Wenzel Krimer], came down very severely on weaklings and usually punished them by his caustic humour or by personal example. Thus it frequently happened that, if he met stragglers along the line of march, he would dismount and proceed on foot, with them walking in front of him. Or he would order them to stick wisps of straw in their shakos and they would then be escorted by cavalrymen to their regiments, decorated as men of straw. [Krimer continued:] Whenever he passed a battalion which he knew to be a brave one, he would not allow his staff to take up the middle of the road. So as not to impede these on the march, he preferred to ride to one side.(31)

Day and night marches brought the Silesian Army to the vicinity of the Elbe at Elster on 1st October. On the same day Napoleon directed the main body of his troops from Dresden northwards towards Liepzig. Bernadotte intimated he would march south to cross the Elbe and join Blücher at Wartenburg; Blücher, in private conversation with his staff, hoped his ally would advance at maximum speed, and the almost untranslatable oath he used underlined his determination to seek action: 'If the dog-of-a-gypsy doesn't come at once may the sacred *Kreuze-Granaten-Bomben-Donnerwetter* grind him to bits' – literally, all the destructive power of grenades, bombs and thunderstorms should descend upon him.(32) Blücher's engineers flung a floating bridge over the Elbe during the night of 2nd October. At dawn next day, Sunday, Blücher's army began to stream across to the French west bank. Bertrand, commanding the opposing forces, rushed reinforcements towards the bridgehead, concentrating his main defences at the village of Bleddin and in Wartenburg itself. Blücher sent his infantry over first, column after column almost running to reach the far bank; after them trotted the cavalry, treading more carefully over the rough damp planks.

'Weapons glanced in the sunbeams,' commented Steffens. 'Host after host was seen coming from afar, till every hill blazed with glittering life.' Once over the river the troops deployed to north and south through the oak woods bordering the bank. Enemy artillery opened fire from further west, with cannon balls crashing through the trees and striking the surface of the river, from which they skimmed upwards to arch high over the water. From the far side of the forest rising fusillades sounded steadily and increasing numbers of cannon-balls thrashed through the foliage. Reports brought to Blücher indicated stubborn enemy defence, especially around Bleddin, where the French benefited from the swampy ground. The bulk of the Silesian Army was engaged by noon, and Blücher rode forward to Bleddin. Not until two o'clock did the village fall; Blücher rallied his men for the advance on nearby Wartenburg. Smoke could be seen rising from the town's chimneys, and Blücher is reported to have called: 'Look my children! The cursed French are baking bread for their breakfast. We'll grab it while it's hot!'(33) But vicious fighting continued, especially around Wartenburg's castle, and not until four o'clock were the first Prussians able to march down the town's main street.

Blücher had opened the allied offensive, and his troops had fought well, especially those under the prickly Yorck – who would become Yorck von Wartenburg in honour of the victory. Bernadotte was moving down from the north; Schwarzenberg had started his advance from the south; Napoleon was being cornered. Blücher ordered a celebration dinner in the great hall of Wartenburg castle where the walls and floor were torn by cannon-balls. He stood to present the toast: 'Thank God we have taken a great step forward towards the liberation of the Fatherland!' At his moment of elation Blücher remembered Scharnhorst; Steffens, sitting amongst the battle-stained officers, wept as he heard Blücher's words in memory of the fallen chief of staff. 'The almost involuntary rush of language was the outpouring of poetry itself.'(34) Blücher wrote a letter to his wife before retiring, and the short, scribbled sentences revealed his exhaustion: 'Today I crossed the Elbe near Listerferde by Elster and beat the French very badly. . . . Tomorrow I pursue the enemy. I and my staff are well. I have rather good news from Franz. He is in Dresden. It is night and I am very tired.'(35)

Leipzig lay sixty-five kilometres to the south. Blücher had thrown Napoleon off-balance, and within twenty-four hours Bernadotte crossed the Elbe on Blücher's right flank. Together their armies totalled 140,000 men. South of Leipzig advanced Schwarzenberg's main allied army, numbering 220,000; on 5th

October the leading regiments reached Zwickau, seventy-eight kilometres from Leipzig, although the tail stretched seventy kilometres back to Komotau. The allied ring around Napoleon steadily closed as Blücher and Bernadotte began to march south on the 5th, with Blücher on the right bank of the Mülde river and Bernadotte on the left. But already disagreements had broken out between these two commanders; both argued that the other army should be the one to cross the Mülde. Nor was Blücher's temper soothed by news from the main army: Schwarzenberg seemed to be advancing too slowly, allowing Napoleon the opportunity to strike.

On 7th October the Emperor despatched orders to Murat: 'Keep the Austrians off to the limit of your power, so that I can defeat Blücher and the Swedes before their junction with Schwarzenberg.' Murat hastened to obey and Schwarzenberg's advance slowed even further. Blücher reached Düben on the 7th, still seeking a satisfactory joint plan with Bernadotte. Napoleon suddenly swooped upon the Silesian Army. But the Emperor lunged just too late: Blücher crossed the Mülde to join Bernadotte as the first French units pushed up the road to Düben; Gneisenau barely escaped in the flurry of skirmishing.

The Swedish Crown Prince suggested a joint move behind the Saale, further west than the Mülde, and thereafter a march southwards to join Schwarzenberg. Blücher agreed after Bernadotte refused his own proposal for a stand near Halle, and he marched towards Wettin on the 10th, where Bernadotte had assured him a bridge would be thrown across the river. Blücher reached Wettin on the 11th to find no bridge. He immediately despatched a curt message to the Crown Prince; since he could not cross before the French arrived, he had no alternative but to march to Halle.

The allies were in complete disorder in both north and south. Austrian advance regiments in Schwarzenberg's army suffered a severe setback when attacked by Murat on the 10th, and on the 11th Schwarzenberg's headquarters remained in total ignorance of the enemy's whereabouts. In the north Bernadotte received Blücher's message with horror, and immediately rushed back a frantic reply: the Crown Prince claimed that four French corps, probably headed by Napoleon himself, were marching on Wittenberg behind Bernadotte's and Blücher's armies, and he, Bernadotte, resolved to retreat back over the Elbe: 'I have not a single moment to lose!' reported the frightened Crown Prince. 'I am hastening the march of my troops in order, if possible, to make the crossing without disaster. . . . I beg you to regard the present writing as a summons to join me with as many of your forces as possible.'(36)

Blücher was presented with a painful choice. Either he must withdraw with Bernadotte and hence lose the long-sought opportunity for decisive battle against Napoleon, or he must face the French alone. Moreover, the Crown Prince attempted to force his hand, ordering one of Blücher's own generals, von Rauch, to lay a pontoon bridge over the Elbe at Aken. He alleged Czar Alexander had given him the requisite authority.

Blücher conferred with Gneisenau at their Wettin headquarters; both agreed retreat was unthinkable. They drafted a reply to Bernadotte. The wording seemed icily polite, but rather than agreeing to the Crown Prince's request to move back over the Elbe, Blücher turned the tables on the other commander. He, Blücher, would move south to join Schwarzenberg; if Bernadotte refused to accompany him, then the Crown Prince would be isolated.

> Your Royal Highness now informs me that you intend to cross the Elbe at Aken. Through this movement I shall be cut off from the Elbe and nothing will remain for me but to join the main army. It is not yet clear to me how Your Royal Highness intends to effect your crossing of the Elbe and how, after the crossing, you will maintain yourself, wedged in as you will be between the enemy, the Elbe, Magdeburg and the Havel.(37)

Bernadotte held a council of war in the castle of Cöthen on the 13th. He urged those present to consider the danger of the present position and the need to cover Berlin by recrossing the Elbe. Even Bülow, most determined of all to protect the capital, dismissed this excuse for withdrawal. Bernadotte pleaded: 'Are we thus to give up everything that is holy and precious to human beings – union with the Fatherland, and our wives and children!' Boyen described the Crown Prince's behaviour. 'Difficult as this may be to credit, he worked himself up to such a pitch that he wept as he continually reverted in his speech to the above-mentioned phrases.'(38)

The war council failed to reach a firm decision, and complete confusion continued. Blücher remained in the vicinity of Wettin, about 20 kilometres north-west of Halle, itself 34 kilometres north-west of Leipzig. Bernadotte's Army of the North was drawn up around Cöthen, to Blücher's north. By 13th October Schwarzenberg's Army of Bohemia had dragged itself forward to Chemnitz, 74 kilometres south-east of Leipzig. Napoleon remained at Düben, 33 kilometres north-east of Leipzig. Each of these blobs on the map represented thousand upon thousand of men, horses, carts, guns, blocking the roads and villages, eating all food from the countryside like plagues of locusts. 'One could scarcely see a piece of ground,' wrote a civilian near Bernadotte's army. 'Everywhere was covered by uniforms and crammed with lances and pikes. On all sides one heard battle hymns, fanfares, drums.' Prussians, Swedes, French, Poles, Italians, Austrians, Russians – somehow these swarming multitudes had to be manoeuvred into position for battle, or for withdrawal.

Napoleon sat in the little castle at Düben, snatching at reports of enemy movements which might allow him the opportunity to strike, then relapsing into lethargy. A staff officer wrote: 'I saw the Emperor waiting for news from the Elbe and completely at a loose end, seated on a sofa in his room in front of a large table on which lay his maps and a sheet of white paper.' Napoleon doodled on the paper, scribbling elaborate and useless Gothic letters.(39) These hours in mid-October comprised the brief lull before the terrible storms; now, suddenly, events quickened into violent climax.

On 14th October advance cavalry squadrons from Schwarzenberg's army clashed with enemy cavalry near Wachau, about fifteen kilometres south of Leipzig; both sides suffered equal losses. On the same day an optimistic message from Blücher reached Schwarzenberg. 'The three armies are now so closely together that a simultaneous attack, on the point where the enemy has concentrated his forces, might be undertaken.' And at last Bernadotte screwed his courage and advanced towards Blücher. The allies began to march down the spokes of the huge wheel radiating from Leipzig. Napoleon sped south to the city, then galloped to the eastern outskirts; he despatched increasing numbers of scouts to north, south and west. 'A camp-chair and table were hurriedly set up in a field and a huge fire lit,' wrote an eyewitness. The weather had turned stormy and the wind tugged Napoleon's map, fixed to the table by multi-coloured pins.(40)

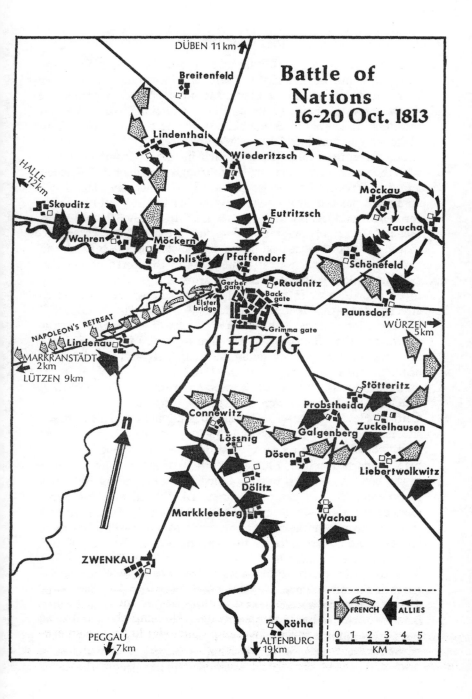

Throughout the 15th his main army moved into position to the east and south of Leipzig, the left wing reaching to the River Parthe and the right to the Pleiss. Marmont's 6th Corps remained to the west of Leipzig, in positions stretching from Wahren through Lindenthal to Breitenfeld, watching the main road from Halle – along which Blücher would advance.

Schwarzenberg intended to launch his attack from the south, with the various regiments striking through the villages of Wachau and Liebertwolkwitz, just to the north of which lay Napoleon's command position at Galgenberg. Another thrust would be made through Markkleeberg and Connewitz. Meanwhile, further west, General Ignaz Gyulai received orders from Schwarzenberg to march his 10,000 Austrians from Markranstädt through Lindenau to block Napoleon's retreat route. Just to the north of General Gyulai would be Blücher's Silesian army and Bernadotte's Army of the North, with instructions from the commander-in-chief to advance down the Halle road. Blücher would remain unsupported by Bernadotte, despite the latter's change of heart about withdrawing to the Elbe: possibly through fears of a flank attack, the Crown Prince moved too far in Blücher's rear and remained out of touch when battle began on the 16th.

Sullen clouds cloaked the sunset on Monday, 15th October. Blücher's headquarters were at Skeuditz, thirteen kilometres from Leipzig. He sat up late with Gneisenau, studying troop dispositions and issuing orders for the following day. Yorck's corps, 21,000 men, would lead the advance towards the enemy along the Halle road. Reports reaching Blücher revealed strong French defences in the villages clustered outside Leipzig: underlined on Blücher's maps were the villages of Wahren, Lindenthal and Möckern. Outside the night sky cleared, although the wind stayed keen and sentries shivered in their thick blue greatcoats. Dawn broke bright on the 16th. Men hurried to their marching formations and weapons were unstacked.

In front the road headed straight towards Leipzig across the flat fertile meadowlands, and on the horizon spread dark patches of forest, tinged by autumn rust. Between eight and nine o'clock faint clouds of smoke rose from beyond the woods to the southeast; guns thumped in the distance. Battle had begun at Wachau in Schwarzenberg's sector. Blücher immediately despatched a rider with orders for Yorck, positioned to the front: the army would strike straight down the main road for Leipzig. A staff officer described the arrival of these orders at Yorck's camp.

Typical of the way he [Yorck] always took care of us, he had got us together for a hot breakfast. Our horses stood ready saddled outside the door. Major Count Brandenburg came in with orders from Blücher. Yorck stood up, glass in hand, and gave us his favourite maxim: 'Beginning, middle and end, Lord God turn all of them to the best.' He drained his glass and put it quietly down. We all did the same. In a solemn and exalted mood we went off to battle. . . .(41)

CHAPTER
8

The Battle of Nations

WITHIN HOURS one third of Yorck's corps, 7,000 men, would sprawl slaughtered or wounded. Blücher's 60,000 troops outnumbered Marmont's defenders over two to one, but, denied support from Bernadotte, Blücher had to keep a considerable force in reserve to guard against a flank attack. Yorck therefore took the brunt of the fighting which erupted round the villages west of Leipzig, and especially at Möckern. The advance to the villages began at about 10 a.m.; sixty minutes later the houses and hedgerows were covered by the usual choking fog of war.

Blücher rode amongst the regiments waiting to attack, calling out to his 'children' and receiving cheers in reply, while to their front these men could see their comrades dropping in scores as they met the murderous French musket volleys.

The battalion with which I stood had to be disbanded . . . because every officer was either dead or wounded [wrote Ludwig von Gerlach of the 1st East Prussian Regiment]. Our first attack was repulsed in bloody fashion . . . The tin star on my shako was pierced and my cloak was holed too. . . . Then I was wounded by a shot in my thigh. My major had his sword shot from his hand, so he rode up to me and accepted mine instead. But he was fatally wounded and died soon afterwards. . . . I collapsed to the ground because my right leg was useless, and I could not get up again....(1)

Such *vignettes* were repeated in their hundreds as Blücher urged his men on over the cabbage-fields. Most of Möckern's houses were by now heaps of rubble, but still the French held, while over

148

to the east the cannonade continued at Schwarzenberg's front and a thick black cloud floated above Leipzig.

Old Blücher came galloping up [wrote an infantry Major, von Hiller], and, pointing at random, shouted to me: 'There is the point you must hold!' . . . We were met with a dense hail of fire from Möckern. I was soon wounded in the hand. The surgeon wanted to take me out from under fire in order to put on a proper bandage. 'We've no time for that,' I told him, 'just patch it up for the time being.' And while he was doing this the poor devil was hit in the head and fell dead on the spot. So, still unbandaged, I re-mounted and led my battalion successfully into Möckern. The battle swayed to and fro, we were driven out and then fought our way in again, four or even five times.(2)

French positions could only be reached by direct frontal attack because the Elster and adjacent marshy ground prevented flanking assaults; the Prussians pleaded for help from Bernadotte, without success. Amongst the appeals went a message from General Sir Charles William Stewart, an Englishman friendly to Bernadotte who served as a military *attaché*: 'Royal Highness! I come from the battlefield of General Blücher! . . . I venture most humbly to beg Your Royal Highness to set out with your army the instant you receive this letter. Not a moment is to be lost. Your Royal Highness has promised me. . . .'(3) But as the bloody afternoon lengthened Blücher was obliged to commit his reserves; he also sent forward Langeron's corps to take Wiederitzsch village. Langeron's assault took longer than expected and only succeeded after three attempts and 1,500 casualties.

Bitter fighting continued at Möckern with bayonets, knives, swords, musket-butts and bare fingers, men struggling at each cottage and barn, surging backwards and forwards through the school-yard and cemetery. Corpses filled the alleys and clogged the ditches. By late afternoon the village had been taken again by Blücher's battered battalions. But at about 5 p.m. Marmont reorganized his regiments; bullets from fresh musket volleys churned the air above the Prussian defenders' heads like strong gusts of wind, then French aims were lowered and the next volleys slapped into Prussian bodies to tear great holes in the ranks.

Marmont threw all his strength into a massive counter-attack;

Yorck's leading division gave way. Maimed men tried to help one
another to safety, and among them hobbled Lieutenant Woyski,
wounded in the shoulder and inside his left thigh:

> I saw dead and wounded men. . . . On all sides arms and legs were
> moving. . . . I found myself in a large cabbage-field: the remaining
> stalks made the going very difficult, and must have made lying
> even more uncomfortable for the wounded. In several places I
> actually saw blood running between the cabbage stalks.

Woyski met a German soldier, wounded in the hand, and with
supporting arms around each other they hurried away from the
French as fast as they could.

> We had gone a few yards like this, side by side, when I suddenly
> heard a dull thud beside me. I fell to the ground, felt myself
> spattered with blood, and saw beside me a leg. Then I heard the
> soldier calling: 'Friend, kill me, for God's sake! Kill me!' One of
> the many cannonballs which were still rolling had struck him from
> behind and torn off his leg just below the belly. I had to leave
> him. . . .(4)

Yorck struggled to rally his forces to stem the French. He
galloped over to the Brandenburg Hussars, shouting out to their
commander as he approached: 'Sohr! Attack!' The cavalry commander appeared to hesitate: his small force would have to face
an overwhelming number of French infantry.

Yorck shouted: 'If the cavalry don't do something now, all is
lost! Sohr, I tell you, attack!'

Major von Sohr pointed with his sword at reserve cavalry
moving in the rear, and pleaded a delay until this help arrived.
Yorck, almost beside himself in desperation, spurred his horse
towards the reserve, snapping orders for an aide to insist upon
Sohr's charge. 'Tell the General,' said Sohr to this messenger, 'I
give him my word of honour I will attack, but will he please allow
me to choose the most favourable moment.'

Ten tense minutes dragged by with Sohr waiting on his horse
and watching the enemy. Then he issued a quiet order: 'Trum-
peter, sound the Trot.'

The bugle blew the command, and the squadrons jingled through
the gaps between the disordered Prussian infantry, and out into

the open. Immediately they suffered heavy enemy musket and artillery fire, and on the flank lurked strong detachments of French cavalry. Sohr despatched an aide to direct the reserve squadrons towards this mounted French threat and continued his advance, horses still moving at a trot. Maintaining this almost leisurely pace the Brandenburg Hussars moved steadily towards the enemy infantry, regardless of musket and cannon fire. Their advance seemed relentless and some French infantry turned and ran; the rest remained with bayonets fixed. But bayonets proved no defence; into the French trotted the hussars. Sabres carved into the massed infantry ranks and lances stabbed forward, and back fled the French. At the same time the reserve cavalry routed the enemy squadrons on the flank, with Yorck leading the charge in person.

Blücher and Gneisenau meanwhile formed improvised battalions from the streams of wounded and bewildered, battle-shocked men flooding back from the front. Still no help arrived from Bernadotte. At this moment Henry Steffens reached the Crown Prince with another urgent appeal. He discovered Blücher's ally in bed. 'The dark Gascon face, with the prominent nose and the retiring chin, was sharply relieved against the white bed-clothes and the laced nightcap.' Bernadotte insisted his cavalry had already started towards Blücher and that his infantry would soon follow.(5) Fortunately they would not be needed. Yorck's brave cavalry charges and the reorganized infantry advance brought intolerable pressure to bear on the bleeding, exhausted French defenders. A French captain, Jean-Louis Rieu, described the situation at Möckern: 'Our position was becoming untenable. Besides the enemy's artillery, which was killing us at point-blank range, an imposing force of cavalry waited a mere twenty yards for us to be put to flight, when they would spring at us, like a tiger.' French troops, crazed with fear, were rebelling against their officers. 'This could not last very long. . . . The men broke and fled.'(6)

Darkness fell with the French retreating towards Leipzig. Yorck had won his victory. Blücher threw his arms around him and the two men rode through the cheering survivors. Now began the most pitiful part of the battle; lit by the lurid glow from the burning villages, men collected the wounded and walked slowly amongst the living and the dead to find fallen friends. Marmont lost about 6,000 killed and wounded, 2,000 prisoners and half his eighty-four guns – and two fingers from his right hand. Surgeons worked throughout the night at bloody, lamp-lit tables, and wounded waited in long lines for limbs to be lopped. These legs and arms filled basket after basket. Blücher stayed up for most of the night. First he issued orders for the following morning, the second day of the battle for Leipzig. Then he tried to help his men. According to his doctor, Bietzke:

> He ordered the wounded to be driven back from the battlefield in his kitchen waggon. He gave them shirts and sheets for bandages. He ordered houses or whole villages to receive the wounded. He himself stayed in the open field near the watchfires, until at last a decrepit empty smithy was found for him to rest.(7)

Steffens reached the area late at night, reporting back to Blücher after his mission to Bernadotte. 'I had to cross the field of battle, and could scarcely get on, the bodies lay so thick.'(8) Other messengers reported to Blücher's headquarters with news of events elsewhere. Schwarzenberg had advanced on the villages south of the city, with 2,000 guns blazing in the biggest artillery duel yet experienced. Allied attacks on Liebertwolkwitz were easily repulsed; four times the allies took and lost Markkleeberg; vain attacks were made on Connewitz, Lössnig and Dölitz. The French therefore clung to their position at tremendous cost, and by nightfall Napoleon's overall casualties numbered about 26,000. But total allied losses were probably even higher, perhaps over 30,000. The slaughter shocked even the hardest veterans: modern war revealed its mass brutality.

Napoleon faced the choice of either retreating on the 17th or renewing battle before allied reinforcements arrived. He did neither. Instead he sat numbed and brooding at the village of Meusdorf. For most of this Tuesday morning, the second day of battle, Blücher reorganized his regiments, pushing men forward to skirmish with the enemy but allowing as many men as possible to rest. They sat in the sunshine amongst the bloated, unburied dead, and they filled their bellies with potatoes and skilly gruel thickened with biscuits. Gneisenau rode across the battlefield with Stosch, his *aide-de-camp*, who commented:

> The corpses of the fallen . . . lay so close to one another that our horses could only get through in single file. I watched Gneisenau's

solemn face, and as he said to me 'Victory was bought with German blood at great cost' a tear trickled down from his eye. It was the only tear I ever saw him shed.(9)

Blücher waited impatiently for orders from Schwarzenberg for a general allied assault on the French. Meanwhile he undertook limited offensives of his own during the afternoon, deploying troops eastwards towards the northern suburbs of Leipzig and especially in the area of Eutritzsch and Gohlis villages. The French advanced some foot units and an artillery battery into the open fields, threatening the Prussian flank. Blücher sat on his horse on a nearby hummock.

'If I were still leading my old hussar regiment,' he commented casually to General Illamon Vasiltshikov, who stood beside him, 'I would attack that infantry from the front, go round the flank and seize the battery.'

Vasiltshikov took the hint. 'If Your Excellency will permit, I'll try with my hussars.'

Blücher grunted his approval and Vasiltshikov cantered off to accomplish the operation, achieving a success which even Blücher in his old hussar days could barely have bettered.(10)

Eutritzsch fell, and soon afterwards Gohlis. But the allied command position at Rötha, 17 kilometres south of Leipzig, showed the usual confusion throughout the day. Czar Alexander and Frederick William remained with the army and continued to add uncertainty and divided counsel. Schwarzenberg, cautious as ever, heard that expected Austrian reinforcements were unlikely to reach the battle area until late afternoon, and Russian reserves under Bennigsen would not arrive until nightfall. The movements of Bernadotte's Army of the North remained a complete mystery. Schwarzenberg therefore decided to postpone large-scale fighting until the following morning, Monday 18th October. The decision soon proved fortunate as clouds thickened over the battlefield and heavy rain began to fall, turning the roads into slurry and the fields into glutinous mud – all of which favoured the defensive. Napoleon also reached his decision during the late afternoon: he would stay and fight again next day. Reinforcements under Reynier amounting to 15,000 men had sneaked through from the east. Yet Napoleon sent Bertrand's corps to the south-east, ready to secure escape passages over the Saale and Unstrut. The Emperor

H.G.—F

then reduced his perimeter, and at 11 p.m. ordered his own headquarters to be moved nearer the city, to a tobacco mill in Stötteritz.

Blücher also shifted his headquarters. During the early evening, as rain drenched his troops, the General received the offer of a pleasant house for his personal use at Wiederitzsch. The house seemed excellent, and Blücher strode through the door. Almost immediately he hurried out again.

'I won't stay there,' he exclaimed. Karl von Raumer, a volunteer, stood nearby.

> I was curious to know what was so repulsive in the house and whether I could find a billet for myself inside. The first room I entered was full of terribly wounded men who in the day's cavalry action had received gaping facial wounds . . . The owner's small library had been scattered all over the floor. The first book I picked up was Hupeland's *Art of Prolonging Human Life*!(11)

Blücher settled down for the night in nearby ruins. Troops prepared themselves for the next day's battle and attended to domestic details: they stripped off their shirts and passed them rapidly through their fires, to shrivel the lice. Then they lay besides the flames which still spat with the rain.

At half-light on the Monday morning French guns fired in desultory fashion and men roused themselves from the damp ground. Bustle increased at Blücher's headquarters. 'Every officer rose and dressed himself leisurely and carefully,' wrote Steffens. He watched them shaving as conscientiously as if preparing for a ball.

> The windows were spread and laid back on the walls, to serve for looking-glasses. Coffee was brought in; some drank from the cups and some from the saucers. Any little difficulty or accident was seized upon to give a cheerful turn to the remarks, but these were never extended to the great event which was impending; they spoke on indifferent subjects, even of happy memories, and a joke was seized on and passed round with thankful eagerness.(12)

Before the end of this terrible day about three out of every ten men in Blücher's army would be killed or wounded; many of those young officers, appearing unconcerned as they completed their toilet, would emerge from the holocaust fearfully mutilated.

Blücher took no part in this headquarters activity. Before dawn he had ridden off to meet his dubious ally, Bernadotte. Some advance units from the Army of the North had reached the Prussians during the previous afternoon, but plans for co-operation between the two forces remained non-existent. Bernadotte had sent proposals – he insisted the Army of the North should move to Blücher's right flank, rather than to the left; this position would place Bernadotte nearer to the retreat route to Halle. But Blücher and Gneisenau had already decided to attack across the Parthe, north of Leipzig, moving via Eutritzsch to swing round on Schwarzenberg's far right. For this movement the added strength provided by the Army of the North would be best placed on Blücher's left, or northern flank. Blücher therefore rejected Bernadotte's suggestion; the latter appealed for a conference, and Blücher now rode to Breitenfeld accompanied by Prince William of Prussia, Frederick William's brother, who would act as interpreter. The meeting took place at dawn. Prince William translated Blücher's insistence upon the attack over the Parthe, and it immediately became apparent that Bernadotte still hesitated to fight.

He exclaimed: 'Don't forget you have to act against the ferocious untameable spirit of a tiger! Consider, it is with Napoleon you enter the lists – who has never yet lost a battle!' Prince William passed over this warning.

Blücher replied: 'Tell his Highness I shall attack the enemy wherever I find him, this morning, and shall beat him. . . . Delay is all we have to fear.'

Finally the Crown Prince promised support – if Blücher gave him additional strength, comprising infantry, cavalry and artillery to total 30,000 men. This astonishing demand was explained to the Prussian commander, who, according to a contemporary account, snapped back:

'If his Highness is afraid – if he doesn't think himself strong enough, I'll let him have Langeron's corps. But by God I'll make a greater impression on the enemy, with my handful of men, than the Prince will with his tens of thousands.'

Blücher is also reported to have said, with malicious glee: 'It shall be an honour to me to lead Langeron's corps myself.' Then he stood and almost shouted: 'Delay will be the devil of us. . . . Let's get on with it!'(13)

Blücher galloped back over the fields, now splashed with colour by the sun which had struggled through the clouds. He called Langeron to him at 6 a.m. On paper the withdrawal of this corps reduced the Army of Silesia by almost a third, yet Blücher's jibe to Bernadotte that he himself would lead Langeron's troops meant in fact that this valuable strength would remain under his control. Blücher still aimed to cross the Parthe, with Sacken's corps in the van attacking Pfaffendorf and Reudnitz, both immediately to the north of Leipzig; Bernadotte would move on Blücher's left to attempt a crossing of the Parthe further north. Langeron would strike near Mockau, aiming for Schönefeld; Bülow's corps would strike via Taucha to thrust from the north-east, with Paunsdorf his objective where a junction could be forged with Schwarzenberg's units.

The armies deployed for battle. Blücher joined himself to Langeron's corps, as promised, and these troops waited for the order to force a crossing over the Parthe. Beyond this river the ground rose slightly.

> There a wonderful spectacle presented itself [stated Steffens]. Over the long distant line of rising ground we beheld the French army in movement, and it soon covered the whole range of hills. . . . The columns continued to emerge from the eastern horizon; infantry, cavalry and artillery glided along in order, and now and then the weapons glanced in the newly-risen sun . . .

Müffling turned to Steffens. 'This is the Battle of Nations,' he declared; and so the conflict became known.(14)

*   *   *

Assaults began on the French at a multitude of points ringing Leipzig. While Blücher's regiments ran forward along the Parthe, Schwarzenberg's divisions advanced towards Dösen, Dölitz, Connewitz, Lössning, Wachau, Probstheida, Stötteritz, Zuckelhausen. Pressure elsewhere compelled the French to relinquish their hold on the bank of the Parthe before Langeron's corps, although not before the surface of the river lay thick with floating dead. Langeron's leading regiments crossed to the east bank near Mockau and the troops forced towards the farms, gardens, orchards and houses of Schönefeld. Blücher and Gneisenau remained on the slight rise just to the rear. From further south along the Parthe came news that the river had been crossed, although Sacken's corps had suffered heavy casualties; scores more Prussians fell at Pfaffendorf, where Marshal Marmont fought ferociously before pulling back his French units.

Pfaffendorf provided an episode of especial horror, even greater than other fearful sights witnessed during the day. A French hospital had been set alight by artillery fire, and the wounded men in the building proved incapable of dragging themselves to safety; Sacken's troops dashed through the flames to rescue as many as they could, but over a hundred had to be left, screaming terribly as the fire engulfed them. One of Sacken's aides wrote:

> I carried on the front of my saddle a young Polish officer, whose nose, jawbone and one eye had been shot away, and yet who clung to life. . . . I handed over my *protégé* to a lightly wounded Russian soldier who was to take him further. Hardly had the two of them gone a few yards than a cannon-ball . . . lacerated them so dreadfully that the bloody shreds of their bodies flew in all directions.(15)

Sacken's soldiers occupied the village; Blücher fed in reinforcements and ordered them on for Reudnitz.

Further north Bülow appeared to be making good progress in his advance round Taucha, but this corps would be unable to outflank the French before mid-afternoon. Meanwhile maximum pressure had to be maintained over the Parthe; despite their weariness and under-strength, Blücher ordered Yorck's reserve into battle. From north to south in front of Blücher's vantage position the whole horizon appeared a mass of boiling black smoke, scorched with sudden flares. Troop formations and cavalry squadrons moved across the fields and through the woods; back from the battle shambled the wounded, sometimes as individuals, sometimes as thick masses when an assault had just taken place.

Then in the early afternoon, a large body of cavalry emerged from the enemy lines and rode down the slope to splash through the river. These troopers proved to be Saxons, seeking to leave the French army and come over to the allies; they sought permission not to fight against their former allies during the battle – their King remained in Leipzig. Blücher granted the request. 'All the events of that day,' commented Steffens, 'from the first, when the great host passed before my wondering sight, up to that last scene, seemed like a splendid act in a Shakespearian drama.'(16)

The situation at Schönefeld resembled Dante, not Shakespeare. The village formed the pivot of Blücher's offensive. French troops under Marshals Ney and Marmont provided perhaps the most stubborn defence of the whole battle. One French brigade lost 1,700 dead out of 2,000 men and a battalion was cut to 180 men and another to 131. A contemporary report described the

> noise and shouting of the troops, the sound of artillery and small arms fire, the landing and explosion of shells, the howling, moaning and lowing of human beings and cattle, the whimpering and calls for help from the wounded and those who lay half-buried alive under masonry, blazing planks and beams. . . . The smoke, dust and fumes made the day so dark that nobody could tell what time of day it was.(17)

Blücher constantly rushed more men towards the flaming village, shouting as they marched past him:

'Fight well my children! Fight well for me and the Fatherland!' He rode amongst the wounded as they staggered back. 'Children, you have been brave, so very brave. I'm pleased with you.' Blücher collected walking wounded and they stood numb before him, filthy uniforms in tatters and stinking of cordite and sweat.

'Come my children – let me see you try again.' And back they went: fewer still returned. It seemed Schönefeld would never fall.

Blücher sat on his horse, watching Langeron's men trying to reorganize themselves. He turned to Steffens.

'Herr Professor,' he said, 'Go instantly to General Langeron. Take him orders to storm that village. He must expect no help by reinforcement, but the enemy must be dislodged immediately.'

Steffens found Langeron amongst the outermost houses and delivered the order. 'My men have fought for many hours,' replied Langeron. 'Their numbers are decimated. They are tired and exhausted. I cannot withstand the enemy without support.' Steffens told him no support existed. The general was silent for a moment, then abruptly turned and gave the command. His men rose slowly to their feet, checked the firmness of their bayonets, and shook themselves into a ragged line.(18)

Blücher could see them from his position by the river: the line advanced over the walls, sometimes breaking as cannon-fire blew ghastly gaps in the ranks, then reforming and walking on again. Behind them lay a trail of bodies. The line disappeared into the charcoal smoke, and Blücher could hear the shouts and screams – and finally the cheers. From the far side of the village fled the French. Ten thousand dead and wounded lay in the streets.

At about the same time reports reached Blücher from other sections of the battlefield. Sacken had advanced from Pfaffendorf to Reudnitz. Bülow's sweep via Tachau had been successful, and at about three o'clock his leading battalions went into action at Paunsdorf, one and a half kilometres from Schönefeld, where the French defence under Reynier had been weakened by the defection of 3,000 Saxons. Allied attacks in Schwarzenberg's area to the south of Leipzig proved less successful, but Benningsen's arrival in the late afternoon caused a further contraction of the French line. Napoleon threw troops against one allied push then another. Realizing that Blücher's advance threatened him most, he scraped forces together for a renewed assault on Reudnitz in the early evening and succeeded in re-taking the village. But his men were completely exhausted; losses had been enormous. Marshal Marmont provided an indication of sweeping casualties in his account:

My chief of staff and his deputy were hit beside me; four *aides-de-camp* were killed, wounded or captured; seven staff officers were also either killed or wounded. As for myself, I had a bullet wound in the hand, a bruise on my left arm, one bullet through my hat and another in my clothes, and four horses killed or wounded under me.(19)

During the evening Napoleon issued the order to retreat west-wards, along the route prepared by Bertrand over the Saale and Unstrut. As night fell silence seemed immense. Napoleon sat on a wooden stool, surrounded by a square provided by the Old Imperial Guard; he fell asleep for a few moments, his hands folded on his chest and his head slumped forward. His generals stood gloomily round a fire. Detachments of retreating troops tramped past. Fifteen minutes later Napoleon jerked awake, called for his horse, and trotted into Leipzig where he supervised the retreat from the Hotel de Prusse. Blücher spent most of the night in the saddle, pulling his forces together for the final assault on

Leipzig the following morning, Tuesday 19th October. Men found whatever shelter they could against the sharp north wind, slaked their thirst from the polluted streams and attempted to satisfy their hunger with mouldy bread and hard, brittle biscuits. Silence continued as dawn broke on the 19th. A thin mist mingled with smoke still drifting from the bivouac fires. Then, an hour after first light, a thunderous barrage opened from the south-east as 1,000 guns began to bombard the retreating French. Soon afterwards the allies launched their offensive against enemy defences at Leipzig which, despite the retreat which had already started, would be stubbornly held. The allied attack comprised five major thrusts: an assault by troops under Prince Hesse-Homburg on the south-west corner of the city, another by Kleist's and Wittgenstein's regiments in the south, Bennigsen's attempt in the south-east towards Leipzig's Grimma Gate, Bülow's strike against the Back Gate in the north-east, and finally Sacken's attempt in the northern suburbs towards Gerber Gate. Langeron's few remaining units would accompany Sacken, and with them would fight Blücher. Allied strength remained insufficient to curl entirely round Leipzig's perimeter: the French escape route to the west stayed open, although perilous. Moreover, the French had made excellent use of the city's old defences. Allied troops began their advance at about ten o'clock. Battalion after battalion edged through the outlying orchards and into the suburbs. Bülow forced back the French from the north-east corner on his third attempt; Hesse-Homburg gained a partial entry; Kleist and Wittgenstein successfully stormed their sectors; Bennigsen prised an opening at Grimma Gate; but the fiercest fighting took place in the northern suburbs, as Sacken and Blücher forced forward for the Gerber Gate and the main street beyond.

Blücher intended to be first inside the walls and first to reach the city centre. 'He felt he owed it to his army to secure this trophy,' wrote his aide, Nostitz. Several attacks by Sacken were thrown back; Blücher sat on his restless horse, regardless of shot and shell, until he could stand the wait no longer. He gathered together a storming party and placed himself at their head, shouting above the battle noise:

'Forward you good Russians! Come on and let them have it!'

The Russians obeyed with bayonets fixed; men of the Eka-terinenburg Regiment, which had distinguished itself at Borodino, clawed their way through the gate; ahead stretched the main street, the Gerbergasse, with each house holding stubborn French defenders. Blücher remained at the front. 'He brought up troops from Langeron's corps,' wrote Nostitz, who rode beside him, 'and led them in person, shouting "Forwards! Forwards, children!" – right up within small-arms range.' 'But still the enemy fought on,' commented a captain in Sacken's corps. 'There was no question of surrender and of laying down arms.' Allied troops suffered heavily from musket fire pouring from the windows; they retaliated by driving inside the houses and slaughtering the French in hand-to-hand fighting on the stairways and in the bedrooms. An unnamed Russian general protested about the personal danger to which Blücher exposed himself; Blücher suspected the Russian feared for his own life and paid no attention, merely continuing to bellow 'Forwards!' to his men. Suddenly Nostitz's horse shied, struck by a bullet, and the Russian General exclaimed that this proved the danger to Blücher. The latter turned impatiently to his aide.

'Is your horse wounded?'

'Not that I'm aware of,' replied Nostitz, and they proceeded even further into the bedlam.

Enemy resistance began to crumble before Blücher's advance towards the Fleischerplatz. His men clambered over the remaining barricade – piled-up ammunition waggons, guns, furniture, and even roped cattle bellowing in fear as the battle raged around them. The last defences fell. Blücher spared a moment to call to his aide:

'That was clever of you Nostitz, telling a lie about your horse's wound. If you'd said "yes", then our good friend would probably have gone to pieces.'

Blücher trotted his horse towards his trophy of being first commander in the city. His action this Tuesday morning earned him the nickname by which he would now be known, coupled with the promotion in rank soon to arrive.

The Russian soldiers had not understood what the General had shouted to them again and again [wrote Nostitz], but when it was translated for them they at once nicknamed him 'Field-Marshal Forwards' – a nickname which epitomized excellently and most suitably the basis of his actions and intentions.(20)

Bitter fighting continued elsewhere. Especially horrible was the scene at the Elster, where Napoleon's units crammed onto the sole remaining bridge. The Emperor crossed, ordering a colonel of the engineers to blow the bridge as soon as the enemy appeared; the fuse was lit too early, trapping the Polish rearguard commanded by Prince Josef Poniatowski on the allied bank. About 20,000 French had still to cross. Some swam to safety, others drowned, including Poniatowski, and about 15,000 fell into captivity. The remnants of Napoleon's army retreated westwards while Blücher stood in triumph in Leipzig's centre. 'This gallant and famous Prussian arrived dripping with sweat,' wrote the Leipzig postmaster, Ulrici, 'and was received by the people of Leipzig with an indescribable shout of joy and delight. . . .'(21)

'We had flowers on our heads, corpses under our feet,' commented Langeron. The Prussians lost about 16,000 men during the four-day battle, the longest Blücher ever fought. Russian casualties totalled 22,000 killed and wounded, and the Austrians about 8,500. Against the allied total of almost 46,000, Napoleon lost about 100,000, including over 20,000 prisoners. In all, an average of about 1,500 men were slain or injured in each hour, day and night, since battle began on the morning of Saturday 16th October. The misery and hellish aspect of Leipzig and its environs were indescribable, and the horrors remained long after the survivors had gone. Arndt visited the area later and the scene reminded him of Vilna in the 1812 campaign: 'Here too were hills of dead bodies, half-eaten by dogs and ravens.'(22) But Blücher could savour his moment of victory. One by one the allied monarchs appeared in Leipzig's market place, and Blücher awaited them amidst the tumult. Next day, 20th October, he sent a letter to his wife:

> Yesterday I could not write. I was too tired, but my friend Gneisenau wrote and told you I am well. . . . We fought the greatest battle, the whole earth has never seen a greater. . . . About two o'clock in the afternoon I took Leipzig by storm. [He continued:] Herr Napoleon escaped but he is not yet safe. This moment my cavalry has brought in another 2,000 prisoners. The enemy's whole army is lost. The Emperor of Russia kissed me in public in the market-place and called me the 'Deliverer of Germany'. The Austrian Emperor heaped praises upon me, and my King thanked me with tears in his eyes. . . .(23)

Blücher addressed this letter from Lützen, scene of the battle the previous year and seventeen kilometres south-west of Leipzig. He had left the city early in the morning; pursuit had already begun. Ahead lay Weissenfels, Napoleon's immediate objective for his retreat, where his army crossed the Saale. Even as the final assault on Leipzig continued, Blücher had despatched cavalry squadrons towards Skeuditz with orders to cross the Elster and combine with forces under Yorck, sent to the Saale the evening before. Yet now Blücher's familiar frustration was repeated: he damned the lack of decisive allied pursuit plans and cursed his own regiments, especially the cavalry. As always he insisted the enemy must be caught and destroyed; as usual his stern demands suffered disappointment. Schwarzenberg had reversed previous orders for strong forces to converge on Napoleon's likely retreat route, because he felt unsure which road the enemy would actually take. Bernadotte, whose forces had suffered least in the battle, insisted upon holding a full-dress parade and failed to move until the 22nd. Everything depended on Blücher and his army, which once again included Langeron's corps. His cavalry closed upon the French rearguard between Weissenfels and Lützen.

> We saw the last of the French troops before us [stated Steffens]. Though in hasty flight, they kept tolerably good order; it was rather a misty morning, and there was nothing to be seen between us and the retreating enemy; all at once we perceived Cossacks in every direction . . . on an instant they were joined into a troop, in another they were down upon the enemy . . .(24)

But this pressure remained insufficient. Blücher arrived just too late at Weissenfels to prevent the enemy crossing the Saale on a bridge of boats. He commanded artillery to be dragged into line and a barrage opened, and although the enemy escaped, retreat became more precipitous. Blücher's units harassed the French back to the Unstrut at Freiburg, eighteen kilometres further west. Steffens commented:

> They were constantly attacked, and fled faster and faster. . . . We witnessed fearful traces of the general consternation. I shall never forget the sight: waggons thrown away to lighten their speed – guns, ammunition waggons, carriages of all descriptions, even some handsome travelling equipages – plainly abandoned because the

tired horses could no longer draw them – remained in close confusion, not only on the road, but in the fields, as far as the eye could reach.(25)

Blücher stayed at Weissenfels until the 25th while his forces maintained the pursuit. He raged at Yorck for allowing Bertrand to secure a crossing over the Unstrut and angrily dismissed his corps commander's pleas that his troops were exhausted; according to Gneisenau, Yorck 'wasted his time in cursing headquarters while Bertrand escaped'.(26) Blücher turned his wrath on his cavalry for failing to attack with sufficient vigour.

'General!' he roared at Langeron. 'I have often told you that your cavalry was bad. I can say the same of my own – yes, it is even worse.'(27)

Blücher's temper was slightly soothed again by a note from Frederick William: 'By repeated victories you roll up your services to the State more quickly than I can follow them with proofs of my gratitude. Accept a new evidence of this in the appointment as General Field-Marshal.'

Napoleon meanwhile remained at the castle of Erfurt and seemed equally displeased with his men. 'They are going to the devil,' he snapped. 'At this rate I shall lose 80,000 men by the time we get to the Rhine.' Reports reached him that 40,000 Bavarian troops under Prince Karl Philippe Wrede were striking from the north. 'Very well then,' he declared, 'we leave tomorrow.' Napoleon took the road for Frankfurt on the 25th.

On the same day Blücher despatched a letter to his wife from Weissenfels: 'I hope that in twelve days, at the longest, the Grand Army will be in Frankfurt.' He spared time to add domestic details in his letter:

As *Frau* Field-Marshal you must live suitably, and don't be too careful about money. I get quite good pay now. . . . [A postscript declared:] I just don't know what to do with all the decorations. I'm covered in them like an old coach-horse. But my greatest reward is the thought that I was the one that subdued the tyrannical upstart.(28)

The tyrant remained far from subdued. Blücher's regiments wilted with weariness as the pursuit continued through Eisenach, reached by Blücher late on the 26th. His men slowed, and Yorck provided this explanation:

> The troops who had taken part in the Russian campaign in Courland were still wearing the clothing issued to them in 1811. The Silesian *Landwehr* jackets made out of coarse cloth had shrunk so badly as a result of wet bivouacs and rainy weather that they were too narrow fore and aft, and too short on top and below. . . . There was a great lack of shoes. . . . Many walked barefoot. There was a shortage of cloaks too. [Yorck continued:] Artillery horses were treated extremely hard, and many were finished.(29)

Blücher angrily dismissed Yorck's complaints, but even Blücher's long-serving Müffling could understand the dwindling speed of pursuit: 'The weather turned so cold and disagreeable that the cavalry searched for stables and the infantry for huts more substantial than those in a bivouac.'(30) Müffling discovered another reason for lack of enthusiasm: 'Nothing could be more unpleasant and disgusting than to follow the wake of the French army. The whole way along the road was strewn with corpses or dying men.' Steffens agreed: 'It was more terrible to me than the violence of the fiercest battle.'(31)

Blücher appeared relentless. He bellowed at the stragglers, praised those in front; he ordered men to be handed rye bread soaked in wine wherever possible to fortify them against the increasing cold. He still hoped to catch the French while Wrede's Bavarian army blocked the enemy from the front. But even Blücher had to admit defeat. Schwarzenberg instructed him to march on a more northerly route via Kassel, while the main army proceeded further south. This move, to ease congestion on the roads, took Blücher away from Napoleon's direct line of retreat. Blücher sent a disgusted letter to his friend von Bonin: 'Had I been allowed to continue I should have reached the enemy.'(32) Wrede reached Hanau at the end of October; Napoleon out-manoeuvred him and slipped through to Frankfurt and over the Rhine into French territory. On the same day Blücher wrote to his wife from Philipps-thal, over 100 kilometres to the north-east: 'I daily hunt the Emperor.' But the hunt had ended. Napoleon's army was reduced to under 50,000 men, yet he would live to fight another day.

Blücher sought to find satisfaction from the outcome of the campaign. 'Now the great enterprise is ended,' he wrote to

Katharina from Giessen, sixty kilometres north of Frankfurt, on 3rd November.

> He [Napoleon] has lost the greater part of his army, especially his artillery, and if we had not made a great mistake, he himself and all his army would have been captured. He will not soon come back to Germany. [Blücher continued:] The day after tomorrow I go to Wetzlar and on to the Rhine, and perhaps across. . . . The roads and weather are miserable.(33)

His regiments rolled forward to the Rhine frontier; the Fatherland had been freed. A nineteen-year-old lieutenant from Silesia described this moment of triumph.

> Oh! What emotions filled my breast as I watched Old Father Rhine flowing by. . . . We have reached *this* goal. . . . Let the whole of France rise up against us. May these bloodhounds poison wells, undermine towns and do whatever else their horrible idol inspires with deceitful design. All this will avail them nothing. We shall wash our hands in the blood of vengeance and cheer loudly if thousands of them whimper and moan in the most hellish agony.(34)

To this blood-thirsty young lieutenant, and to his seventy-year-old Field-Marshal, the first stage of the campaign had been concluded; now the next must be opened, even bloodier than the last.

CHAPTER
9

Invasion

NOVEMBER OPENED WITH blustery north winds and with
Blücher still condemning the allied mistakes which had allowed
Napoleon's escape, but still optimistic with the thought of an early
invasion of France.

> It is true that we accomplished much [he wrote to a relative], but
> not nearly as much as we might have done. By rights, Napoleon
> ought not to have come through, and God forgive those whose
> tardiness and laziness were to blame. But the devil is ever at work
> and envy is not idle! If they had left me on my pursuit path which
> I took after Leipzig, then things would have been very different.

Gneisenau agreed: 'If the monarchs and generals had not lost
so much time with feasting in Weimar, rather than giving orders
to the troops, and if Yorck had not been so slow at Eisenach,
nothing of the French army would have been able to escape.'
These 'ifs' belonged to the past; now Blücher intended to allow
his men just forty-eight hours of rest at Geissen before pushing on.
He admitted on the 4th:

> We have lost men not against the enemy but those who had to stay
> behind exhausted. But they will come back again . . . Our people
> are especially short of boots, shoes and trousers. But their goodwill
> is unshaken. . . . When I come out in the morning, they greet me
> with cheers. . . . The day after tomorrow I shall move forward.(1)

A letter from Blücher to Bonin stressed the Field-Marshal's
feverish desire for the offensive.

We want to conquer Brabant and Holland and drive [the enemy] out so strongly that he will have to sue for peace. This is my suggestion, which I have sent to higher places. . . . The discontent of the [French] nation is rising and Napoleon will have to end his reign. This is my belief. The next letter which you will receive from me will be written from the other side of the river, in which we shall wash off the slavery.(2)

But Blücher's scheduled two days of rest extended to seven. His troops then moved forward, but only to the bank of the Rhine. Worse followed. On the 17th Blücher received his orders – he would command an army of 100,000 men, yet this force would only operate in the Frankfurt area. The Field-Marshal, to his and Gneisenau's complete disgust, led an army of observation; the allies as a whole were to consolidate their position on the east bank of the Rhine. Opportunity for a rapid, full-scale invasion of France was thrown away, and only in the north, in Holland, was limited offensive action to be attempted. Blücher was given instructions to establish his headquarters at Höchst, seven kilometres to the west of Frankfurt.

The allied monarchs converged on Frankfurt in mid-November to discuss the next campaign. Disagreements broke out immediately. Austria and Prussia clashed over schemes for the future of a united Germany, each struggling for a dominant position. Czar Alexander demanded invasion of France, and wanted the Emperor to be replaced by Blücher's frail partner at Leipzig, Bernadotte. With France removed as a potential counter-balance to Russia, the Czar reckoned he could over-awe Prussia and become master of Poland, and having thus strengthened his European frontier, the Czar could turn to the conquest of the Near East. But this Near Eastern policy clashed with Austria's interests. Chancellor Metternich therefore opposed the Czar, and the Emperor Francis, Napoleon's father-in-law, supported his minister. Frederick William displayed his customary hesitation, merely considering that the primary aim had been accomplished – the Fatherland had been restored. Whilst the convoluted merry-go-round whirled away in Frankfurt, no further military operations could be organized; indeed, on 10th November tentative and abortive peace proposals were despatched to Napoleon. Only mopping-up actions were attempted and on 11th November came the capitulation of Dresden.

Blücher fretted and cursed, but remained helpless. Instead he found pleasure wherever he could, amidst the reorganization of his army. As usual, his desire for activity drove him to alcohol and the cards; his dinner-parties lasted well into the early hours, and his capacity for Rhine wine grew. Not surprisingly, he felt greatest sympathy for Czar Alexander who also sought invasion of France, although for different motives. 'Alexander is cleverer than all his generals,' he wrote to his wife. 'On top of that he is the noblest of all men. He said to me, "Blücher, it would be good if you were twenty years younger, but your good health will get you through." '(3) Blücher displayed his vigour at the Frankfurt balls. He responded well to flattery, especially from women. One particular lady, the young, fragile and fair-haired sister of a hussar, endeared herself to Blücher by calling him 'the German Suvarov'. Blücher immediately showed his delight at being compared with the great Russian general by chucking the lady under her chin and exclaiming: *'Das esse ich am liebsten'* – 'this is my favourite dish'. He celebrated his 71st birthday on 16th December with a dinner and ball, at which he entertained his guests with a very sprightly quadrille. Blücher, as always, played as hard and as enthusiastically as he fought. But beyond his immediate noisy circle the gaiety of Frankfurt seemed contrived and tawdry.

The British diplomat Sir George Jackson described the atmosphere in his diary entry for 17th November.

In the evening I assisted at a ball given by the town of Frankfurt to the Allied Sovereigns. Little expense was incurred in preparations for it, the ball-room being but poorly decorated and no supper provided. . . . Besides the King of Prussia we had His Majesty of Bavaria – a good, jolly, farmer-like fellow, crossed with the heaviness of a German Prince, and who formed a principal object of curiosity and attention in this motley crowd. . . . Bonaparte's papa-in-law [Francis] sneaked about as he always does, as if he were ashamed of himself. His brother Emperor [Czar] Alexander, though for the second time only that I have seen him wear shoes and stockings since he was invested, did not condescend to wear the Garter [highest order of English knighthood]; at which I felt in such a rage that I almost wished I could have had it to strangle him with. His Imperial Majesty sauntered about *faisant le joli coeur* with every pretty woman he met. [Sir George continued:] The venerable Marshal Blücher was present, covered with his well-earned honours. . . . As to the women, I never saw at any *réunion* less beauty or more vulgarity. . . . Even a town hall in Hull could hardly show a collection with less distinction.(4)

Blücher, feeling increasingly stifled in this suffocating atmosphere, spent time settling domestic affairs with his wife. 'I am still waiting for news of you,' he wrote on 23rd November, 'and of what you have decided to do – whether you want to stay in Breslau or go to Berlin. It is entirely up to you and it doesn't make any difference where you spend your money, but nevertheless it is important that as the wife of a Field-Marshal you take on another servant and generally live well. Let me know if you can manage on 3,000 thalers.'

This letter provides a glimpse of another facet of Blücher's character. Besides being a rough, tough, roisterous and bloodthirsty soldier, he was also a patient and somewhat paternal husband to Katharina. The tone of his letters to his young wife showed her to be frequently demanding attentions; she complained of the inconveniences caused by his absence; she seemed to seek presents at every available opportunity; she nagged him for more letters. Blücher, not normally the most tolerant of men, responded with sympathy and gentleness. During campaigns he snatched time amidst the pressures and hardships to scribble notes to her. Now, at Frankfurt amidst his worry for the future, he wrote: 'I look hourly for a letter from you, but unfortunately none has arrived. I only hope that illness is not preventing you from writing.' He continued his attempt to ensure that Katharina would have adequate money. 'I gave instructions for 6,000 thalers to be paid to you in Breslau; write and tell me if you received them.' Blücher wrote again on 12th December: 'Dear wife. . . . You complain that you are not receiving any letters from me, yet I write every fortnight.' He advised her to move to Frankfurt if she did not care for Berlin: the mail situation would be better because even if he crossed the Rhine the military couriers would take back letters. He continued: 'My financial situation is quite good at the moment. I get over 20,000 thaler a year. I don't spend much.'(5)

Blücher assured his wife of his good behaviour. 'Since I left Strehlen I haven't had a card in my hand', although he made no mention of drink or dice. He had one especially happy item to report to Katharina during these weeks of waiting. With the capitulation of Dresden on 11th November large numbers of allied prisoners were released, amongst them Blücher's eldest son. 'Franz is free now,' he wrote on 5th December, 'and is in Weimar. But as he is still weak the Duke of Weimar will not let him travel.' Two days before Christmas he wrote: 'You can imagine how glad I was yesterday when Franz stepped unexpectedly into the room – quite sound and well. He looked better than ever. He will stay here a few days and then go to Erfurt where his Regiment is. God has freed me from this anxiety.' However, concern would soon rise again following evidence of Franz's mental ill-health.(6)

Letters to Katharina also revealed mounting impatience with the allied situation and with the glittering gallery of monarchs and their advisers at Frankfurt. 'Herr Napoleon is being cornered,' he wrote on 23rd November, 'and if he isn't saved by any stupid moves on our part he will be forced to make peace.' Blücher added: 'All the "Grand Gentlemen" are in Frankfurt. I go there now and again, but I can't abide this sitting here, idle.'(7) He complained to Bonin: 'Envy is rife here. . . . In Frankfurt there is a whole army of monarchs and princes and this assembly spoils everything. The war is not being conducted with energy any more, and I fear we will dream a lot away. If someone had listened to my plans we would have been in Brussels today.'(8)

The allied leaders counted on Napoleon becoming increasingly unpopular with the French people; thus a proclamation issued in Frankfurt on 1st December declared war was being waged not on the French population but merely in defence of the Fatherland and Russia. For a moment it seemed the policy might be successful. One by one the states of Napoleon's Confederation of the Rhine deserted to the allies – Baden, Bavaria, Berg, Frankfurt, Hesse, Westphalia, Württemberg. In Paris, Talleyrand declared: 'He's got nothing left to fight with. He's exhausted. He'll crawl under a bed and hide.'(9) Yet Napoleon still enjoyed immense support in the towns and villages of France; in the call-up of autumn 1813 he had asked for 160,000 volunteers and 184,000 came forward.

Even in Frankfurt it became clear that war would have to be waged over the Rhine if Bonaparte was to be toppled from power. Czar Alexander's party achieved predominance, and from the first week of December onwards the discussions shifted away from peace negotiations. Military talks proved equally confused and hesitant. Blücher declared at a dinner on 6th December: 'There are certain people who believe that, just because we have had some important successes, we should now fold our hands on our laps.' Plans were discussed and rejected in rapid succession; tempers frayed. General Joseph Radetzky, Schwarzenberg's chief of staff, received a summons from the Russian Emperor, who declared: 'If you don't stop sending me your plans. . . . I'll have you imprisoned or made a head shorter.'(10) But by mid-December the plans seemed nearer completion. Gneisenau wrote to his wife on the 11th: 'If we conduct operations intelligently, in strength and quickly, then we shall have enforced peace within three months.'(11)

Almost immediately after this letter Gneisenau joined with Blücher in condemning the latest allied schemes as grossly inefficient. As before, three allied armies would take the field: Bernadotte's 60,000 men were to advance through Holland and across the lower Rhine, while Blücher, with 75,000, advanced across the middle Rhine and up the Moselle Valley into Lorraine. But the third and main army, totalling 210,000 under Schwarzenberg, would make a detour south to enter France via Switzerland. This far-flung sweep threatened to split the allied offensive, and weakened chances of maximum effort being placed in a direct drive on Paris, as Blücher and Gneisenau sought.

Military grounds for the Switzerland detour seemed slender. The route gave access to the high plateau of Langres, and near Langres itself rose several large rivers. Proponents of the plan declared it would be easier for the army to cross these rivers at their source than lower down. The plateau of Langres was termed the 'commanding position' for the campaign in France, but to critics of the plan such terminology smacked of methods of waging war which had been rendered outdated by Napoleonic developments. Clausewitz, for example, condemned the old-fashioned type of general who believed in 'algebraic actions' rather than in the new forms of flexible warfare on a mass scale. Clausewitz probably had Schwarzenberg in mind when he criticized those who worshipped the 'sacred relics of military erudition.'(12) Blücher, lacking Clausewitz's education, expressed himself in more forceful fashion. He declared that the only advantage he could see in taking the Langres plateau, which also happened to be the watershed of France, was that if he stood on the summit and

urinated, half would trickle down into the Mediterranean and half into the Atlantic.

Behind criticism of the plan's outdated methodology lay another reason for objection. It seemed that the Austrian point of view had emerged the strongest: advantageous peace should be sought, rather than the complete destruction of Napoleon. By advancing into France on three separate lines, the population would be affected to a greater degree than through a single concentrated push for Paris. The French people would be more likely to turn against Napoleon. Yet Blücher, Gneisenau and those like them believed the fundamental objective remained to destroy the enemy army and its commander. Gneisenau wrote to Stein in January 1814:

> We must take revenge for the many sorrows inflicted upon the nation, and for so much arrogance. If we do not, then we are miserable wretches indeed, and deserve to be shocked out of our lazy peace every two years and threatened with the scourge of slavery. [Gneisenau continued:] We must return the visits of the French to our cities by visiting them in their's. Until we do our revenge and triumph will be incomplete.(13)

Blücher and his supporters therefore believed that the military objective – destruction of the enemy main force – must come first, even above diplomatic considerations. Yet Schwarzenberg had no chance to avoid these other diplomatic factors, surrounded as he was by a multitude of monarchs, ministers and diplomatic advisers.

'It really is inhuman what I have to tolerate,' exclaimed Schwarzenberg, normally mild-mannered, 'surrounded as I am by feeble-minded people, fools of every kind, crazy project-makers, intriguers, asses, loud-mouths. . . . I often think I shall collapse under their weight.'(14)

Metternich warned Schwarzenberg that the allies must advance 'cautiously' in order to 'utilize the desire of the common man in France for peace by avoiding warlike acts'. To Blücher and Gneisenau only 'warlike acts' could end the war.

Dangerous differences therefore existed amongst the allies even before the campaign began. Moreover, Blücher's army had still to recover completely from the hammering endured at Leipzig. Fresh recruits filled the gaps, but these lacked training and experience, and the recruiting material seemed less promising than in previous months. At least six out of every ten conscripts were too young to shave and Blücher's favourite name for his troops, 'my children,' assumed greater relevance. But Blücher still sifted optimism from this apparently gloomy situation. His spirits revived as he sat in his draughty quarters at Höchst. War lay ahead; problems would sort themselves out. 'What our march is going to do only time will tell,' he wrote to his wife on 12th December. The same letter revealed that the allied headquarters would be moving from Frankfurt to Freiberg, together with the monarchs and their accompanying hosts. 'I am glad that all the "Grand Gentlemen" are leaving, because they inconvenience me.'(15)

Events quickened as the New Year approached. On 21st December Schwarzenberg's main army began to cross the frontier into Switzerland, prior to the invasion of France. 'It is impossible to say how wearing it is to see such an immense number of men march by,' commented Lady Priscilla Burghersh at her home near Basel. 'They were going by this house from eight o'clock till past two, without a moment's cessation.'(16) At the same time Blücher moved his headquarters sixty kilometres west to Kaub, where the cold grey Rhine lapped the gardens of the houses.

Whatever the policy of the allied monarchs, Blücher and his chief of staff seized upon the salient factor in the new situation: simply by advancing across the Rhine the allies would switch from a defensive to an offensive war. Blücher and Gneisenau aimed to underline this transfer in their own forceful fashion. Schwarzenberg intended Blücher's Army of Silesia to operate slightly to the rear of the main army's advance, but with allied headquarters moved from Frankfurt, Blücher immediately altered the emphasis. 'I am not circumscribed and can act as I see fit,' he wrote to General von Rüchel. Rather than staying back, he would lead the advance.

Blücher told Stein: 'Forward it shall be, that I promise you!'(17) He would set the pace, and would strike while the main army still proceeded cautiously through Switzerland. On Boxing Day orders reached Yorck, once again commanding a corps in Blücher's army:

I beg humbly to inform Your Excellency that on 1st January, at dawn, I shall cross the Rhine with the army. [Blücher's message continued:] The disposition for the troops will follow tomorrow. In order to keep secret my design I shall, on the 29th of this month, move my headquarters to Frankfurt and take measures to make it seem as though I intended to stay there for some time.(18)

Blücher returned to Frankfurt as planned. He wrote to a relative: 'At daybreak on 1st January I shall cross the Rhine with the whole army, but beforehand I want . . . to wash away all servitude in this proud river. . . .'(19) For forty-eight hours he occupied himself with ostentatious dinners and theatre parties for the benefit of French agents, whilst his army stole forward in three columns towards crossing places over the river at Kaub, Mannheim and Coblenz. By New Year's Eve, clear and starry with a touch of frost, the regiments stood ready on the bank of the Rhine.

*   *   *

'Up to this moment 4,000 infantrymen have crossed in barges,' wrote Blücher to a friend during 1st January, 1814. 'The bridge will be ready by midday, then I shall follow with the whole corps.' In the evening he wrote to his wife: 'I crossed the proud Rhine. The banks echoed to sounds of joy, and my brave troops receive me with jubilation. The resistance of the enemy was inconsiderable.' He added: 'I go forward at once.'(20)

Blücher spent the night of 1st January on the west bank at Bacharach. The army continued to cross next day while he advanced over his old campaigning area of the 1790s. For all Blücher's optimism, the passage over the Rhine nonetheless proved slow and tedious: currents ran swift, thickened by ice-flows, yet maximum speed had to be maintained to prevent a determined French counter-attack. None came, and as Blücher commented later: 'The whole crossing was at a cost to me of 300 men. . . . No army of 80,000 ever crossed it so cheaply.' He issued stirring proclamations, composed for him by Gneisenau, aimed at obtaining the support of the locals. 'See in the hosts of the confederate Sovereigns, the friend of humanity, whose only enemies are the enemies of peace.'(21) Caulaincourt, Napoleon's roving envoy, complained about these declarations: 'They damage us even more than their guns.'(22)

Blücher pushed rapidly towards Metz, while further south

Schwarzenberg's main army moved more slowly through the Belfort Gap towards the plateau of Langres. By 7th January Blücher had reached Lauterecken. 'I am fairly well and expect soon to be far into France,' he told his wife. 'With God's help I think we shall finish it in four months and Herr Napoleon will have to make peace.'(23) 'Blücher enjoys the most perfect health,' commented an officer on his staff. 'He undertakes all the toils of the campaign, which hardly seem to bother him, with such youthful energy that those around him are astonished.' Blücher spent the whole of each day in the saddle, rested for an hour or so in the evening, then appeared for dinner refreshed and hearty. His dinner conversation remained as vigorous and salty as ever, so much so that when the English *attaché* Sir Hudson Lowe sought a translation, Prussian officers were too embarrassed to oblige.(24)

Marmont's blocking force of 10,000 men pulled back on Blücher's approach, and on 11th January he could write to Katharina: 'I am only eight hours away from Metz today. Tomorrow I hope to appear in front of the fortress.' He said the local people were half-starved, diseased and demoralized. 'If we avoid silly mistakes the best is to be expected. I do not know much about the other armies and mind my own business.'(25) The advance continued on schedule. 'Today I arrived with the Silesian Army before Metz,' he reported to Schwarzenberg next day, 12th January.(26) Two days later the enemy pulled back from Metz, withdrawing towards Verdun. 'So we are off to Paris!' wrote Blücher to Rüchel. 'Unless we do something foolish we shall carry all before us.'(27)

The Prussian columns moved steadily down the icy roads. 'Just one more harsh battle, which we must and will win,' Blücher told Katharina, 'and peace will come.' By 18th January he had reached Nancy. 'I wish you could eat oysters with me to-day, which are very good.' He believed his Silesian army would be the first to see the spires of Paris.(28) Onwards went the Prussians towards Châlons, about 150 kilometres from Napoleon's capital. Yet even Blücher knew his army alone could not destroy the main French forces which would block the road ahead; Schwarzenberg must also advance. Opinion at the allied headquarters still proved against the push on Paris. Emperor Francis and his powerful minister, Metternich, joined with Frederick William and his chancellor, Hardenberg, in believing a complete defeat of Napoleon should still be avoided, for political reasons. Knesebeck, Frederick

William's adviser, favoured manoeuvring for a fortnight while diplomatic discussions opened with the enemy.

Blücher and Gneisenau vehemently disagreed. 'Should the main army advance far enough to enable us to effect a junction,' wrote Blücher to Schwarzenberg, 'I believe we shall be quite strong enough to strike an absolutely decisive blow.'(29) But the main army dallied at Langres. Schwarzenberg cursed the mad-cap Prussian Field-Marshal and his equally hot-headed chief of staff. He wrote an angry letter to his wife:

> Blücher, and still more Gneisenau . . . are urging the march on Paris with such perfectly childish rage that they trample underfoot every single rule of warfare. Without placing any considerable force to guard the road from Châlons to Nancy they rush like mad to Brienne. Regardless of their rear and of their flanks they do nothing but plan *parties fines* in the Palais Royal. That is indeed frivolous at such an important moment!(30)

Blücher and Gneisenau preferred to bend the rules of war and continued to suspect Schwarzenberg's rigid adherence to the text-book. Moreover, rather than neglecting their rear, they relied upon the main army to perform this function for them. Yet arguments continued at Langres for almost two vital weeks; Blücher continued to press forwards for Châlons, but he advanced unsupported.

In Paris, Napoleon completed his preparations and on Tuesday, 25th January, he bid farewell to Marie Louise. 'I shall beat *papa François* again. Don't cry. I shall soon be back.' Next day he reached his army at Châlons. His troops shivered in the icy wind: many were young, pink-cheeked teenagers known as Marie Louises, who were handed uniforms and taught hurriedly how to load and aim a musket just before being prodded forward to fight.(31) They would find themselves vastly outnumbered – if only the allied armies could combine. But such a junction remained unaccomplished. Amongst the allied leaders only Alexander continued to support Blücher and his chief of staff. Stein, visiting the allied headquarters, wrote to Gneisenau on the 27th: 'I always show your letters to the Czar, who alone stands there strong and noble and spurns the counsels of the weak and of the despicable.'(32)

The monarchs finally reached a compromise solution on Friday, 28th January. In answer to Austria's demands, a congress of ministers would meet at Châtillon to discuss peace possibilities, but military operations would meanwhile continue. The main army, now totalling 120,000, was to march to Troyes and thence towards Paris, while Blücher's 75,000 troops advanced on its present route past Vitry and Châlons. The allied decision came too late. By this Friday, 28th January, Blücher had reached Brienne, further forward than Schwarzenberg anticipated. A gap yawned between Blücher's Silesian army and the main allied forces; Napoleon stabbed forward to seize his opportunity. News reached Blücher as he wrote to his wife during this Friday: 'I must close, as a report has come that Napoleon has arrived at Vitry which is only a short distance from here. So up and to horse!'(33)

This latest report proved false: Napoleon was even nearer, at Blücher's northern flank around the village of Maizières, less than ten kilometres away. The bulk of Blücher's units had already advanced west from Brienne, and now they had to hurry back. French guns began to shell Brienne early on Saturday 29th January, while Blücher and his staff ate their breakfast in the castle behind the town: a cannon-ball crashed into the upper floor and plaster showered the officers in the dining room below. Blücher calmly finished his breakfast 'as if music was playing for his entertainment'.(34)

He had ordered his regiments to stay on the defensive, his primary aim being to hold Brienne and allow the main army a chance to move up from the east. Fighting on the 29th therefore stopped short of full-scale battle; French troops continued to probe forward and were repulsed by strong Prussian defences, and Napoleon lacked sufficient strength to launch an all-out attack. Musket fire and artillery roars subsided during the early evening. Blücher returned with Gneisenau to the castle; he climbed the stairs to survey the surrounding area from the roof, ordering his horse to be unsaddled and led to the stables.

Shots suddenly rang out from the castle courtyard. French troops had crept unnoticed into the castle. Blücher and Gneisenau clattered down the winding stairs and fortunately found their horses still in the yard. They threw themselves into the saddles and galloped through the gate, bullets humming behind them. Sounds of firing came from Brienne itself, mingled with shouts and bugle calls: French cavalry had launched a surprise assault.

Night had fallen, but the enemy cavalrymen were clearly visible against the burning houses. Blücher tried to rally his men, and insisted upon riding through the streets until Gneisenau demanded to know whether he wanted to be led in triumph as a prisoner to Paris. But at about 10 p.m. Blücher ordered his troops into a counter-attack, and they drove the French from the town again, only to withdraw once more as Blücher pulled back towards the main army. About 3,000 men had been lost by each side during the day's fighting.

During the night Blücher accomplished one of the most difficult military manoeuvres, and by doing so stole the march on Napoleon. Despite the dark and dangers of a French attack, and the weariness of his troops, he disentangled the army from Brienne, marched south through the difficult terrain by the river Aube, and by dawn on 30th January had drawn up his forces in perfect order on the hills above Trannes. This movement at last allowed junction with Schwarzenberg's main army, advancing from Langres, and defeated Napoleon's intention to 'pursue the enemy as far as Bar-sur-Aube.' All the French could do was to occupy La Rothière below Blücher's positions.

For two days both sides stood within a short distance of each other, with Napoleon not daring to attack Blücher's excellent defensive line in the hills, despite the Emperor's anxiety over the imminent arrival of Schwarzenberg's main force. Blücher, on the other hand, again tussled with the allied headquarters. The Austrians still sought to avoid battle, and Schwarzenberg agreed. Discussion on the 30th and 31st eventually resulted in another unsatisfactory compromise. Blücher was given chief command of the forces to be engaged in battle with Napoleon, but Schwarzenberg restricted the number of these forces to about 53,000 men, about 8,000 more than the French but far less than could have been deployed, and he insisted upon controlling the disposition of reinforcements during the battle. Blücher was therefore denied the opportunity of inflicting decisive defeat on Napoleon. Moreover, he was informed on the eve of battle that as soon as it had finished he must separate his forces from those of the main army. The latter would remain on its present road, marching towards Troyes, while Blücher followed the right bank of the Marne past Vitry and Châlons. All the value of merging the two armies would thus be thrown away.

Snow swirled across the wooded hills and fields around La Rothière on Tuesday 1st February. Blücher rode to his command position at 7 a.m. and peered through the white scurries at the village. Below him black lines of Prussian and Russian infantry waited to advance from the Trannes heights against the French; at mid-morning the drums beat their staccato rolls and the battle of La Rothière began. Fighting continued throughout the day, concentrating on the village itself and on another hamlet called Chaumésnil and in La Giberie wood. Blücher spent the morning on the Trannes heights, puffing at his pipe and directing forces first to one point and then another.

Battle intensified during the afternoon and Russian troops seized La Rothière; French counter-attacks were repulsed. Blücher had ridden forward with the successful advance, and now trotted amidst the burning timbers and splintered slates, bellowing his customary encouragements at his men. Snow continued, sizzling and spitting in the fires. The French fell back across the whitened fields; as night came down Blücher ordered his troops to start the pursuit. For the first time in his career Napoleon had suffered defeat on French soil, and now his demoralized, frozen troops pulled back first to Troyes and then to Nogent, a distance of over seventy kilometres. Blücher advanced to Brienne and reoccupied the castle, where the monarchs joined him to toast his success with champagne.

'Blücher,' exclaimed the Czar, 'to-day you have set the crown on all your victories. Mankind will bless you!'

Blücher grunted his thanks and retired exhausted to bed, to sleep five hours. Both sides lost about 6,000 men in the battle on 1st February. Blücher had earned his victory, which stemmed from the excellent use of ground worked out with Gneisenau, but the success would have been far greater if he had been able to use all available allied troops. Once again Napoleon had survived.(35)

Blücher wrote to his wife later on the 2nd:

The great blow is over. Yesterday I met Napoleon . . . The battle lasted into the night and, about 10 o'clock, I had driven the Emperor out of his positions . . . Now he is retreating on Paris . . . My staff send their respects. To their astonishment they are all unhurt . . . I tremble so that I can't write more. [But he added:] If he keeps the Crown he must look upon it as a present from the hands of our Monarchs.(36)

Schwarzenberg still dallied over full pursuit; snowstorms hindered Cossack cavalrymen chasing after the French, and as Gneisenau commented: 'We have destroyed the last but one fortress of the enemy – but the last one will have to be destroyed too.' Napoleon rallied his regiments to block the road at Nogent. Renewed allied arguments broke out. A council of war held at Brienne castle on the 2nd decided that

> the allied forces shall separate anew; that the Silesian army of Field-Marshal Blücher shall at once march from here to Châlons, unite there with the scattered divisions of Generals von Yorck, von Kleist and Count Langeron, and then press on along the Marne, past Meux, to Paris; while the main army turns towards Troyes, and likewise presses on to Paris along both sides of the Seine.(37)

Although the respective routes to Paris lay parallel, a distance of about eighty kilometres stretched between them, and Napoleon lurked in the centre at Nogent. Moreover, the Austrians still wished to obtain peace without further battle. 'I am rather sad,' admitted Metternich after Brienne, 'that it didn't turn out to be a small defeat for Blücher.'(38) On 6th February, as Blücher advanced from Châlons towards Étoges, about 150 kilometres east of Paris, ministers met at Châtillon to discuss possible peace, and in Stein's words: 'Schwarzenberg relaxed his military operations.'(39)

Blücher's isolated army moved through increasingly hostile countryside.

> We felt for the first time thrown back wholly on our own resources [wrote Henry Steffens]. I now perceived that the face of a hostile land wears a mask to the invader – every house and thicket conceals a danger – every object has an ominous meaning, and this character it never loses.(40)

Yet Napoleon's troops suffered even greater depression, so accustomed to victory and now experiencing the violation of their country. Their uniforms were saturated, their stomachs empty; the infliction of another defeat could transform Napoleon's army into a panic-stricken rabble. Events reached a climax on the night of 7th February. Napoleon lodged in a private house at Nogent, and there he received one dismal despatch after another. Parisians were fleeing from the city; churches were holding special services to pray for deliverance; Murat, Napoleon's friend for two decades, had deserted.

'I hope to live long enough to take my own and France's vengeance!' exclaimed the Emperor. He feared for his life and for another lost battle. 'It is possible,' he scribbled in a note to his brother Joseph, 'that I shall make peace soon.' He slumped on his couch and tossed restlessly as he sought sleep. Then, in the early hours of the 8th, another messenger burst into his room. Napoleon tore open the despatch and shouted for his maps. He spread the maps on the floor and began sticking pins here and there: Marmont had discovered the fatal gap between Blücher and Schwarzenberg.

'Plans are completely changed,' exclaimed Napoleon. 'At this very moment I'm just about to beat Blücher. . . . Peace can wait!'(41)

Napoleon knew Blücher's whereabouts, but Blücher had been completely misinformed by Schwarzenberg over Napoleon's position. The allied commander had declared that the Emperor was 'to an almost complete certainty' concentrating at Troyes for an attack on the main army. On 9th February Blücher received a frightened request for Kleist's corps to be despatched as reinforcement for Schwarzenberg. Blücher obliged not only with Kleist's troops but also with the corps of the Russian generals Kapzewitsch and Olsufiev. Yet at that moment Napoleon was hurrying north to Sèzanne, ready to pounce upon Blücher's scattered columns, and within hours Blücher's scouts reported the advancing French. Hurried orders were despatched for the Silesian Army to concentrate; Yorck, further north pursuing French detachments under Macdonald, was told to link with Sacken's corps at Montmirail. But confusion rapidly increased and Yorck delayed in marching south.

Napoleon struck. First he fell upon Olsufiev at Champaubert on 10th February and overwhelmed this small force. Next day he engaged Sacken's unsupported corps at Montmirail, and as Sacken retreated northwards towards Yorck, Napoleon continued to pound the Prussians and tangled with Yorck's corps as well. Blücher, situated near Étoges with the remainder of his army, appealed to Schwarzenberg for help: the main army must strike north to threaten Napoleon's rear. Blücher called back forces sent to reinforce the main army, and now had about 20,000 men, but Yorck and Sacken were retreating past Château Thierry in the Reims direction, leaving 3,000 casualties behind.

Schwarzenberg failed to act. Instead he continued to condemn Blücher's offensive policy.

My old Blücher is so eager again to reach the Palais Royale [he wrote to his wife during the day], that he is pressing on madly without considering that although the enemy before him is certainly weak, the enemy army is at his flank. It will be a miracle if this dissipation of his strength does not bring about a catastrophe for him.(42)

Schwarzenberg had been guilty of greater dissipation through separating the allied armies, leaving Blücher unsupported, yet his criticism had some justification. Blücher, typically, indeed decided to fight forward, especially as a captured Frenchman assured him that Napoleon had now turned back towards Paris to defend the capital.

I have had three bitter days [he wrote to Katharina on the 13th]. Napoleon attacked me three times . . . but he has not gained his purpose and to-day is retreating to Paris. Tomorrow I pursue him; then both of our armies unite and a battle before Paris will decide everything. Don't fear that we shall be beaten; that is out of the question unless unheard of mistakes are made.(43)

Blücher advanced from Étoges early next morning, 14th February, heading towards Montmirail. Even Gneisenau advised caution. Later in the day reports reached the Field-Marshal that Yorck and Sacken had been driven back across the Marne, and therefore remained too far away for early reunion. Gneisenau urged Blücher to withdraw, and the Field-Marshal reluctantly agreed.

Almost at this moment, Napoleon attacked. Reports of his retreat towards Paris had been false, perhaps deliberately planted by the Emperor himself, and now he swooped upon the out-numbered Prussians. Blücher, with less than 20,000 men, found himself in the most desperate situation of his career. Line after line of French infantrymen closed upon him; massed cavalrymen awaited the order to charge; shells exploded on the road to front and rear.

A horseman close to me was struck [wrote Steffens]. I looked involuntarily round, and saw him fall with his head frightfully shattered. . . . I was with Blücher and his staff, who, separated from the main body and escorted by only a few troops, brought up the rear. Then we saw the enemy on the hills on both sides. Grenades burst close to us; cannon-balls fell thicker into the midst of us; the musketry began to be destructive as the enemy approached; and even some single cavalry soldiers tried to hew their way into the midst of us. They were wrapped in white cloaks, and wore immense bear-skins, which half-covered their faces.(44)

Step by step Blücher's army retreated. Enemy infantry attacks were repulsed, but the cavalry inflicted severe casualties. Blücher, so often the leader of a cavalry charge, experienced the effect of such attack. He insisted upon staying with the rearguard, provided by the Russians, and he bellowed at these troops to stay steady. Only rigid formation could offer defence against the cavalry assaults; once the lines became dispersed the enemy would slash through the ranks. Blücher frantically organized and re-organized the men, encouraging troops back into position, striving to keep them calm despite the thundering shell fire and repeated cavalry charges. Nostitz, Blücher's aide, pleaded in vain for him to seek some safety; Blücher shouted above the din that if all was lost he would rather die than be captured.

'Words fail me to express my admiration for the fearlessness and discipline of the troops,' wrote the English *attaché*, Sir Hudson Lowe, and he stressed the example set by Blücher 'who was everywhere and always in the most exposed positions.'(45) By nightfall the army had struggled back to Étoges. Blücher had managed to extricate his force, but eye-witnesses described him looking 'desperately grim'. In less than a fortnight he had lost 14,000 men, and Napoleon still blocked the road to Paris; Blücher's army remained scattered, and allied co-operation seemed as unattainable as ever.

Peace-seekers at the allied headquarters would receive support from Napoleon's successes, and for this reason Blücher and

Gneisenau made light of the setbacks. 'We tried to act as though we had not been beaten,' confessed Gneisenau later.(46) Instead they urged even greater action. Blücher rejoined forces with Sacken and Yorck on the 16th and reorganized his regiments to the west of Châlons. He explained his plans in a letter to Hardenberg, in which he permitted himself a single side-thrust at Schwarzenberg:

> My three corps, Yorck's, Sacken's and Kleist's have all three fought separately with Napoleon. Many have fallen, but I have accomplished my purpose and detained the Emperor here for five days. If, during this time the main army has accomplished nothing, while it was practically unopposed, then it is a matter for regret. The hour has struck; a decisive battle must take place as soon as possible. If we stand still and wait we exhaust our supplies and render the people here desperate; they will rise *en masse* against us. [Blücher continued:] On the 19th I make straight for the enemy, on that you can pin your faith. But the main army *must* go forward or things may turn out badly. . . .(47)

Blücher's pledge to advance on the 19th remained unfulfilled. Allied confusion reached new levels, and for the next two weeks chaotic manoeuvring continued east of Paris, while the allied commanders talked of peace. Napoleon struck at the Austrians near Monterau on the 18th. Schwarzenberg ordered Blücher to march south and join him, saying a battle would be fought at Troyes on the 21st. But rather than risk such a battle, Schwarzenberg retreated from Troyes on the 23rd; Napoleon entered the town the following day. The allied monarchs sought an armistice, to which Napoleon sent no reply.

'At the first stroke of misfortune,' he commented to Joseph, 'these poor wretches fall on their knees.'

Instead Napoleon wrote to his father-in-law, Emperor Francis, offering to make peace on the basis of France's 'natural frontiers': the Alps and the Rhine, including Belgium. The conditions would clearly be unacceptable, but meanwhile the possibility of peace hindered military operations. Blücher had received reluctant permission to march forward from Arcis-sur-Aube towards Paris, then, on 24th February, he received further orders from Frederick William: 'As negotiations for a truce with the Emperor Napoleon are in progress, and this truce will very likely soon be effected, the case is altered with regard to the order to assume the offensive which the army under your command received. . . .'(48)

This order, and subsequent instructions from Schwarzenberg to march south to join the main army, came as a shattering blow to Blücher. He considered the situation with Gneisenau at their Esternay headquarters, 110 kilometres from Paris, and they decided to continue regardless.

Yesterday my vanguard drove the enemy as far as La Ferté Gaucher [wrote Blücher to Schwarzenberg on the 25th], and is drawn up in face of that position. Were I to turn back I could under no circumstances effect my junction with your Grace within the stated time and should expose the army to the gravest perils. By moving on Paris, on the other hand, and operating in the rear of the Emperor Napoleon, I hope to secure for your Grace the most effectual relief.(49)

Blücher and Gneisenau flaunted the orders of both Schwarzenberg and the King of Prussia. By advancing without plans for support from the main army they risked encirclement and destruction – and they also risked upsetting possible truce talks. As far as the first danger was concerned, Blücher hoped that if he led the way, Schwarzenberg would follow. And, with the second danger, he banked on the armistice discussions coming to nothing. The gamble paid off. Word reached Blücher late on the 25th that the negotiations had failed. Fresh orders came allowing him to advance, but he would still be unsupported – the main army would draw back and gather reinforcements.

The expected truce has not come to pass [wrote Frederick William]. Accordingly my orders to you of yesterday lose their validity. It has now been decided that Prince Schwarzenberg's army . . . shall continue its retreat. Henceforward the outcome of this campaign depends on you.

'Press on grenadiers,' shouted Blücher to his troops. 'Now we are off to Paris!'

But dangers surrounding him were immense. Although outnumbered, Napoleon might attack at any moment; Blücher could only hope that the main army might lure the French from his flank. Before him lay Marmont's force of 8,000; around him spread cold, unfriendly countryside; his men were ragged after the constant marches and battles over the last two months. Marmont withdrew north-westwards on the 26th, eluding Blücher's cavalry who immediately suffered their commander's wrath. The Silesian Army had also to toil northwards, both to chase Marmont and French forces under Mortier, and also to effect a junction with supporting regiments under Bülow and Wintzingerode, striking down towards Soissons from Laon.

Manoeuvring continued during the last days of February and in the first week of March. Blücher's army crossed the frozen Marne on 27th February, harried by French detachments. Kleist's corps lost 1,000 men on the river bank. Enemy pressure increased on the 28th as Blücher tried to turn west towards Paris. Napoleon had left 40,000 men under Macdonald to chase Schwarzenberg, and hurried north to fend off Blücher. The Silesian Army was subjected to repeated attacks on the flank and rear, and Blücher was forced to continue north. Soissons fell to Bülow, and Blücher joined forces with him at the beginning of March. His army now totalled about 100,000 men, twice Napoleon's strength, but the Prussians and Russians were exhausted and denied supplies.

'The army is nearly starved,' exclaimed Frederick von Bülow. 'All discipline and order are dissolved, and I confess to our shame that it looks not unlike a band of robbers.'(50)

Blücher stayed cheerful, despite the gruelling manoeuvring. He pestered Gneisenau to ensure his 'champagne waggon' kept up with the army, and asked him one night if this store remained safe.

'Why that I don't know, Your Excellency,' replied Gneisenau.

'Surely you put it on a safe road?' asked Blücher, to which Gneisenau replied: 'There isn't any safe road.'

'God forbid the French should get it,' exclaimed the Field-Marshal.

His chief of staff retorted: 'I wish they had it already, then we could stop bothering about the damned thing.'

Wenzel Krimer, a surgeon in the army, described another of Blücher's nightly pleasures which continued even amidst the campaigning slog.

A drum had to be brought over, and he would throw dice with the first officers who came along. If he won a few thalers, he was as delighted as a child and would stroke his grey moustache and grin;

while if he lost (and he often lost a great deal of money) he would laugh at himself.(51)

Napoleon also remained optimistic and cheerful. On 5th March he struck northwards from Reims. '*Mon amie,*' he wrote to Marie Louise at ten o'clock that night. 'I have delivered Reims, taken 4,000 prisoners and 600 baggage waggons. Tell them to fire 30 guns . . .'

The armies converged. Now, at the end of the first week in March, Blücher turned for battle. Napoleon crossed the Aisne at Berry-au-Bac, about thirty kilometres south-east of Laon; Blücher's army lay on the plateau of Craonne, immediately to his front. Blücher spent the night of 6th March sitting in a chair in a house at Braye, fifteen kilometres west of Napoleon's position. North of Craonne the uneven plateau spread almost to Soissons, sloping to the Ailette in the north and descending sharply to the Aisne in the south. At the easterly end of the high ground, towards Craonne itself, the plateau tapered to a ridge. This area of high land, deep gulleys and rushing streams, would provide the battle-field. But Blücher would only employ a part of his army.

Considerable disagreement had broken out amongst his senior officers over whether to fight on offensive or defensive lines. The difference of opinion had even spread to Blücher and his chief of staff. The Field-Marshal, inevitably, wished to clash with Napoleon in offensive battle; Gneisenau advised great caution in view of supply shortages and the weariness of the troops. Finally a compromise was reached on 6th March: some regiments would continue to Laon and take up strong defensive positions at this city, while troops under Woronzoff, Kleist, Langeron, Sacken and Wintzingerode would engage Napoleon The compromise held serious risks because Prussian superiority of numbers would be reduced and difficulties of command would be increased. A decisive battle might not be possible. Moreover, the lack of clear opinion led to greater strain upon Blücher himself and now his health began to fail. By the morning of 7th March the Field-Marshal was suffering from a temperature, nagging ear-ache and sore eyes. His seventy-one years, the constant campaigning in wet and dismal conditions, suddenly began to tell.

Nevertheless, the Army of Silesia had already been put in motion for battle. On the evening of the 6th Blücher despatched orders to Wintzingerode: he must move across the Ailette and march south-east with his 10,000 cavalry to fall upon the enemy from the rear. Napoleon had begun to march along the high road leading over the plateau from Berry-au-Bac to Laon. At the same time Woronzoff and Sacken were ordered to engage the enemy from the front; Kleist and Langeron would sever any enemy retreat. The plan seemed bold, but it was also complicated, allowing too much possibility of error by an individual commander, and from the start the scheme collapsed.

Wintzingerode advanced too slowly on the evening of the 6th and then inexplicably decided to camp for the night. So, when Napoleon clashed with the Prussians and Russians on the ridge next morning, Sacken and Woronzoff found themselves unsupported and rapidly pressed back. Only the speedy arrival of Wintzingerode's cavalry behind the enemy could rectify the situation, and Blücher himself rode off to find his errant subordinate. He ignored his fever and pains, and hurried as fast as he could, but not until 2 p.m. did he manage to locate the flanking force. By this time the regiments on the ridge were reeling backwards, outnumbered by the concentrated French. A messenger rushed to Blücher with a despatch from Sacken. 'I beg most urgently that Your Excellency hasten the operation against the right wing. . . . The enemy has drawn up all his artillery against us.'(52)

But the roads over which Wintzingerode's cavalry had still to travel were sheeted with ice, the horses were ill-shod through shortages of horse-shoes, and already the March afternoon had started to darken. Blücher could only order withdrawal. Back fell the Prussians and Russians on the plateau. French cavalry and infantry pressed hard after Blücher's retreating men. At one point the way was so narrow that Russian cavalry had to halt under heavy fire while infantry filed through the gulleys. But the Russians maintained perfect order, 'as if on the parade-ground' according to one eye-witness, and by nightfall the survivors moved behind the Laon defences. Both sides suffered about 6,000 casualties during the day. Blücher, with pains in his eyes, his fever unabated, and his temper vile, cursed the missed opportunity; Gneisenau, for all his plea for caution, agreed that 'if Wintzingerode had done his duty the destiny of France would have been decided.'(53)

'*Ma Bonne Louise*,' wrote Napoleon at 7 a.m. next day, 8th March. 'I attacked yesterday and completely defeated the Russian

army commanded by Wintzingerode. They were 30,000 men. . . .
I march on Laon. My health is good, though rather tired. It is
very cold. . . .' Blücher's temperature remained high; his brother-
in-law, Major Colomb, described him on the 8th as 'feverish and
apparently rather unwell, but full of spirit with regard to the
coming battle.'(54) Blücher's army totalled about 90,000, over
twice as many men as Napoleon commanded; the positions at
Laon had been strengthened, and the town itself occupied a very
strong natural position on a chalky hill rising at a forty-five degree
angle from the surrounding plain. Only Napoleon's under-
estimation of Blücher's remaining strength could have persuaded
him to launch such a reckless offensive.

At five in the morning, 9th March, the outnumbered French
ran forward in suicidal charges against the Prussian and Russian
defences. It was a clear bright spring day. Blücher had ordered
wicker chairs to be brought to the edge of the cliff which surrounded
the town, and there he sat to watch the battle. The sun shone on
his tired face; he constantly shaded his inflamed, blood-shot eyes
with his hand. The view from his vantage point was superb:
rolling fields, distant villages, white roads leading towards the
blue horizon. Across this beautiful vista spread the horrors of
battle. Blücher sat watching his 'children' slaughter the French.
'We saw all with perfect ease,' wrote Steffens, who stood beside
him.

Hour after hour the clash continued. Messengers constantly
reached Blücher's command position and he issued new orders.
Later in the day, as his weariness increased, he frequently waved
away the messengers for Gneisenau to deal with them. All the
while the ant-like men fought on the sunny plain below.

On one place a Russian square was furiously attacked [commented
Steffens]. They were shot at with musket balls, while a mass of
cavalry tried to hew a road into the midst of them; but they were
not to be broken; they waved every way, and curved and bent, but
always drew closer again into a dense mass as if they had been one
single living body. It was a grand, a wonderful sight!

Within this anonymous mass were multiple incidents of personal horror and heroism. One cavalryman had a miraculous
escape when a shell tore into his mount, entering near the animal's
shoulder and burying deep into the body. The horse shrieked and

leapt high into the air with a convulsive jerk, throwing the rider; then the shell exploded, spewing bloody limbs and entrails over the cavalryman, who staggered to his feet unhurt. Nor were Blücher and his staff entirely safe. A shell whistled over their heads and crashed into a mill just behind them, scattering burning timbers. Some officers, including Blücher's aide, Nostitz, were wounded by splinters, but the Field-Marshal sat unscathed.(55)

Fighting died down at dusk. French attempts to seize the Laon suburbs had been repulsed, and only the nearby village of Athies, where Marmont's troops had driven out Prussian defenders, had fallen into enemy hands. But Marmont's soldiers, young, inexperienced, many of them under fire for the first time, slumped where they had fought without taking necessary precautions against counter-attack. 'Overcome by fatigue, stiff with cold, weak with hunger,' wrote the French historian Houssaye, 'they slept around their camp-fires like a drove of sheep huddled together.'(56)

Such negligence proved fatal against Blücher's hardened veterans. Both Blücher and Yorck had the same idea: emissaries from each met between Laon and Athies, both carrying proposals for a night assault on the village. Yorck issued his orders: 'Not a shot shall be fired. The attack is to be made with bayonets.' Zieten would lead cavalry to block retreat. Yorck's troops slipped forward through the dark in four columns to surround the village and edge amongst the houses. All units crept successfully to their positions. 'All at once,' wrote von Schack, one of Yorck's officers, 'all the division's trumpets, horns, and other instruments were sounded; one hurrah after another rent the air, and panic and confusion spread throughout the hostile army.' Hordes of bewildered French soldiers, most of them teenagers, were rounded up into captivity; probably as many as 2,000 were killed or taken prisoner. Blücher clapped Yorck's adjutant on the back and exclaimed: 'You Yorckists are trustful and brave chaps. If I couldn't rely on you, then heaven would fall.'(57)

Within hours this trust and reliance on Yorck would falter and heaven nearly fell. Blücher, with Napoleon almost on the run and with the gates of Paris just over the horizon, suffered mental and physical collapse. His entire position as Field-Marshal and commander of the Silesian army was thrown into jeopardy; even relations with Gneisenau threatened to founder. This sad situation developed rapidly during 10th March, the day after the main fighting at Laon. Napoleon attempted other attacks during the morning of the 10th, but soon withdrew. Blücher had issued orders for the pursuit late the previous night, but by the morning of the 10th his health had deteriorated to such an extent that it seemed his judgement could no longer be trusted.

The old Field-Marshal made a valiant attempt to rally his strength and to hide his real condition. His brave deception was revealed in a letter to his wife, dated this Tuesday, which opened with a huge white lie. 'Nothing out of the way has happened,' he told his anxious wife. His letter was written under stress; the writing appeared even more illegible than usual, and his memory played him false. He mentioned a bullet snick he had received in his leg, but said this had happened five days before; in fact the incident had occurred on 22nd February, sixteen days previously. The letter remained unfinished.(58) Blücher slumped on his bed, his room darkened to ease his painful eyes.

> His extremely inflamed and thickly swollen eyes made it absolutely necessary for him to wear a bandage [wrote Nostitz], since every ray of light caused violent pains. Confined to his room on a strict diet, unable to take his usual exercise, and with his heart full of vexation at seeing himself doomed to inactivity just as the last decisive blow was on the point of being struck: all this taken together had not only undermined his health, but had also most strongly affected his temper, and put him in a condition of mind that was apt to go with his bodily sufferings.

Nostitz, with him almost day and night, described his rapid decline. Blücher was

> . . . constantly thinking of death and fearing it, bearing pain with anything but fortitude, torturing his mind by always imagining he had found new symptoms, thinking of himself alone, indifferent to all that went on around him, even to the greatest and most important events. . . .(59)

His hallucinations returned and his speech slipped into incoherence.

Gneisenau inevitably shouldered a greater burden of command, and Blücher's chief of staff had already decided that a defensive policy should be adopted. On 10th March he reversed Blücher's orders for the pursuit, and instead reorganized the Prussian and

Russian forces for the final cautious manoeuvring before Paris. Almost immediately cohesion began to collapse amongst the Army of Silesia. Fusion of multiple nationalities and highly individual commanders into one whole had always been amongst Blücher's principal abilities and now, without Blücher's powerful personality, splits appeared. Rumours spread that the Field-Marshal was finished, insane, about to quit the service. Yorck, already furious that the pursuit order had been cancelled, had his travelling coach prepared for departure and his baggage packed. He sent a curt message to headquarters declaring he was laying down command through ill-health; he climbed into his coach and left. 'As the coach drove away,' wrote one of his officers, 'we stood as if paralysed.'

Three of his officers rushed to the main headquarters, where they were initially refused admittance. Blücher lay in bed, and Gneisenau and Müffling were also ill. Yorck's officers appealed to Nostitz who hurried them in to Blücher. The Field-Marshal pulled himself up on his couch to write an appeal to his departing corps commander. Nostitz had to guide his hand over the paper and the words were scrawled huge and wavering. 'Old comrade,' declared the faltering note, 'history should not have to relate such things of us. For God's sake be sensible. Come back. Don't leave the army now that we're at our destination.'(60)

A fast rider galloped after Yorck's carriage and Blücher's appeal proved successful. The message indicated that Blücher's mental condition had not collapsed, as Yorck feared, and he replied: 'Your Excellency's personal letter is a reprint of your honest heart which I always did and always will esteem. . . . I have returned to my post. I will continue to fight as long as there is need.'(61)

Yet the situation remained unsettled. Gneisenau insisted that horses and men must be rested: stiff battle lay ahead. Napoleon's army lurked to the rear of Blücher's forces. Schwarzenberg remained stationary in the Troyes region, and had written before Blücher's battle at Laon: 'I have no news and I confess that I tremble. If Blücher suffers a defeat how can I myself give battle? For if I am conquered what a triumph for Napoleon!'(62) Czar Alexander continued to urge an advance. 'I believe we would still be stuck in the Bohemian muck,' he wrote, 'if Field-Marshal Blücher had not pulled us out of it with the crossing of the Elbe. I am quite certain that he will once again carry us with him.'(63)

News of Laon reached Schwarzenberg and, at long last, the main army began to move. But now the Silesian army remained stationary, virtually without a commander. For over a week Blücher lay helpless, and his illness drove all interest in the campaign from his shaken mind. Nostitz wrote: 'Every announcement, every report, no matter from whom or about what, was disgusting and loathsome to him.'(64)

Discussion took place behind Blücher's back on a possible replacement for the ailing Field-Marshal. According to Prussian regulations the next most senior general should assume control if the commander became incapacitated; but this would have been Langeron, serving with the Russians, and he declared that under Russian regulations the chief of staff should take over – Gneisenau. The latter, and Müffling and Nostitz, agreed that none could assume Blücher's place, even if the Field-Marshal were no more than a figurehead to rally the troops. Even Langeron declared: 'For God's sake let's carry this corpse along with us!' Blücher therefore continued to be nominal commander, despite the fact that he lay tossing upon his bed, sweat streaming from his forehead, moaning nonsensical sentences.(65)

Yet Napoleon also suffered rapid decline during mid-March. The two great adversaries simultaneously lost their touch and their will for victory.

It became too much for him [wrote Napoleon's biographer, Vincent Cronin]. Suddenly he was no more than a weary, red-eyed man in a grey overcoat huddling out of the bitter cold, with too few troops to halt a tide of invaders. It was then that Napoleon resolved to die if he could. He desired one thing only, to fall in battle.(66)

On 20th and 21st March he clashed with Schwarzenberg at Arcis-sur-Aube and proved unable to prevent the outnumbering Austrians from pushing steadily forward. Napoleon deliberately exposed himself to death during the two days of fighting. When a delayed action shell landed in front of him, he urged his horse forward to meet the explosion: the shell burst, killing his horse and hurtling Napoleon to the ground. But he rose unhurt. He plunged deeper into the fighting; shrapnel and case-shot ripped his uniform, yet he survived to lead his army back in retreat. 'I did all I could to meet with a glorious end,' wrote the Emperor. 'I continually exposed myself, bullets rained all round me, my clothes were full of them, yet not one touched me. I am condemned to live.'(67)

News of Arcis-sur-Aube snapped Blücher from his depression. Schwarzenberg's army now lay within a day's march. All Blücher had longed for seemed within his grasp. He clambered from his couch on 23rd March, his eyes still inflamed, and called for his maps. At the same time he received a captured letter, written by Napoleon to his Marie Louise and displaying exaggerated claims – and details of the Emperor's next moves.

> *Mon Amie*. All these last days I have been in the saddle. On the 20th I took Arcis-sur-Aube. . . . I have decided to march on the Marne and their communications so as to push them away from Paris. . . . This evening I shall be at St. Dizier. *Adieu, mon amie!*

The letter had been written earlier in the day. Blücher hurriedly summoned a war council – and also ordered the letter to be sent on to Marie Louise with respectful greetings, and, according to some reports, accompanied by a bunch of spring flowers.

Napoleon reckoned on the allies falling into a panic by his threat to their communications. Yet he completely misunderstood the character of his principal adversary, Blücher: a move towards his rear would merely induce 'Field-Marshal Forwards' to strike for the open gates of Paris. So it proved. By the evening of the 23rd the Silesian army had begun to move. Too ill to mount a horse, Blücher lay in an open carriage, wearing a woman's green poke-bonnet on his head to shade his eyes. First he manoeuvred south towards Châlons, to shift closer to Schwarzenberg and to threaten Napoleon's own communications to St Dizier. Meanwhile he also prepared for the dash on Paris. He would thrust alone, if necessary; then, on the 24th, the happiest message of the whole campaign reached his camp from Schwarzenberg: 'The enemy has marched by way of Vitry and St Dizier to cut our communications, *therefore* it has been decided to march on Paris with the full force of all our armies by the shortest route.' The Austrian commander told his Prussian colleague that he would reach Ferre Champenoise on the 25th, Treffaux on the 26th, Coulommiers on the 27th, and the following day Meaux or Lagny, barely forty-five kilometres from Paris, and where Schwarzenberg suggested the allied forces should at last combine.(68)

The great march on Paris began before dawn on 25th March. Columns of Prussian, Russian and Austrian troops advanced steadily down the roads towards the French capital, squadrons of cavalry streaming across the fields, waggons and carts raising a cloud of dust into the fresh spring air. The programme proceeded according to plan. Schwarzenberg's forces swept aside the outnumbered corps of Marmont and Mortier at Ferre Champenoise on the 25th. The march continued with the two armies moving in parallel lines about fifteen kilometres apart. Napoleon flung his forces backwards and forwards across the allied rear, severing supply lines, but Schwarzenberg and Blücher forged ahead. All depended upon the people of Paris: if the capital offered strong resistance, then the allies would be trapped.

'Give me four days,' prayed Napoleon, 'and I have them. God delivers them into my hands.'

But on 28th March the allied armies merged into one; next day they approached so near the capital that their rumbling cannon could be heard by the citizens. Parisians lacked the will to resist. At 11 a.m. on the 29th a convoy of glittering vehicles sped from the city, carrying Marie Louise in her coronation coach on the road for Rambouillet. Napoleon received a message from the Minister of Posts, Lavalette: 'The presence of the Emperor is necessary if he wishes to prevent his capital being handed over to the enemy. There is not a moment to lose.'(69) As the allied monarchs slept in the chateau of Bony on the night of the 29th, with the lights of Paris twinkling in the distance, Napoleon abandoned his army and galloped through the darkness, flogging his horse to reach his capital in time.

The battle for Paris began on 30th March. Marmont and Mortier had hurried back to scratch together all available resistance, amounting to about 30,000 men; against them marched about 110,000 allies. Unlike Paris civilians, these last-ditch military defenders proved determined to fight. Battle continued throughout the day, with casualties steadily mounting on either side. Especially bitter was the struggle at Montmartre. Blücher flung off his female's bonnet, climbed from his coach and into a saddle, and directed the attack on the hill of Montmartre with his customary daring. By late afternoon these heights had fallen; Blücher ordered cannon to be dragged to the summit ready to bombard Paris should negotiations fail.

But by two o'clock in the morning of 31st March the last allied conditions had been made and accepted by the French. Marmont and Mortier would retire from the city. French troops began to evacuate Paris as a prelude to capitulation. Napoleon received the news during the night when he reached the last staging post at La Cour de France. Within three hours came fresh news: the capitulation had been signed, and the keys of Paris were in the hands of Czar Alexander. Napoleon drove slowly and sadly to Fontainebleau, his head sunk in his shoulders and his limbs aching and leadened. Seventeen kilometres away Blücher shut himself in a darkened room in Montmartre, his eyes streaming again and his head reeling. Victory had been gained; the war was virtually over, but all Blücher's acute depression and wretchedness had returned.

CHAPTER 10

Interlude

BLÜCHER AND NAPOLEON, victor and vanquished, suffered similar mental and physical collapse. The French Emperor awaited his fate at Fontainebleau, a solitary figure sitting for hours in his first floor study, with its walls of green striped silk, its mahogany bookshelves and gloomy huge desks. The Prussian Field-Marshal crouched in the corner of his bare room in Montmartre, half-blind, brooding over his condition and fearful of death. Outside his windows the troops celebrated in the streets, and the allied monarchs made their triumphant entry into Paris.

Frederick William and Czar Alexander rode into the city during the morning of 31st March. The Czar sat on the white stallion which Napoleon had given him in the days of their alliance. The monarchs received a rapturous welcome from the fickle Parisians.

It was difficult to make room for the victors [wrote a contemporary]. All the windows of the splendid apartments were filled with shouting spectators, the ladies in their most elegant costumes. White handkerchiefs fluttered from the casements; a rain of lilies fell from every storey. . . . One would have thought a victorious French army had annihilated a dangerous enemy.

Behind the monarchs marched the troops, heavily stained by war and criticized for their appearance by Frederick William. 'There was not one whole garment on our bodies,' wrote Blücher's son Franz. 'No stockings, no shoes, our feet wrapped in rags.' Alexander's guards, by contrast, strutted in splendid uniforms; Frederick William looked in vain for his own élite troops. 'Have you seen my Guards?' he asked Yorck. The latter pointed to the tattered regiments which had fought with Blücher and replied: 'Your Majesty, those are your Guards.'(1)

Blücher refused to move from his room. 'Everyone rode up to him and urged him to march in with the troops,' stated Nostitz. Blücher merely answered: 'What have I to do with the Parisians? What is Paris to me?'(2) On 1st April, as the allies opened talks with Talleyrand for the political overthrow of Napoleon, Blücher consented to ride from Montmartre and take up quarters in Paris, but next morning his condition deteriorated still further. 'That day a deadly illness fell upon me,' he wrote later to Bonin, 'and they feared for my eyesight on the 3rd, and for my life. For six days I lay blinded.' Bietzke, his doctor, described how Blücher imagined himself to be suffering all kinds of dreadful ailments: dropsy, failing heart, tumours, cancers. He begged Nostitz and Bietzke to stay by his bedside, so that he should have company in his final moments. The old warhorse was blown, his incredible energy sapped by the struggle with enemy and allies alike.

While Blücher lay prostrate and sightless, Napoleon's reign reached its temporary close. On 11th April the Emperor abdicated unconditionally. Forty-eight hours later he lay writhing on his bed, his body icy then burning hot, rigid then torn by convulsions, his teeth clamped tight shut to stop himself spewing out the poison he had taken.(3) The suicide attempt failed; Napoleon recovered, ready for his exile on Elba.

Blücher's health began to return on about the same day. The yellow seeped from his cheeks and the red from his eyes, his hands ceased to tremble, and his voice became boisterous – and belligerent – again. As before, his recovery proved as rapid as his descent into illness had been, but he still wanted an end to military service.

> The King and the Czar came to see me [he wrote to Bonin]. I laid the command of the army at the King's feet and asked to retire. He would not hear of it, but finally said: 'Well, in God's name rest and take care of yourself. You may choose your own place of residence.'(4)

Blücher chose Berlin and made ready to depart. He sought escape from the lengthy peace negotiations, and feared these discussions might rob the allies of adequate victory. One evening he presented a toast at dinner which warned: 'May the fruits won by the swords of the army not be thrown away by the pens of the Ministers.' Blücher made a last request to the King that his troops should be properly rewarded. 'I regard the army as my family, and it would be painful for me to leave it forever without seeing it in possession of the inheritance which it is my sacred duty to secure for it.' Frederick William promised to oblige and Blücher began to say his emotional farewells.(5)

His plans suddenly changed. 'Dearly beloved wife,' wrote Blücher on 22nd April. 'I was just about to leave here when I unexpectedly received an invitation from the Prince Regent of England to go to London to see him.' Frederick William virtually ordered him to accept, but Blücher believed the visit would not unduly delay his reunion with his wife in Berlin. 'I shall leave for London in eight days. I can be there in three days, I will not stay long.' He finished this letter: 'I can't write much because of my eyes, so I'll just mention that I'm looking forward so much to seeing you, and pressing you to my heart.'(6)

The eight days before departing for London stretched into almost eight weeks. The King and Czar also decided to visit England, and insisted Blücher must accompany them. A longer period had to be spent in preparation, and in the final diplomatic discussions of the monarchs in Paris. During these weeks of April and May, while the blossom littered the Paris boulevards, Blücher realized the fame which now surrounded his name. He grumbled at the mobs which greeted him and the admirers who constantly pestered him, but lapped it up nonetheless.

> The City of London has awarded me a sword of honour which is to be presented to me there [he told Katharina on 28th April]. The sword I received from the Czar Alexander is estimated by the jeweller here to be worth 20,000 thalers; another sabre like it is coming from St. Petersburg. What the devil shall I do with all these bejewelled weapons?(7)

On 6th May he told his wife: 'Over a hundred Englishmen have come here just to see me. . . .'

Steffens described a meeting with Blücher at Véry's one morning.

> As I made my way out two Englishmen approached me respectfully . . . and asked timidly if that was really the great hero? – a great

number of English had come to Paris on purpose to look at him. When I answered in the affirmative they turned towards the table where he sat, and were lost in contemplation; an Ah! of admiration was all that I heard from them; they folded their hands, and I never saw such a picture of silent veneration . . .(8)

By now Blücher's health and zest had fully returned. Schwarzenberg's jibe during the campaign proved correct: he frequented the Palais Royale at every available opportunity. His gambling stakes reached new heights, and he was reported to have collected winnings totalling 19,000 thaler. He ate and drank as heartily as he gambled: Steffens commented on his appetite for champagne and oysters for breakfast.

Celebrations in Paris reached fever-pitch at the beginning of May. On the 3rd the new Bourbon monarch returned to the city: Louis XVIII, brother of Louis XVI, rode in triumph down the boulevards, by courtesy of the allies. Next day Napoleon reached Elba. Also on the 4th, Wellington rode into Paris, fresh from his Peninsular victories; he had been gazetted Duke just twenty-four hours before. 'Yesterday the famous Lord Wellington came here,' wrote Blücher to his wife on the 5th, 'and I have been invited to spend three days with him, but I must watch my drinking.'(9) Blücher and Wellington, the first old enough to be the other's father, immediately struck up a warm and understanding friendship. Crowds surrounded them at their historic introduction, and they stood quietly, while someone translated the usual courtesies, Wellington listening attentively and Blücher stroking his long grey moustache. Language difficulties would always prevent intimacy, but the two leaders had characteristics in common: frankness, eagerness, the ability to drive their men almost beyond endurance. Each would prove the other a worthy partner on the field of Waterloo.

'Damned fine fellow,' commented Wellington of his Prussian ally. But Blücher remained anxious to retire in peace to Berlin. The days dragged on and still he could not leave Paris for London. 'I am now completely well,' Blücher wrote home on the 16th, 'but unfortunately I must still wait here. . . . I dislike this intensely.'(10)

Diplomatic discussions finished towards the end of May, leading to the First Treaty of Paris on the 30th. The settlement did nothing to please Blücher. Intent upon making France a force for international stability, the allies negotiated a moderate treaty that imposed no indemnity, gave France roughly the boundaries of 1792, and restored some former colonies. France would remain a great power. The seeds of dangerous international rivalry were again being sown, and talks about the new European balance of power would continue in the capitals throughout the summer, prior to the general congress in Vienna in late September.

But with Paris negotiations successfully concluded, the Kings could depart and Blücher's journey to England began. He received one more honour as he left French soil. 'The gratitude which the State owes you still continues,' declared Frederick William in a document dated 3rd June, 'and as proof of it, I hereby raise you to the dignity of Prince Blücher of Wahlstatt, and your heirs to peers of the realm, as Counts Blücher of Wahlstatt.'(11) The honour failed to find Blücher's favour. Initially the King intended him to drop his own name in the princely title, but Blücher raised strenuous objections. 'I was expected to change my name to Wahlstatt,' he wrote to a cousin, 'but this I positively refused to do; so now I am to be called "Prince Blücher of Wahlstatt". Everything will depend on the sort of principality I am to receive in Silesia. Under no circumstances will I consent to add one more to the horde of sickly, hungry princes.' By July he had found that Wahlstatt referred to the cloister and village of the same name near Liegnitz, on the River Katzbach, and under pressure he agreed to remove his final opposition. 'I was obliged to consent,' he wrote, 'because they insisted that I must do so for the sake of the nation. Yet it is as "Blücher" that the crowds cry out to me.'(12)

On 3rd June Blücher addressed a letter to his wife from Boulogne. 'I am stone deaf from all the cannon-fire and nearly deranged from all the formal bowing. If this continues I shall go mad in England.'(13) Forty-eight hours later Blücher stepped ashore at Dover. For the next few weeks his favourite adjective would be 'indescribable' and no word could have better summoned up his welcome. Thousands crammed the quayside and the narrow Dover streets to see the distinguished party from France: the Czar, described by one irreverent teenager as '*horridly* Pink & Pudding-like' with his poodle scampering at his heels; the King of Prussia, wall-eyed and with the semblance of a smile twitching his otherwise sullen face; scores of glittering generals and handsome aides with their tight breeches, fur and froggings; but most of all the crowds loved Field-Marshal Prince Blücher. He beamed and bowed and raised his hat high in greeting; he climbed into an open carriage, and the crowd immediately unharnessed the horses and dragged the vehicle themselves. Women clamoured for locks of his silvery-grey hair.

'Ladies, ladies,' he protested, 'were I to give each of you just one hair I should have none left.'

'I can't believe I'm still alive,' he wrote to his wife. 'The people nearly tore me apart.'(14) Next day he reached St James's Palace in London; the capital was illuminated for three nights, and a vast mob surged round Blücher whenever he appeared in public. When he entered the opera-house on the 9th all singing was abandoned and the whole house rose to thunder their 'hurrahs!'

For over a month Blücher plunged into a mad whirl of parties, dinners and social functions. The Lord Mayor of London gave him a State banquet in the Guildhall; the navy and army were reviewed; there was a thanksgiving service at St. Paul's and a private dinner at Windsor with the Prince Regent, who gave him a fine stallion and exclaimed: 'Believe me you have no truer friend on earth than I.'(15)

The public contributed £100,000 for the sufferers in the villages around Leipzig, to which Parliament added another £100,000. In his speech of thanks Blücher declared: 'Had I not had a wife and children, whose inclinations and convenience it is my wish and duty to consult, I swear to you I would never leave this blessed country . . .'(16) Cambridge University conferred the Degree of Doctor of Civil Law upon him and entertained him at a magnificent dinner in Trinity College. In turn Oxford awarded him the degree of Doctor of Law. He went further afield, to Edinburgh, and everywhere the people warmed to his buoyant personality. His rough, earthy talk, bringing with it the tang of military life, provided a fascinating contrast to the usual artificial and often inane conversation at court and at society dinners.

At one function he sat next to a powdered, bewigged lady who tried to engage him in conversation while he spooned his soup. Finally he wiped his whiskers and said, through an interpreter: 'Madam, what beautiful white hands you have', to which she simpered that she wore calf-skin gloves to protect them. 'Lady,' he reportedly replied, 'I wear calf-skin breeches but they don't do a thing for my arse.'

It became the fashion to relate the most incredible stories about

Blücher's social triumphs and exploits: that he was besieged by ladies who refused to leave him alone until he bestowed his whiskery kisses; that his servant sold the feathers from his helmet, and countless feathers not from his helmet, at an exorbitant cost; that one morning the crowd of ladies outside his door at St James's Palace became so great that the door burst open, revealing his aide, Major Colomb, in his night attire. The Major scuttled behind his four-poster to complete his dressing. The most sparkling social event took place at Burlington House on 1st July in honour of Wellington. Two thousand people were present, including Blücher, and the ladies now had two heroes to admire. Wellington danced a polonaise; Blücher joined in, not to be outdone, and later brought cheers and claps from the crowd by 'skipping down the room with Lady Burghersh in a German country dance'.(17)

The hectic pace threatened to become too much for him. 'The French could not succeed in killing me,' he wrote on 30th June, 'but the Regent and the English are in a fair way to doing it.'(18) Earlier, on the 12th, he had written to his wife: 'I am inhumanly exhausted. I am being painted by three painters simultaneously.'(19) He feared his health might break down – barely two months had passed since he lay seriously mentally and physically ill.

'It will be a miracle if I don't go crazy,' he exclaimed in London. 'I have to watch myself that I don't make a fool of myself.'(20)

By early July he became increasingly anxious to depart. The monarchs had already gone, and on the 11th he left the cheering crowd at Harwich as his ship sailed for Holland.

> I have come out of England alive [he wrote to Gneisenau], but worn and weary. Words fail to express how they treated me; no one could have had shown to him greater kindness or goodwill. . . . As far as concerns drinking in England I had great fears; but they did not force me. I had declared from the beginning that I drank no other wine than Bordeaux and I kept to it.(21)

Fresh crowds awaited him in Germany. 'In every village,' wrote his doctor, Bietzke, 'the Prince was most heartily greeted and was adorned with flowers by the most beautiful girls.' He entered Berlin in triumph on 7th August for the reunion with his wife and family, and for a renewed round of banqueting. On one occasion he stood to make a special toast, tears in his eyes. The crowd hushed as he declared: 'Art thou present, spirit of my friend, my Scharnhorst? Then be my witness that without thee I could have accomplished nothing.'

Blücher slipped away to his Silesian estate at Krieblowitz, seventeen kilometres from Breslau. He rested in his seventeenth-century castle, took out his long pipes and occupied himself with leisurely farming and with planning a garden. Although he officially remained a serving soldier, his military days seemed over.

*   *   *

Worries soon began to cloud Blücher's attempted retirement. The health of his son Franz deteriorated during the summer. At first Blücher believed him to be merely a hypochondriac and asked Gneisenau to help. Gneisenau obliged with a cheerful letter telling Franz not to worry so much about his health. 'Leave that to us old folk, or even better take as your model the constant cheerfulness of your father.... I often model myself on him if I am tempted to succumb to depression.'(22) But Franz's illness was diagnosed as mental, caused by the head wound received earlier in the war, and by the end of the year he had to be admitted to an institution.

Other, non-domestic, anxieties crowded in. By the time autumn began to crisp the linden leaves on his estate, Blücher had hurried to his house near Berlin's Brandenburg Gate. Diplomats and dignitaries had converged on Vienna for the Congress called to settle the future of Europe, and it soon became clear to Blücher that their deliberations might make a mockery of all he had fought for against Napoleon.

'They neglected their opportunities in Paris,' he declared to Bülow. 'France's tone is growing too assured. They should more effectually have clipped her wings.' He started to mutter: 'We're only having a day of rest.'(23)

Preliminary discussions at the Congress of Vienna opened on 22nd September. Wellington later arrived in the Austrian capital as Britain's First Plenipotentiary. But Blücher was not invited, to his intense dissatisfaction. His anger rapidly increased when news of the proceedings reached Berlin. Bickering immediately broke out between the five big powers: Russia, Prussia, Austria, Britain and France, with the latter represented by Napoleon's former Grand Chamberlain and Foreign Minister, Charles Maurice de Talleyrand. Prussia, represented by Hardenberg, wished to end the weakness caused by the wide spread of her separate possessions; both Austria and Prussia wanted to play the leading role in German affairs. Britain's Lord Castlereagh and Wellington sought to restrict Russian authority, while Czar Alexander put forward his semi-mystical attempt to base the peace on a Europe united by Christian principles.

This 'Sacred League' contained one practical demand. The Czar proposed to swallow Poland, compensating Prussia with independent Saxony while Austria would help herself to Italy. Britain, Austria and France feared the powerful position which might be occupied by Russia, allied to Prussia, and on 3rd February 1815, these three concluded a secret treaty, promising to fight together if any of them were attacked by Russia or Prussia. On 17th February Berlin newspapers reported the official preliminary results of the Congress, and Blücher was thrown into an almost uncontrollable rage. France emerged still a great power; Blücher believed his campaign to have been in vain, and the deaths of thousands of his 'children' to have been wasted. Prussia renounced her old provinces of East Friesia and Ansbach-Baireuth, and in return only received a strip on the left bank of the Rhine, plus part of Saxony, the inhabitants of which had fought alongside Napoleon and detested the Prussians.

'It honours and rejoices me to have shared in the war that is ended,' wrote Blücher to Gneisenau, 'but my chief satisfaction is in not having shared in the peace that has been concluded.' He condemned the Vienna Congress as a cattle-market. 'We drove in a fine bull and have got in return a dried-up old cow.'(24) His relationship with Hardenberg, chief Prussian negotiator at Vienna and formerly his friend, faltered through his bellicose complaints of the minister's work. Even more serious, his friendship with Gneisenau suffered a reverse. Blücher proclaimed that he alone had brought a victorious conclusion to the 1814 campaign – 'if I had not prevailed with the Czar we would never have seen Paris' – and his chief of staff objected to Blücher giving himself sole credit. 'The ingratitude of my commander-in-chief which was revealed in Berlin filled my heart with bitterness,' wrote Gneisenau to Hardenberg.(25)

The Field-Marshal informed his chief of staff on 17th February, the same day he received news of the Vienna conclusions, that he intended to quit the army completely. Gneisenau wrote back within hours of receiving Blücher's letter: 'Permit me to make the following observations about your proposed step.' Firstly, he declared, Field-Marshals were not allowed to resign; secondly, even if it were possible, it would be unwise, since details of the peace terms had still to arrive; thirdly, Blücher's resignation would reflect badly on the Chancellor, Hardenberg. 'The Chancellor is a good friend and has plenty of enemies just waiting for a chance like this.'(26) Blücher refused to change his mind or to quieten his opposition to the Vienna terms. Relations with Gneisenau and Hardenberg had still to be repaired, and the King had still to reply to Blücher's resignation appeal, when shattering news reached Berlin.

Gneisenau woke Blücher in the middle of the night, 8th March 1815. Napoleon had slipped from Elba on 26th February, and had landed in France on 1st March.

Blücher exclaimed: 'It is the greatest piece of good luck that could have happened to Prussia! Now the war will begin again! The armies will fight and make good all the faults committed in Vienna!' He called for his uniform; some tried to stop him and General Kalkreuth reminded him of his age.

'What silly nonsense are you gabbling?' snapped Blücher, despite the fact that he had celebrated his seventy-second birthday the previous December. 'I have not been able to grant your request to be discharged,' wrote Frederick William on the 15th, and two days later a letter arrived at Blücher's home bestowing upon him the command of the Prussian army.

'Napoleon Bonaparte has placed himself beyond the protection of the law,' declared the Vienna Congress powers on 13th March, 'and rendered himself subject to public vengeance.' On the same day this outlaw received his most valuable public support so far in his journey from Provence to Paris – Marshal Ney joined Napoleon in Auxerre, thereby casting aside his promise to King Louis to drag Bonaparte to him in an iron cage. King Louis fled from his capital on the night of the 19th, heading for Brussels and suffering further indignity *en route*. Someone stole a suitcase from his baggage waggons.

'What I regret most,' he moaned, 'are my bedroom slippers. They'd taken the shape of my feet.'

Next evening Napoleon's coach rattled over the Paris cobbles; he walked slowly up the wide steps of the Tuileries, savouring the moment. 'His eyes were shut,' wrote an observer, 'his hands stretched forward like a blind man's, his happiness showing only in a smile.'(27)

The Hundred Days had begun; the allies prepared for war. On 25th March Wellington was appointed commander-in-chief of the British and Dutch-Belgian forces in Flanders. The Duke left Vienna for Brussels, where he arrived on 4th April. Blücher left Berlin at the beginning of April and reached the Rhine on the 7th. By the 16th he had arrived at Coblenz, where he wrote to his wife: 'Tomorrow I go to Lüttich, where I shall find my headquarters. Hostilities have not yet begun. They cannot be long delayed. . . . Everything here is in the most beautiful blossom, and the weather is incomparable.'(28)

But clouds floated on Blücher's horizon. Gneisenau remained in an ill-humour; some generals criticized Blücher's appointment; Blücher himself arrived at the Prussian camp on the 17th in a foul temper. Gneisenau had hoped for independent command, and instead returned to his old appointment as Blücher's chief of staff, overshadowed by the Field-Marshal's fame and personality. Hardenberg, who also remained angry with Blücher, sympathized strongly; he wrote to Gneisenau on 1st April:

All the good you do will be boasted about by someone else. . . . The King will not deviate from the seniority list, or it would be you who would be in command of the army. Now in actual fact you are in command, but old Blücher lends his name to it. Not many people will be misled by this.(29)

Others besides Hardenberg thought Blücher the wrong choice as commander. Even Müffling, who had fought with him so many loyal years, considered him too old and senile. 'The old Prince, who was past seventy, understood nothing at all about leading an army – so little, indeed, that when a plan was laid before him for his approval, even if it had only to do with some minor operation, it conveyed no clear meaning to him.'(30) Kalkreuth had dared to warn the Field-Marshal before he left Berlin that he must be prepared to forfeit all the fame he had won in the last campaign. This remark still rankled when Blücher reached his headquarters near Liège on 19th April, and he immediately growled at his staff that the army must not lose a single battle.(31)

Other problems loomed. Blücher's army was short of money,

and as late as 25th May, three weeks before Ligny and Waterloo, Gneisenau wrote to Hardenberg: 'We are in such financial straits here that the Field-Marshal almost had to pawn his whiskers.'(32) Even more serious was a disturbing question of loyalty within the army. For the first time Blücher felt unable to trust some of his regiments. These units were Saxon, amounting to about 14,000 men, who came from the portion of their country now allotted to Prussia. Orders arrived from Berlin that Saxon regiments should be segregated from the rest of the army, so that a closer watch could be kept upon them. Riots broke out immediately and Saxon mutineers surrounded Blücher's house. For a moment it seemed he might be murdered, but Blücher escaped through a back door after having been persuaded not to attempt a fighting defence. He told his wife: 'The mistake was that the people have not been treated with kindness, but with severity.'(33)

The remark was typical: Blücher always believed men should be persuaded to display loyalty through respect and affection, rather than through strict discipline. Yet Blücher always reacted firmly against those who took advantage of his apparent leniency; thus his actions after the Saxon mutiny also proved characteristic. 'I am sorry that I have to shoot four persons as rebels tomorrow,' he told Katharina. 'But the Saxons must learn to respect my name.' The executions duly took place, and one battalion was condemned to the disgrace of having its standard publicly burnt, even though this standard had been embroidered by the Saxon Queen herself. General von Borstell, a Prussian corps commander, objected to this last punishment. Blücher immediately suspended him from command, despite their long acquaintance. Borstell was court-martialled and imprisoned. Blücher warned Frederick Augustus, King of Saxony: 'I shall restore order by force even though I be compelled to shoot down the entire Saxon army.'(34) Eventually only part of the Saxon cavalry was found sufficiently reliable to serve in the coming campaign.

Yet despite these problems, despite his aching old limbs and rheumy eyes, Blücher responded once more to the army atmosphere. Gneisenau's loyalty returned; he began to call Blücher 'my Prince' again in his letters. The chief of staff realized that Blücher remained incomparable and irreplaceable. Müffling, in the midst of his exaggerated criticisms, unwittingly provided the reasons. Blücher, he wrote, was '*merely* the bravest in battle, the most tireless in enduring fatigue, the one who set the example and who through his fiery addresses understood how to rouse enthusiasm'. Müffling also admitted: 'You can reckon on it that if the Prince has given his word to engage in a common operation that word will be kept, even if the whole Prussian army be annihilated in the process.'(35)

This unshakeable dependability would be the key-note of the imminent campaign. Only through Blücher's ability to keep a promise, come what may, would Napoleon be defeated and the British army be saved. On 3rd May, just twenty-four hours after putting down the rebellion in his own army, Blücher rode from his camp to meet his allied partner, the Duke of Wellington.

Ligny

BLÜCHER MET WELLINGTON on 3rd May at Tirlemont, half-way between Brussels and Liège. Their armies now held a front of nearly a hundred miles. The Duke, with his headquarters in Brussels, drew his supplies from Ostend and Antwerp, while the Prussians, with Blücher's headquarters in the process of shifting from Liège to Namur, stretched their line of communications in the opposite direction to Coblenz on the Rhine. In the event of disaster to either army, or both, their natural lines of retreat would therefore carry them further apart. The difficulty would be to protect the joint or hinge between the two armies at Charleroi. Further south lay Schwarzenberg's Austrians, while in central Germany a Russian army under Barclay de Tolly moved slowly westwards.

Altogether the allies totalled 592,000 men: 95,000 in Wellington's Anglo-Dutch army, 120,000 Prussians, 210,000 Austrians and 167,000 Russians. The broad plan was simply to advance into France and overwhelm Napoleon through sheer force of numbers: the French frontier was to be crossed by all armies between 27th June and 1st July. Details of this plan were settled at Tirlemont, and Blücher and Wellington decided to concentrate their armies on the line Quatre Bras–Sombreffe. In the event of a threat to the vulnerable central hinge around Charleroi, Wellington agreed to close up eastwards to his left; Blücher, in turn, agreed to warn his ally of the first signs of such an attack.

Napoleon, studying his maps and his intelligence reports in Paris, summed up the situation correctly. His forces would be outnumbered. Despite another display of incredible energy since returning to France, the actual number of men he would take to battle totalled about 124,000 – around 90,000 less than the British and Prussians combined. Napoleon's only chance would be to strike before Blücher and Wellington could each draw their forces up in forward concentration. He aimed to drive a wedge between the two allied armies at Charleroi and destroy both in turn. All depended upon the allied speed of concentration. Napoleon guessed that Blücher would be ready before Wellington; as General Gaspard Gourgaud, one of Napoleon's brightest young officers, declared: 'The hussar habits of Marshal Blücher, his activity and decided character, formed a strong contrast with the cautious disposition, the deliberate and methodical manner of the Duke of Wellington.'

Napoleon therefore decided to fix his attentions upon the Prussians before the British. Another reason for choosing the Prussians first again stemmed from the characters of the respective allied commanders. 'I felt sure when I attacked the Prussians,' Napoleon later told Gourgaud on St Helena, 'that the English would not come to their assistance, while Blücher, who is hot-headed, would have hastened to support Wellington, though he had only two battalions.'(1) The Prussians would be annihilated, then outnumbered Wellington would be dealt with.

By the end of May the four Prussian corps were in position, before the completion of Anglo-Dutch concentration. The 1st Corps, 32,692 men under General Count von Zieten, had its headquarters at Charleroi itself. On its left, to the east, lay the 2nd Corps, 32,704 men commanded by General George Ludwig von Pirch, who had replaced the disgraced Borstell. His head-quarters were at Namur. To the south-east stretched the 3rd Corps, 25,000 men under General Johann von Thielmann, based at Ciney. Finally the 4th Corps, Bülow's 30,000 men, lay at Liège. Blücher had organized his dispositions so that all four corps could be collected at their respective assembly points – Fleurus, Namur, Ciney and Liège – within twelve hours, ready to face a French attack once the direction of this thrust was known. If the French crossed the Sambre at Charleroi, the most dangerous point, Blücher intended to shift his army into final concentration before Sombreffe, on the Namur-Nivelles road. There he would be within twelve kilometres of Quartre Bras, Wellington's final point of concentration in such circumstances.

Wellington experienced a number of difficulties. His forces were placed on Dutch soil, and not until 3rd May did King William I of the Netherlands agree to Wellington becoming commander-in-chief of the Dutch regiments in his army. Moreover, as long as 'peace' officially continued, Wellington was not allowed to send cavalry patrols to investigate French-held territory. Further, Wellington proved dissatisfied with his regiments. 'I have got an infamous army,' he wrote on 8th May, 'very weak and ill-equipped, and a very inexperienced staff.'(2)

While he struggled to prepare this army he found himself hampered by conflicting reports of Napoleon's whereabouts. On 11th May Wellington heard that Napoleon was believed to have reached Lille three days before; on 6th June reports declared that Napoleon had just left Paris for Laon. Added to faulty intelligence was the danger stemming from a poor relationship between some sections of the Prussian command and Wellington; chief among these critics of the British commander was Gneisenau. Müffling had been appointed liaison officer at the British headquarters. He wrote: 'General von Gneisenau warned me to be much on my guard with the Duke of Wellington, for that by his relations with India, this distinguished general had become so accustomed to duplicity, that he had at last become such a master in the art as even to outwit the Nabobs themselves.'(3)

But Blücher's friendship with Wellington continued and apparently, unlike the British commander, he admired the British army. On the 28th and 29th May the Field-Marshal visited Brussels, where Wellington arranged a march-past. 'Wellington has shown me 6,000 men of his most beautiful cavalry,' wrote Blücher to his wife; he told Hardenberg that this cavalry seemed almost too beautiful to be used. Wellington also entertained him to dinner, proposing a toast to the allies – and to Blücher's support. The Field-Marshal tried to reply in French but soon broke into German, which few could understand; his emotion and enthusiasm transmitted the message and his speech ended with a tremendous drumming of glasses on the tables. Wellington's confidence also increased. One day shortly before hostilities began, Mr Thomas Creevey met the Duke in the park at Brussels.

Creevey said: 'Will you let me ask you, Duke, what you think you will make of it?'

Wellington casually replied: 'By God! I think Blücher and

myself can do the thing.' And he repeated: 'I think Blücher and I can do the business.'

Yet as May swept on, it became increasingly possible that Napoleon would attack before the allies started their own offensive. Blücher's impatience rose. As early as 17th May he wrote to his wife: 'Nothing has happened yet, but we are close to the enemy and fighting may begin any day.' On 3rd June Blücher told Katharina that he expected action in ten days at the most. He also asked her to instruct their landlord to keep the Berlin house open for them, because he would be back by winter.(4)

Next day he displayed his impatience in a report to Frederick William: 'The enemy grows in strength relatively far more rapidly than we. . . . I must humbly ask Your Majesty to hasten the beginning of hostilities as much as possible.'(5) An even stronger appeal left Namur for Hardenberg. 'I beg you, my dear Sir, will you see to it that we soon come to operations? Our lingering can have the greatest disadvantages.' He urged an advance over the frontier. 'If orders to advance do not arrive and the unrest in France increases, I shall do as I did in Silesia and go to battle. Wellington will probably accompany me.'(6)

Wellington had finished his preparations. But he insisted an offensive should await permission from Blücher's old dilatory ally, Schwarzenberg. 'The Marshal Blücher is ready and very impatient to start,' wrote Wellington to the Austrian commander at the end of May, 'but I have made it known to him today that we shall have to wait for the day when you order us to begin.'(7) Then, in early June, the allied commanders changed their minds over Napoleon's likely intentions. Disturbances had increased in France; it now seemed likely that Bonaparte would delay his advance. This assessment further increased Blücher's desire to strike into France. 'Napoleon does not attack us,' he wrote to his wife. 'For that we could wait another year. His affairs do not stand brilliantly.'(8) Gneisenau wrote on 9th June: 'The enemy will not attack us but will retire as far as the Aisne, Somme and Marne in order to concentrate his forces.' He added on the 12th: 'The danger of an attack has almost vanished.'(9) Wellington apparently agreed: on the 13th he believed that Napoleon's departure from Paris was 'not likely to be immediate. I think we are now too strong for him here.'

In fact Napoleon had left the capital the day before. By evening on the 13th he had joined his army at Avesnes, fifty-two kilometres down the main road to Charleroi and Brussels. By nightfall on the 14th he had moved his headquarters twenty-six kilometres forward to Beaumont, his army tightly concentrated around him. The Prussians had begun to react. Forward p. trols observed French camp fires at Beaumont on the night of the 13th, and Zieten, corps commander at Charleroi, despatched warnings to Blücher and Wellington. Almost immediately the character difference between the two allied commanders became noticeable. Blücher's natural inclination was to advance – perhaps for this reason the vital bridges over the Sambre at Charleroi had not been blown. Wellington, on the other hand, feared Napoleon might be attempting a sweep round the Anglo-Dutch flank to cut communications to the sea, and Wellington preferred to wait until Napoleon's intentions became plain.

'We are still standing here idle,' wrote Gneisenau on the 14th, 'while the enemy is increasing his strength.' He added, 'The blame for this lies in our cautious policy.'(10) Yet Blücher and Gneisenau now threw caution to the winds. At noon on the 14th Blücher began drawing in his more distant regiments. At 11 p.m. on the same day, Gneisenau issued vital orders for the final concentration of the army in the Sombreffe-Fleurus area. Unlike Wellington, he believed the direction of the French thrust had become obvious, and that the enemy should now be blocked, far further forward than the British considered safe. Gneisenau issued these orders on his own initiative – Blücher had gone to bed and was undisturbed – but the plan had been pre-arranged. Thielmann's 3rd Corps began marching forward from Ciney to Namur, Pirch's 2nd Corps from Namur to Sombreffe, while Zieten's 1st Corps was to prepare for the French advance on the Sambre, and then gradually fall back to Fleurus. Less than four hours after Gneisenau had issued these instructions, Napoleon's main army started to flood across the Belgian frontier near Charleroi.

Prussian regiments force-marched during the 15th. But Bülow failed to move his 4th Corps to Hannut as instructed and would arrive too late for battle. This mistake stemmed from an unhappy relationship existing between Bülow and Gneisenau. The two men had quarrelled in the past and disliked each other; Gneisenau had therefore worded his instructions in polite terms to avoid further friction, so blunting the urgency of the summons. 'I have the honour humbly to request Your Excellency to be kind enough to concentrate the 4th army corps under your command tomorrow, the 15th. . . . Your Excellency had doubtless better make Hannut your headquarters.' Bülow's corps was tired after a recent night march and the General decided to rest them for a further day.(11)

Zieten's troops meanwhile attempted to slow Napoleon's advance to provide time for the rest of the army to reach Sombreffe and Fleurus. Napoleon's offensive on Zieten's defences at Charleroi had begun early in the morning on the 15th; for the rest of the night and morning the Prussians in the 1st Corps made a fighting withdrawal to Fleurus. Blücher left Namur at about 1 p.m. on the 15th, finding time to scribble a note to his wife: 'At this moment I have received the report that Bonaparte has engaged my whole outposts. I break up at once and take the field against the enemy. I will accept battle with pleasure . . .'(12)

A Prussian officer 'all covered with sweat and dirt', reached Wellington two hours later and the Duke was informed that Zieten had been attacked and the Prussian outposts driven in at Thuin. Wellington hurriedly consulted his maps. Thuin lay to the south-west of Charleroi: Napoleon might still be intending to strike westwards via Mons to sever the Anglo-Dutch communications to the sea. Further reports reached Wellington soon afterwards which seemed to strengthen the Duke's fears of such a move: The French had attacked Binche, even closer to Mons, although gunfire had also been heard at Charleroi. Between 5 p.m. and 7 p.m. the British commander therefore ordered his regiments to take up positions between Grammont and Nivelles – even though this would incline the Anglo-Dutch army away from the Prussians and expose the hinge between them. Critics later blamed Blücher for this British mistake, claiming Wellington had been ill-informed of the attack on Charleroi. But Wellington, like Blücher, without doubt had numerous reports of French moves at a variety of points; from the confusion Blücher picked out Charleroi as the most important, while Wellington was influenced by his fears of a French sweep via Mons, and failed to reach a similar conclusion. Now a dangerous opening had been created for Napoleon between the two allied armies.

Another explanation for this error stems from Wellington's lack of realization that Blücher was already concentrating as far forward

H.G.—H

as the Sombreffe-Fleurus area, and the British commander believed
his own moves would link with those of the Prussian army.

> If the enemy do not straightway attack Nivelles [declared a message
> from Müffling, received at Blücher's headquarters at 7 p.m. on the
> 15th], the Duke will be in the neighbourhood of Nivelles tomorrow
> to support Your Highness; or should the enemy have already
> attacked Your Highness, to fall on his flank or on his rear as shall
> have been agreed. I imagine Your Highness will be pleased with
> this explanation and with the Duke's activity.(13)

At about the same time this message reached Blücher, a note
arrived in Brussels from the Prussian commander. This finally
informed Wellington of the intended forward concentration at
Sombreffe and sought information of Anglo-Dutch support plans.
Wellington told Müffling that the main French attack might still
come through Mons; he made no alteration to his plans.

Napoleon continued to thrust forward at maximum speed,
aiming at the junction between the two allied armies. Zieten's
battered corps retreated through Fleurus and scrambled into
positions on the road to Sombreffe. Should Napoleon burst
through, the French might be able to stab straight towards
Brussels. But behind Zieten's weary Prussians the 2nd and 3rd
corps were hurrying over the dark roads to throw in their much-
needed support. And at last Wellington learnt his mistake. He
entered Müffling's room just before midnight on this Thursday
15th June.

'I have got news from Mons,' he declared, 'from General
Dörnberg, who reports that Napoleon has turned towards
Charleroi with all his forces.'

The Duke had already issued orders for his army to concentrate
between Nivelles and Quatre Bras, rather than between Nivelles
and Grammont, thus reducing the gap between the Anglo-Dutch
and Prussian armies. Yet the hinge remained weak and Wellington
failed to appreciate the speed of the French advance. By now
Charleroi had fallen and the French had pushed beyond. Wellington
believed nothing more could be done for the moment.

He told Müffling: 'Let us therefore go all the same to the
Duchess of Richmond's ball; after which, about five o'clock, we
can ride off to the troops assembled at Quatre Bras.'(14) At the
famous ball two more items of information arrived; together, they

revealed that the French had split forces at Charleroi, with Napoleon leading the bulk of the army towards Fleurus while other French regiments streaked towards Quatre Bras. Wellington learnt that the Prussians had already retired beyond Fleurus.

'Napoleon has *humbugged* me, by God!' exclaimed Wellington. 'He has gained twenty-four hours' march on me.' He added: 'I have ordered the army to concentrate at Quatre Bras. But we shall not stop him there; and if so, I must fight *here*.' He swept his finger over the map to a position south-west of an unknown village named Waterloo.(15)

As Wellington's officers galloped through the night to organize desperate defences at Quatre Bras, Prussian regiments from Pirch's 2nd Corps and Thielmann's 3rd Corps ran along the roads and through the fields to reach Zieten's bedraggled units. These troops had flung themselves into the villages five kilo-metres north of Fleurus. The position stretched in a salient along the Ligny brook with the right flank at Wagnelée, the centre at St. Amand and the left flank at Ligny village. Early in the morning of Friday 16th June, Thielmann's troops began to deploy to Zieten's left between Sombreffe and Le Mazy, while Pirch's regiments bolstered Zieten's rear. At about this time Bülow received news that battle was about to begin at Ligny.

'My God!' he cried, 'why was I not informed of that before?' His corps still lay seventy kilometres away. Blücher could therefore only fight with about 84,000 men at Ligny. Napoleon's force totalled 78,000 with 242 guns – 16 more than the Prussian artillery. The battlefield area covered the junction of roads from western and northern Belgium and from Germany and the Rhine. It was vital to destroy Napoleon's attempt to drive a wedge between the allied armies; defeat at Ligny would throw Wellington into a highly dangerous position.

Blücher's plan at Ligny had therefore to be defensive, and for this he could make use of the villages clustering the valley-bottom – St Amand, La Haye, Wagnelée and Ligny itself – each with stout stone houses enclosed with walls or thick hedges. Nevertheless, force of circumstance had placed the Prussians in a tactically weaker defensive position. The French-held ground behind Fleurus rose higher than the hills on the north of the valley, where Blücher's main regiments were situated, giving Napoleon easier observation and allowing his guns greater range.

Moreover, the folds of the land in the valley offered excellent dead ground for the French assaults. Antoine Henri Jomini, the Swiss military historian, described the Prussian positions as 'detestable', and Wellington expressed his unease when he rode over to confer with Blücher during the morning. The two commanders met at the mill of Bussy, between Ligny and Bry. Wellington wore a simple blue overcoat without decorations and an ordinary three-cornered hat. Blücher wore his Field-Marshal's jacket, flapping open to reveal his white waistcoat and the broad orange sash of the Order of the Black Eagle; his untidy white hair sprouted from beneath his peaked cap.

'We noticed in the distance a party of the enemy', wrote Colonel Ludwig von Reiche, Zieten's chief of staff, 'and Napoleon was easily distinguishable in the group. Perhaps the three greatest military commanders were looking at each other.' Wellington swept the Prussian positions with his spy-glass.

> I told the Prussian officers [he wrote], that according to my judgement, the exposure of the advanced columns and, indeed, of the whole army to cannonade, standing as they did displayed to the aim of the enemy's fire, was not prudent. . . . I said that if I were in Blücher's place with English troops, I should withdraw all the columns I saw scattered about in front, and get more troops under shelter of the rising ground. However, they seemed to think they knew best. . . .(16)

'Our troops like to see the enemy,' snapped Gneisenau, referring to Wellington's preference for keeping his forces on the hidden slope until the last moment. Wellington, repeating his fear that the Prussians would be 'damnably mauled', rode off to his own battle at Quatre Bras. He promised to send help – if he himself was not attacked.

Napoleon planned to contain the Prussian left between Sombreffe and Le Mazy, while the Prussian centre was battered by troops under Vandamme and Girard aiming at St Amand, and by Gérard's corps at Ligny. He hoped Blücher would be obliged to commit all his reserves. Ney would meanwhile engage Wellington at Quatre Bras, and after defeating the outnumbered Anglo-Dutch, would thrust forward to encircle the Prussian right wing. Napoleon therefore delayed the start of the offensive at Ligny until he heard the sound of Ney's initial cannonade at Quatre Bras. Ney dallied during the morning, allowing Wellington more time to prepare, and not until 2 p.m. did the distant sound of the guns reach Napoleon's position at Ligny. Minutes afterwards he ordered the attack to begin.

Troops on both sides almost welcomed the opening of battle. For seven hours they had waited in position, their stomachs heaving with fear, their mouths parched, their limbs trembling despite the fierce sun.

> A dense cloud of dust enveloped us and made breathing difficult [remembered a French sergeant]. The heat was stifling, there was no breeze to cool one's face, and the sun was right overhead. . . . By means of a dozen handkerchiefs tied together and suspended over a ring of piled arms, we erected a sort of tent, which provided a little shade.(17)

Now the French collected muskets from these piles and moved into line along the edges of the yellow corn fields, which shimmered in the sun. Blücher's troops could hear the drums and the shouts of command from across the valley, and then, at about 2.30 p.m., the French lines began to walk forward through the corn towards St Amand, held by three Prussian infantry battalions.

At the same time a massive artillery bombardment clouded the village of Ligny in dense grey smoke; other shells exploded on the grassy hills beyond. The Prussian guns replied, and missiles screamed over the sunlit valley. French infantrymen ran yelling over the last few yards at St Amand and Ligny; once, twice, they were thrown back; on they rushed for a third attempt. Some houses fell. Blücher was positioned on the hill beyond, and he rushed in reinforcements from Thielmann's corps, among them a recruit named Franz Lieber:

> The village was intersected with thick hedges, from behind which the grenadiers fired upon us, but we drove them from one to the other. . . . I stepped round and a grenadier stood about 15 paces from me; he aimed at me, I levelled my rifle at him. 'Aim well, my boy,' said the sergeant-major, who saw me. My antagonist's ball grazed my hair on the right side; I shot and he fell; I found I had shot through his face; he was dying. This was my first shot ever fired in battle.(18)

French skirmishers swarmed across the open ground between the villages, fighting along the edge of Ligny stream until the brook was dammed by floating bodies. Horse-artillery hurried from one point to another, desperately trying to smash opposing columns of infantry as they advanced towards the burning houses. Acres of fields were churned into powder as grape-shot and shells scythed into the French marching through the corn. But still more French ran forward against the Prussian defences. One French soldier wrote: 'From every hole in the old ruin, from all the windows and loopholes in the houses, from the hedges and orchards and from above the stone walls, the muskets showered their deadly fire upon us like lightning.' The Frenchmen flung themselves behind cover, soaked with sweat and sobbing for breath. Then they rose, reorganized themselves, filled the gaps in their ranks, and advanced again.(19) St Amand fell to the French. Girard's division took the ruins of La Haye.

Pirch sent his Prussians down the slopes from Bry to counter-attack, but terrible French artillery fire smashed into these battalions; survivors scrambled to their feet and struggled on; scores more fell as they came within range of vicious French musket fire from the houses of La Haye. Still the Prussians pressed on. One after another the houses were wrenched from the French, but back came the enemy. Girard himself was killed, yet his Frenchmen fought on and the Prussians retreated up the hillside. Blücher waited them. He ordered them to stop, turn about, reform and advance once more into the hell below.

He stood in his stirrups and shouted: 'My sons! Carry yourselves bravely, don't let that nation be your master again! Forward! Forward in God's name!' The blood-stained Prussians responded. '*Vorwärts!*' they screamed.

From down in the village came the answering French call: '*Vive l'Empéreur! Vive Napoléon!*'

The Prussians still shouted Blücher's battle-cry as they advanced down the hill again, straight into the blazing French guns to slaughter the defenders and once more occupy the useless, stinking buildings. Other Prussians ran on to drive the French from nearby Wagnelée, but they came under deadly fire from French *tirailleurs* hidden in the waving corn. Ligny experienced the fiercest fighting. Men slithered on the blood-wet cobbles as they grappled hand-to-hand.

'The dead in many places were piled two or three deep,' said a French officer. 'The blood flowed from under them in streams.

Through the principal street the mud was red with blood, and the mud itself was composed of crushed bones and flesh.'(20) Over the houses hung a misty black veil, pierced by the cries of the wounded, the death rattle of musket fire, booming artillery salvoes, harsh coughing from the howitzers, crashing timbers and tinkling slates from the roofs. Alleys and doorways were choked with dead and dying, showered by debris and sparks.

Prussian bullets swept us away by the dozen [wrote Erckmann-Chatrain in Gérard's Corps]. The drums kept up their *pan-pan-pan*. It was a thousand times worse inside the houses, where the screams of rage mingled in the uproar. We rushed into a large room already packed with soldiers, on the first floor of a house. It was dark because they had covered the windows with sacks of earth, but we could see a steep wooden staircase at one end, down which the blood was running. We heard musket shots from above, and each moment the flashes showed us five or six of our men sunk in a heap ... and the others scrambling over their bodies with bayonets fixed, trying to force their way up into the loft. The room was full of dead and wounded, the walls splashed with blood. Not one Prussian was left on his feet.(21)

Blücher rode backwards and forwards through the cannonfire on the slopes beyond the villages, white waistcoat and white hair streaked with black powder stains, his voice almost hoarse from bellowing encouragement at his men. Both opposing commanders awaited help: Blücher from Wellington and Napoleon from Ney. Both were disappointed, for the same reason. Ney had failed to overrun the British at Quatre Bras, but Wellington was too heavily engaged to send assistance to his Prussian ally. A message reached Blücher from Müffling during the afternoon to inform the Field-Marshal that no immediate help would be forthcoming. Gneisenau never forgave the British commander. 'The Duke of Wellington had promised to attack the enemy in the rear,' he wrote later, 'but he did not come, because his army, Heaven knows why, could not concentrate.'

Even without Ney's support, Napoleon still expected assistance: French troops under Jean-Baptiste d'Erlon marched within striking distance and, about 6 p.m., word reached Blücher that these reinforcements might soon reach the French. Yet to Blücher's astonishment and great relief, this new French column abruptly halted and began to march away again. D'Erlon, desperately wanted by both Ney at Quatre Bras and by Napoleon at Ligny, wandered between the two and finished by helping neither.

But the Prussians were beginning to crumble beneath the relentless weight of the French offensive at Ligny. At all sections of the seven-mile front the defences neared collapse. Thielmann's corps was slashed to a quarter fighting strength; few other reserves remained. Despairing reports reached Blücher. Troops at La Haye had exhausted all ammunition, even the rounds in the pouches of the dead, to which Blücher replied that the soldiers must fight with their bare hands. Another messenger said Ligny could hold no longer. Gneisenau insisted it must, if only for another thirty minutes. Now, at 8.30 p.m., Napoleon launched his final attack. He still had over 10,000 reserves uncommitted, including the élite Guard, and these troops swept forward towards Ligny. They shattered the fragile Prussian defences, surged over the bodies and debris, flowed through the streets and into the houses. Blücher's centre regiments retreated, still in reasonable order, and formed squares on the slopes between Ligny and Bry. Artillery fire reached a new crescendo in the fading light; horses and infantrymen clashed again and again as the French tried to disrupt these blocking Prussian squares.

In the gathering darkness Blücher reverted to the days of his youth. Defeat and retreat stared him in the face, and he responded in typical fashion: he would attack. He became the young hussar officer again, rather than the seventy-two-year-old Field-Marshal. He bellowed cavalrymen to form into line and he trotted to their front, and charged.

'Forward!' he shouted. 'Forward my children!' Down the slope thundered Blücher and his cavalrymen, jumping the ditches and corpses in a swaying, clattering wave. Blücher had made score upon score cavalry charges in his life, each time risking death or ghastly mutilation: the sound of thudding hooves, the creaking of leather, the sickly scent of human and animal sweat, the feel of the horses between his thighs and the sabre in his fist – all were intensely familiar. This would be old Blücher's last charge, and he barely survived. A shot gouged into his mount's left flank near the saddle-girth, inches from Blücher's knee. The horse, a fine grey stallion given him by the Prince Regent of England, galloped a few more yards, then Blücher could feel it falter beneath him. The stallion lurched again and began to fall. 'Nostitz!' shouted Blücher. 'I'm done for now!' His horse rolled, legs kicking high in its death throes, and Blücher lay pinned unconscious beneath the body. Prussian and French cavalrymen clashed around him, the hooves of their horses milling about his head. But Nostitz had thrown himself from his own saddle and stood over the fallen Field-Marshal, sabre in one hand and his horse's bridle in the other. The French cavalry swept past, so close that they collided with Nostitz's mount, but Nostitz flung his cloak over Blücher to hide his medals, and the enemy charge continued in the noise and darkness. Back came the French, streaming to left and right of Blücher and his aide, and behind them galloped the Prussians once more. Nostitz grabbed the bridle of a Prussian *Uhlan's* horse and stopped others who were following. Half a dozen troopers lifted the body of the dead stallion, dragged out the unconscious Blücher, threw him over a saddle and fled, just before the French rushed back again. Staff officers carried the inert Field-Marshal back from the battlefield and laid him amongst the dead and dying at a rough field hospital.

Gneisenau assumed command of the reeling Prussian army. He could only take one decision: to retreat. Upon him lay the whole responsibility. Indeed, for a while during this terrible night of Friday 16th June, Blücher was lost. The whole area behind Ligny covered by confused, broken battalions, splintered cavalry squadrons and artillery columns. Drummers scattered over the fields to beat their different rallying rolls, calling their respective regiments, while down in the valley sporadic skirmishing continued until just before midnight. The French offensive diminished, with Napoleon's troops almost as exhausted as the Prussians. Fires spluttered from the villages; long lines of wounded stumbled and crawled from the battlefield, and those too weak to move shrieked and moaned in the darkness together with the pitiful whinnying of dying horses. About 16,000 Prussians had been killed, wounded or captured, almost one-fifth of the entire army; a further 10,000 Prussians deserted during the night, mainly troops from provinces which had recently been part of the French Empire. But Bonaparte's losses were also heavy, probably about 12,000 men.

Blücher's chief of staff, himself shaken by a fall from his horse,

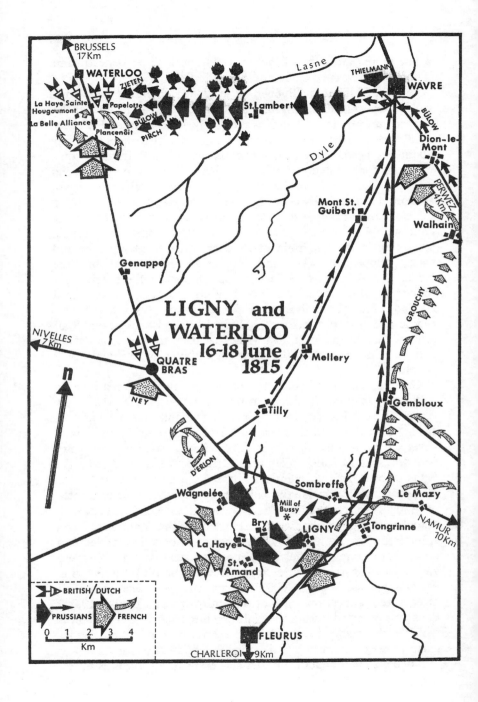

worked throughout the night to sort some semblance of order from the confusion. Corps commanders and their deputies rode backwards and forwards across the battlefield, forming men into line, bringing in stragglers, counting their losses. 'All our troops were scattered and we could only find them again with great difficulty,' wrote Clausewitz, Thielmann's chief of staff. 'I believe my hair turned grey that night, and I only dismounted my horse once, to write my report for the Field-Marshal.'(22) Somewhere to the rear, among the wounded, lay Blücher. The improvised hospitals provided the most horrific sights of all: men propped against the walls, bleeding to death; soldier upon soldier with crushed legs, arms, chests; other men wandering aimlessly about, their eardrums shattered by artillery blasts, their eyes blinded by the flashes.

A retreat route had to be chosen for the Prussian army. It was at this moment that Gneisenau's dislike and suspicion of the Duke of Wellington had potentially disastrous effect. Two main possible routes existed for the Prussians to take. One lay almost due north towards Tilly and Wavre, and the other headed eastwards towards Liège. The first would run in a parallel line to a British withdrawal from Quatre Bras and would cover Brussels; the second moved back along the Prussian communications to the Rhine – and away from the British. Gneisenau now had to select one or the other. A senior Prussian officer gave a glimpse in his diary of Gneisenau during the night as he pondered his choice.

> The village had been abandoned by its inhabitants, and every building was filled with wounded. No lights, no drinking water, no rations. We were in a small room, in which an oil lamp flickered dimly. Wounded men lay moaning on the floor. The General himself was seated on a barrel of pickled cabbages; only four or five people clustered round him. Disorganized troops filtered through the village throughout the night: no one knew whence they came or whither they were going. . . .(23)

In this desolate, nerve-racking situation, Gneisenau's feelings against Wellington took control. His rage increased over the lack of British support, either directly through Anglo-Dutch regiments arriving at Ligny, or indirectly by presenting sufficient threat to the French at Quatre Bras to make Napoleon divert forces from Ligny. Gneisenau even maintained that Wellington's alleged promise given during the morning had been the major factor in deciding to fight the battle. He wrote: 'On the 16th of June in the morning the Duke of Wellington promised to be at Quatre Bras at 10 o'clock with 20,000 men. . . . On the strength of these arrangements and promises we decided to fight the battle [at Ligny].'(24) But reports reaching Gneisenau during these hectic hours confirmed that the Anglo-Dutch concentration at Quatre Bras had been far too slow: instead of 20,000 men in the area by 10 a.m., the battle began at 2 p.m. with only about 8,000 Anglo-Dutch troops confronting 21,000 French. Not until evening could Wellington's strength be raised to 30,000.

Gneisenau, as he sat amongst the debris of battle during this Friday night, blamed Wellington for the lack of allied victory at Ligny. He considered the Prussians had played their painful part: concentration had been quick and decisive. Napoleon's advance had been blocked and severe casualties inflicted upon the French – while Wellington had hesitated and finally engaged the enemy with only a small proportion of his army. Moreover, Gneisenau believed Wellington had been kept fully informed of the Prussian situation throughout the day. Blücher had sent a messenger during the afternoon; Gneisenau had despatched another soon afterwards. The first rider, Major von Winterfield, had been severely wounded by French troops *en route*, but the second, von Wussow, reached Wellington in the early evening. He told the Duke that the Prussian positions were still holding, but added:

> The most we can do is to hold the battlefield until nightfall. Any greater success is not to be looked for. Perhaps a strong offensive by the English troops could prevent Napoleon from turning his full force against the Prussian army. [Wussow's account continued:] The Duke instructed me to tell Marshal Blücher that so far it had been extremely difficult for him to resist the heavy attacks made by superior French forces, but that with the reinforcements that had just arrived – he believed he now had about 20,000 men on the ground – he would try to launch a powerful attack which would benefit the Prussian army.(25)

Wellington did launch a general advance, and by 9 a.m. the battle was over with both sides having suffered about 4,000 casualties. But the outcome came too late to help the Prussians.

And slowly, fatefully, Gneisenau's choice of retreat route swung towards Liège – abandoning the British to face Napoleon alone, outnumbered. But almost at this moment staff officers found Blücher in farm buildings at the village of Mellery, seven kilometres to the north of Ligny. The Field-Marshal had regained consciousness and lay on a camp-bed. He reeked of brandy, gin, rhubarb and garlic, all of which had been rubbed into his bruises. He had demanded brandy for internal use, but the doctor had refused, leaving him with a magnum of champagne instead. Now Blücher considered himself fit to fight again, despite a throbbing right shoulder. Gneisenau hurried in to see him. And Blücher refused to consider a retreat away from the British.

'We've had a blow and now we must straighten out the dent,' declared Blücher. He ordered beer to be brought in, carried in stable buckets, and urgent discussions continued almost till dawn. According to Sir Harry Hardinge, British liaison officer:

> I was told that there had been a great discussion that night in his rooms, and that Blücher and Grolman carried the day for remaining in communication with the English Army, but that Gneisenau had great doubts as to whether they ought not to fall back to Liège and secure their own communications.(26)

Hardinge himself had been severely wounded. 'I passed that night with my amputated arm lying with some straw in his (Blücher's) anteroom, Gneisenau and other Generals constantly passing to and fro.' Early in the morning of the 17th Blücher called for Hardinge; the British officer found the Field-Marshal dressed for renewed battle. From him wafted the stench of the weird medicaments used on his battered body. He threw his arms round Hardinge, despite the latter's recent amputation, and roared: '*Ich stinke!*'

Hardinge wrote: 'He said to me . . . that he should be quite satisfied if in conjunction with the Duke of Wellington he was able now to defeat his old enemy.'(27) Blücher refused to consider resigning his command on account of his injuries; according to his aides he had declared that 'no matter what his condition he would rather have himself tied to a horse than resign', and 'a thirst for bloody vengeance had taken possession of his will and of his intelligence'.

Wellington had still to be told the direction of the Prussian retreat. The British commander sent a messenger to seek information; this officer, Captain Alexander Gordon, returned to the British positions at 7.30 a.m. on the 17th and found Wellington standing by a fire at the chilly Quatre Bras crossroads.

The Duke turned to his staff: 'Old Blücher has had a damned good licking and gone back to Wavre, eighteen miles. As he has gone back, we must go too.' Wellington rightly considered the decision to retire to Wavre as crucial and correct. 'It was the decisive moment of the century,' he wrote later. The moment belonged to Blücher.(28) Wellington issued his orders and by 10 a.m. the British withdrawal had begun: the Anglo-Dutch army would retire level with the Prussians – to the village of Waterloo.

Once again the allies were moving in unison. But both armies, and especially the Prussians, remained in acute danger of a strong French offensive while they organized themselves and retreated. Blücher's forces were still in a chaotic state when dawn broke on the 17th.

> The men looked terribly worn out after the fighting [wrote one Captain]. In the great heat, gunpowder smoke, sweat and mud had mixed into a thick crust of dirt, so that their faces looked almost like those of mulattos, and one could hardly distinguish the green collars and facings of their tunics.

The last regiments retreated from the battlefield at about 9 a.m. Not only had the men to be organized into fighting formations again, but they had also to be helped to regain their confidence, and for this a superb leader of men was needed, rather than a skilled tactician or strategist – a Blücher, not a Scharnhorst or a Gneisenau. Blücher rode among his retreating regiments; his troops, who had feared he might be dead or taken prisoner, cheered with revived strength.

> He had had his bruised limbs bathed in brandy and had helped himself to a large *schnaps* [wrote a Westphalian captain], and now, although riding must have been very painful, he rode alongside the troops, exchanging jokes and banter with many of them, and his good humour spread like wildfire down the columns.(29)

Fortunately, the French failed to launch rapid pursuit. The Emperor had managed to have only just over twelve hours sleep in the fifty-one hours between 3 a.m. on the 15th and 6.30 a.m. on the 17th. His body was frequently racked by pain. After the battle of Ligny he threw himself on a bed in the château of Fleurus and fell asleep while the Prussians reorganized and began to pull back. Durutte's division lay near the Prussian line of retreat, but failed to act. Despatches reached the French headquarters from Marshal de Grouchy, commander of the 1st and 4th French corps, but by that time Napoleon was in a feverish sleep and no one dared wake him. The Emperor himself added to the mistake on the 17th: reports were presented to him which indicated the Prussian columns were moving towards Wavre, but he refused to believe that Blücher would dare to move across the French front to join Wellington. He apparently forgot words he had spoken to his English warder on Elba, describing Blücher: 'That old devil always attacked me with the same vigour. If he was beaten, he would, a moment later, show himself ready to fight again.'(30)

Not until midday did Grouchy receive orders to pursue the Prussians. At last Napoleon realized that both the Anglo-Dutch and Prussian armies had made good their escape, and might soon merge to oppose him with overwhelming numbers. He hurried over to Quatre Bras, found Ney had also delayed his pursuit, and exclaimed: 'France has been ruined!' The allies continued to slip away. The weather, which had clouded over during the morning, deteriorated rapidly. Rain sluiced upon the roads, making conditions miserable for pursued and pursuers alike: men waded through the mud, waggons and guns were pushed and heaved through the mire and slime, and cavalry horses floundered. But the Prussians proved tougher.

Grouchy halted his infantry corps for two hours, and lost control of the situation. Local inhabitants informed him that at midday Thielmann's Corps had entered Gembloux, ten kilometres south-east of Wavre; other reports revealed Prussian forces at Perwez, even further east. Grouchy therefore sent a despatch informing Napoleon that the Prussians seemed to be withdrawing in two directions, with some going to Wavre and others to Perwez. This message, received by Napoleon at two o'clock in the morning of the 18th, continued: 'Perhaps it may be inferred that one portion is going to join Wellington, while the centre, under Blücher, retired on Liège.' Grouchy therefore divided his forces to conform with this mythical enemy split. His report was based on a serious error. Prussian regiments at Perwez belonged to Bülow's corps, which was now moving towards the rest of the Prussian army at Wavre. By the time Grouchy wrote his despatch in the late afternoon of the 17th the bulk of the Prussian army had already concentrated again. Blücher, who had reached Wavre earlier in the day to establish fresh headquarters in the town, considered his army to be ready for battle, and he sank on his couch for welcome rest.

'If Napoleon proposes another similar battle, he and his army will be finished,' wrote Blücher to his wife. 'My troops fought like lions, but were too weak because two of my divisions were not with me. But I've collected them all round me now.'(31) He visited his regiments; his shoulder still ached abominably but he remained cheerful, although he talked frankly to his troops. The infantry had battled bravely, he declared, and he also expressed satisfaction with the artillery, but advised them to advance more resolutely next time. The cavalry, as so often, failed to receive his congratulations; instead Blücher demanded more boldness and perseverance. Blücher believed he might be allowed time to correct faults: he told his wife that 'in a few days it will be possible to come to a battle again'. Within hours he learnt this breathing space would not be granted.

A rider reached the Prussian headquarters at Wavre, and Nostitz roused Blücher from his bed at 11 p.m. this Saturday night. The messenger had been sent by Müffling and declared that the Anglo-Dutch army had reached a position in line to the Prussian army, over to the north; the French seemed likely to attack. Wellington requested Prussian assistance of at least one corps. Blücher immediately called Gneisenau. Staff officers waited outside, among them Hardinge, the British liaison officer. Blücher's chief of staff came out of the room, then Hardinge was summoned.

'Gneisenau has given in,' said the Field-Marshal. 'We are going to join the Duke.' Blücher handed the British officer the draft of his reply to Wellington: 'Bülow's (2nd) Corps will set off marching tomorrow at daybreak in your direction. It will be immediately followed by the (4th) Corps of Pirch. The 1st and 3rd Corps will also hold themselves in readiness to proceed towards you.' Blücher would therefore send double the help requested by Wellington, with the possibility of more to follow.(32)

Blücher confirmed this promise at 9.30 a.m. the following day, Sunday, 18th June. He drafted another message to Müffling, which declared:

> Ill and old though I am, I shall nonetheless ride at the head of my troops to attack the enemy's right flank as soon as Napoleon makes any move against the Duke. But if today passes without any enemy attack, then in my opinion tomorrow we should attack the French army together.

So Blücher insisted that if both allied armies combined, they should take the offensive. Gneisenau was still intensely suspicious of the cautious Wellington, and sought to ensure this offensive policy: Nostitz showed him a copy of Blücher's draft, and Gneisenau added a few words: 'Müffling, I beg you to discover very carefully if the Duke really intends to do battle in his position, or if these are only demonstrations which could be of great inconvenience to our army.'(33)

Blücher's shoulder still gave him considerable pain. He nevertheless refused to allow Dr Bietzke to smear fresh ointment on his bruises, saying it made no difference to him whether he went 'anointed' or 'unanointed' into eternity. 'If things go well to-day,' he commented, 'we shall soon all be washing and bathing in Paris.' The fields and meadows around Wavre bustled with troops preparing to march. The previous night had been miserable, with rain drumming on the improvised tents or on the greatcoats of the men attempting to sleep in the open. They rose before dawn, stiff, sodden and starving. Now the drums began to beat again and they shuffled wearily into line.

'I shall once more lead you against the enemy,' declared Blücher's Order of the Day. 'We shall defeat him *for we must!*' The Field-Marshal stood by the roadside in the drizzle as the first troops marched past him on the road to Waterloo.

CHAPTER 12

Waterloo — The Last Battle

LESS THAN FIFTEEN kilometres separated the Prussian and Anglo-Dutch armies on the morning of the 18th, but Blücher's movement to join Wellington nevertheless presented acute problems and dangers. Regiments were weary and still suffering from the battle of Ligny; this meant that Bülow's 2nd Corps, not present at Ligny, would lead the way. Yet Bülow lay further away from Wellington's army than the others, and Pirch's 4th Corps could not move until Bülow had passed. This caused delay and endangered the Prussians: if Marshal Grouchy had been more active, Blücher's army might have been attacked while the delicate and complicated manouevre continued. But while the Prussians struggled into marching order, the French Marshal delayed at Walhain, eating a breakfast of fresh ripe strawberries. Bülow advanced from Dion-le-Mont, through Wavre, and on to the road for Chapelle St Lambert. His corps had taken its vanguard position by mid-morning, and Pirch began to follow, with Zieten next to move. Blücher and his staff rode out at 11 o'clock; Gneisenau left later after having helped Thielmann to organize his corps, which would remain at Wavre to block Grouchy. Within minutes of Blücher's departure from Wavre sullen booms echoed from over the hills in front. The battle of Waterloo had begun.

Recent rain made the going almost intolerable for the Prussians. At each rise, no matter how slight, troops had to put their shoulders to the gun carriages and ammunition waggons; already wet from the downpour the previous night, the men now became coated with slime. Some lost boots in the muck, but continued to slog forwards; they slithered and fell, but climbed to their feet again.

> Sunken lanes cut through deep ravines had to be negotiated [wrote Colonel von Reiche in Zieten's corps]. Almost impenetrable forest grew on each side, so that there was no question of avoiding the road, and progress was very slow, all the more so because in many places men and horses could get through only one at a time. The column became very split up and wherever the ground allowed it, the heads of the columns had to halt so as to give time for the detachments to collect themselves again.(1)

Always from the front rumbled the cannons of Waterloo. By midday Blücher had overtaken Pirch's Corps and reached Bülow at Chapelle St Lambert, halfway to Wellington's army, but before them loomed the thick forest known as the Bois de Paris, and beyond that the steep slopes by the river Lasne. At 1.30 p.m. a renewed bombardment sounded from the battle ahead.

This latest cannonade was fired by the French upon the forward slopes of Wellington's positions. So far the battle had centred upon the Château Hougoumont to the right of the Anglo-Dutch line, which spread east-west along the hillside behind La Haye Sainte and Papelotte, south of Waterloo village. Now d'Erlon's four divisions thrust for La Haye Sainte and Papelotte; Wellington's infantry stood from their cover on the reverse slopes of the hillside to block the advance. At about the same time reports reached Napoleon that troops had been seen on the heights of Chapelle St Lambert, seven kilometres to the east; after some disbelief these soldiers were identified as Prussian advance patrols. Napoleon immediately rushed orders to Grouchy at Wavre: 'Hurry, there isn't a moment to lose', and he intensified his attack upon Wellington's defences. Wellington in turn threw in his cavalry to support the infantry against d'Erlon's advance, and the French reeled back. A lull fell over the battlefield.

Increasing numbers of Blücher's troops were dropping from sheer exhaustion. They sprawled face down in the mud while waggon wheels rolled slowly over them and while comrades tramped across their bodies. The dank eerie Bois de Paris threatened further hardship: the French might have laid ambushes along the narrow, water-logged lane. But Blücher's scouts reported no sign of enemy activity; the Field-Marshal ordered the march forward again. Never before had he relied so much on his close relationship with his men, and never before had their response been so apparent; Nostitz noticed how private soldiers slapped the Field-Marshal's knee as he rode passed, calling out: 'Bring us lots of luck today Father Blücher!' Then came the hardest part of the march: the long, slippery grind up the steep hill beyond Lasne river. Cannons skidded and threatened to overturn in the mire; cavalrymen dismounted to drag their mounts by their bridles; troops could barely lift their mud encrusted boots.

'Forward boys!' shouted Blücher. 'I hear some say it can't be done. But it must be done! I have promised my brother Wellington. Would you make me a liar?'(2) One by one the battalions struggled to the summit and men flung themselves down to rest. But now they had to fight a battle.

'I first saw the Prussian vedettes about half past two,' commented Wellington later, 'and never in my life did I observe a movement with such intense interest. The time they occupied in approaching seemed interminable; both they and my watch seemed to have stuck fast.'(3) Those last four kilometres would take over two hours for the exhausted Prussians to cross.

Meanwhile Ney ordered the French cavalry to attack the British lines, without instructions from Napoleon. Over 5,000 horsemen pounded the British squares, charging, reforming, charging again a dozen times or more. British musket balls drummed on the enemy cavalrymen's breastplates like hail upon a window; squares collapsed and were overrun, and the survivors ran together to reform before the next dreadful charge. One officer after another reported to Wellington that their units were so decimated they doubted if they could hold much longer. Wellington scraped together all available reserves, and still more were needed; even divisional generals began to mutter about retreat. If the British could hold, then Napoleon's position would be extremely precarious with his cavalry depleted; conversely, a determined French infantry advance against the fragile, bleeding British defences in the centre threatened to be the finish. 'Night or the Prussians must come,' the Duke was heard to say.

Blücher arrived first. He had ridden ahead to a vantage point overlooking the chaotic battlefield. Troops from Bülow's corps

were rushed forward in almost immediate attack, and at about
4.20 p.m. the first Prussian guns roared from the fringe of the
woods to the east.

'The battle is mine!' exclaimed Wellington. Already Napoleon
was obliged to divert reinforcements from Ney to face this new
threat, and these regiments attacked Bülow's corps as soon as it
reached the battlefield. The leading Prussian units were driven
back by French troops under Count Georges Lobau, but the rest
of Bülow's corps pressed on towards Plancenoît, thereby threatening Lobau's right. Plancenoît fell to the Prussians; further French
battalions, including two from the Old Guard, counter-attacked
at about 5.30 p.m. and drove out Bülow's men. Napoleon turned
his attention back to the Anglo-Dutch centre, believing he had
blocked this Prussian threat to his flank. Marshal Ney led the
wreckage of d'Erlon's corps against La Haye Sainte, and the
garrison finally fell after having clung to the battered buildings
since battle began. Capture of La Haye Sainte exposed Wellington's
troops in the centre to close-range French musket volleys; at the
same time Ney brought up a battery of horse artillery and this,
at 300 yards range, smashed into the remaining British squares.
Several formations started to give way. 'At every moment the
issue of the battle became more doubtful,' wrote a senior staff
officer.(4)

But Zieten's corps now followed Bülow's on to the battlefield.
Colonel von Reiche, Zieten's chief of staff, reached the area with
the advance guard; Müffling galloped over to him. 'I learnt that
the Duke was anxiously awaiting our arrival and had repeatedly
declared that time was running very short, and that if we did not
arrive soon he would have to retreat.' Almost at the same time
another rider dashed up to von Reiche. This officer, Scharnhorst's
son, served on Bülow's staff, and told von Reiche that Bülow
urgently needed assistance at Plancenoît. Two sections of the
battlefield therefore demanded the immediate arrival of this
Prussian corps: the British in the centre, and fellow-Prussian
battalions on the flank. Von Reiche hesitated, and during the
momentary delay the column moved further along the road away
from the British centre. Nearby British troops believed the
Prussians to be withdrawing, and a minor panic spread. But then
Zieten himself arrived; von Reiche explained the dilemma;
Zieten immediately ordered the corps to advance in support of the

British centre, and by 6.30 p.m. these Prussian regiments were moving into position.

Napoleon lost his final chance of victory. Preoccupied by the Prussian pressure on his right, where Bülow was now being strengthened by the arrival of Pirch's corps, he delayed too long in launching his last and most powerful weapon at the allied centre – the Imperial Guard. Wellington's line had been strengthened, but Napoleon tried desperately to recover. He ordered the Guard to advance and placed himself at the head, at least until these magnificent troops reached La Haye Sainte, where he handed over to Ney. The time was just after 7 p.m.

> One hundred and fifty bandsmen now marched down at the head of the Guard [wrote a French colonel, Octave Levasseur], playing the triumphant marches of the Carousel as they went. Soon the road was covered by the Guard marching by platoons in the wake of the Emperor. Bullets and grapeshot left the road strewn with dead and wounded.(5)

At this moment word reached Blücher from Wavre: Thielmann's corps had come under heavy attack from Grouchy. If this rearguard should fall, Grouchy would be able to strike behind the Prussian army, and Thielmann requested urgent reinforcements.

'Not a horse's tail shall he get,' answered Blücher. All depended on the outcome at Waterloo. Gneisenau was even more explicit in his refusal of Thielmann's appeal. 'It doesn't matter if he's crushed as long as we gain the victory here.'(6)

Gunfire subsided to comparative silence as the Guard advanced. Napoleon made his last bid for victory and survival. Drums rapped out their staccato beat; British troops peered through the murk to see them come. Ney took over command from the Emperor. Michael Ney, Prince of Borodino, had lost five horses during the battle and now walked, dwarfed by the giant Guardsmen with their long blue greatcoats, huge epaulettes and red plumes waving on high, hairy bearskins. In their haversacks they carried ceremonial uniforms for the victory parade into Brussels. Six thousand of them marched steadily forward, breaking step as they trudged through the mud and over the bodies, then advancing up the hillside in close-packed, highly disciplined ranks, carrying with them their famous nickname of the 'Immortals' and their reputation for invincibility. The distance between them and the British narrowed. One hundred paces, eighty, sixty, fifty, towards Wellington's 1st Brigade of Guards lying behind the ridge.

'Stand up, Guards!' barked the Duke. About 1,500 British troops suddenly rose from cover. 'Fire!' The head of the French column seemed to jerk bodily back as 1,500 musket balls struck simultaneously. Three hundred French flung up their arms and fell.

'Now's the time my boys,' yelled the commander of the British 1st Foot Guards, and forward they ran. British bayonets plunged into Napoleon's hand-picked troops; the line wavered, and then the French gave. An appalling cry ran through the French army: '*La Garde recule!*' More British regiments carved forward despite flank attacks from enemy cavalry. More French regiments retreated. The tide of battle had finally turned. On swept the British; Wellington threw in his last cavalry reserve, and these joined with Prussian squadrons. Three squares of the French Guard were hurriedly formed on the main highway to cover Napoleon's retreat, but Prussian and British cavalry smashed into these formations and by nightfall the road lay open; Napoleon took to his carriage, then abandoned it when Prussian cavalry swooped near, and fled on his mare down the track for Charleroi.

Behind him the British bands played 'God Save the King' and hundreds of Prussian voices joined in singing the Lutheran hymn: '*Herr Gott, Dich loben wir*' – 'Lord God we praise you.' At 9.15 p.m., according to the Prussians, Blücher and Wellington had their historic meeting outside La Belle Alliance inn, used by Napoleon for his headquarters before the battle. Blücher leant forward in his saddle to embrace the Duke. '*Mein lieber Kamerad!*' he exclaimed. '*Quelle affaire!*'

Wellington later denied both the site and timing of this incident. 'It happens that the meeting took place after ten at night, at the village of Genappe.' The difference of opinion stemmed from conflict between the two commanders over the name for the battle. Blücher suggested at the meeting that the most suitable name would be La Belle Alliance; Wellington made no comment at the time, nor did he when Müffling repeated the suggestion later in the evening. He preferred the battle to be called after the site of his own headquarters, Waterloo – a Belgium name, rather than French, and one perhaps which underplayed the Prussian part in the conflict. Wellington prevaricated over paying credit to the

Prussians for their help. His despatch after the battle first seemed
to deal out generous tribute, but his next sentence took away much
of the acknowledgement.

> I should not do justice to my own feelings, or to Marshal Blücher
> and the Prussian army, if I did not attribute the successful result
> of this arduous day to the cordial and timely assistance I received
> from them. [But then Wellington added:] The operation of General
> Bülow upon the enemy's flank was a most decisive one, and, even
> if I had not found myself in a situation to make the attack which
> produced the final result, it would have forced the enemy to retire
> if his attacks should have failed. . . .

Wellington therefore still insisted that he 'made the attack that
produced the final result.' He ignored Zieten's presence to bolster
the British centre, and he overlooked Bülow's value in diverting
French forces from the main attack and in delaying the advance
of the Imperial Guard, allowing Wellington time to recover. The
Prussians were even more partisan. According to the official report
written by Gneisenau but signed by Blücher, their arrival 'decided
the defeat of the enemy. His [Napoleon's] right wing was broken
in three places; he abandoned his positions. Our troops rushed
forward at the *pas de charge*, and attacked him on all sides, while,
at the same time, the whole English line advanced.'(7)

The Prince of Orange, although by no means a reliable witness
and over-fond of praising himself, agreed with the Prussians. 'We
had a magnificent affair against Napoleon today. . . . It was my
corps which principally gave battle and to which we owe the
victory, but the affair was entirely decided by the attack which the
Prussian's made on the enemy's right.'(8) Blücher found time
during the night to scribble a note to his wife. 'What I promised
I have kept. On the 16th I was forced to retire a short distance;
the 18th – in conjunction with my friend Wellington – completed
Napoleon's ruin.'(9)

Blücher's words, written with trembling, tired hand, seem the
most just. Both armies fought in conjunction, to both went the
honours of victory. Blücher always considered the name Waterloo
to be an insult and continued to insist upon La Belle Alliance, and
perhaps this title remains correct. Neither army beat Napoleon
alone. But whatever the part played by Prussian troops in the
actual moment when the Imperial Guard was repulsed, it is

difficult to see how Wellington could have staved off defeat, when his centre had been almost shattered, his reserves were almost all committed, the French right remained unmolested and the Imperial Guard intact.

'It has been a damned nice thing,' admitted Wellington, 'the nearest run thing you ever saw in your life'.(10) Blücher may not have been totally responsible for victory over Napoleon, but he deserved full credit for preventing a British defeat. Certainly Blücher's army suffered a heavy share of the casualties: despite the fact that the Prussian corps were engaged for only a third of the duration of the battle, their dead and wounded totalled almost half those in the Anglo-Dutch army – 7,000 compared with 15,000. French losses on the battlefield itself numbered about 25,000.

Thousands more French were to fall during the next few days. To the Prussians went the role of pursuers. Wellington halted his troops by La Belle Alliance and accepted Blücher's offer for his units to undertake the chase 'as long as they had a man and a horse able to stand'. First the Prussians had to disentangle themselves from the horrible chaos around the battlefield itself: troops tried to organize themselves during darkness, amidst the dead and dying, while skirmishing continued with pockets of French. Prussian and British fired upon each other as troops of various nationalities made mistakes in the confusion and night. But by the early hours of 19th June the main Prussian pursuit had begun. Blücher, exhausted and aching, stayed at Genappe; Gneisenau led 4,000 soldiers on for 'the finest night of my life', chasing and cutting down the panic-stricken French.

For the next two weeks the Prussians advanced via Charleroi, Avesnes, Guise, St Quentin and then to Compiègne, while the Anglo-Dutch army followed a slower and more westerly route through Nivelles, Mauberge, Cambrai and Péronne. The Prussian path was smeared by blood and destruction, to an extent which horrified their British allies.

We perceived, on entering France [wrote Ensign Rees Howell Gronow of the 1st Guards], that our allies the Prussians had committed fearful atrocities on the defenceless inhabitants of the villages and farms which lay in their line of march. . . . We found that every article of furniture in the houses had been destroyed in the most wanton manner . . . and, on the slightest remonstrance on the wretched inhabitants, they were beaten in a most shameful manner, and sometimes shot.(11)

Prussian ruthlessness and cruelty stemmed from four main factors. First, and most immediate, was sheer blood-lust generated by the frenzy of battle. In this respect the Prussians behaved no worse than Wellington's troops on some occasions in the Peninsular War, notably at Badajoz in April 1812, when a British captain declared: 'The infuriated soldiery resembled . . . a pack of hell-hounds vomited up from the infernal regions for the extirpation of mankind.' Secondly, unlike the British, the Prussians had seen their own country invaded and violated. Thirdly, Blücher's army pressed forward at maximum speed, and therefore faster than their supply system. They suffered exhaustion and starvation.

'We went incessantly by forced marches,' wrote Clausewitz. 'The effort we had to make was such that some people shot themselves in despair. Others fell dead.'(12) The troops had to live off the land, and Wellington himself knew that his own army would probably have behaved in similar fashion in this situation. Pressed by Müffling to hasten the British pursuit, Wellington replied:

> I tell you, it won't do. If you were better acquainted with the English army, its composition and habits, you would say the same. I cannot separate from my tents and supplies. My troops must be well kept and well supplied in camp, if order and discipline are to be maintained.(13)

The final factor contributing to the character of the Prussian pursuit was the attitude of Blücher and Gneisenau. None sought revenge more eagerly than they; none glorified more in the defeat of Napoleon. On the day after Waterloo, Blücher's brother-in-law, Colomb, found the Field-Marshal at Quatre Bras, proudly wearing Napoleon's hat and with the Emperor's sword strapped to his waist. 'How do you like me?' boomed the triumphant Blücher.(14) He insisted his troops should drive on as far and as fast as possible, despite his own weariness and a lame leg which forced him to ride in a carriage for some of the way. Snipers shot two horses from under Blücher during the pursuit, and his soldiers often met stiff opposition, yet he refused to listen to those who suggested that the army needed time for reorganization and rest. This time he would allow no allied intervention; victory must be made complete. 'The first shock can do a lot to the Frenchmen,' Blücher declared in his orders to the regiments immediately after the battle. 'One has to be bold now and not work according to theories and books.'(15)

He dictated a letter to his wife on the morning of the 20th, with his headquarters near Beaumont. 'I don't expect to come to a big battle very soon and perhaps not any more. Our victory has been the most complete which has ever been achieved. Today I am going into France.'(16) Napoleon reached Paris on the morning of the 21st and struggled to rally support. Blücher intended to maintain such pressure that this support would be unobtainable and the people would rise against their former ruler; he urged the army on, and his determination increased still further when rumours began to circulate of a possible armistice.

But the strain on Blücher began to have effect. He told Hardenberg on the 21st that his strength was waning. 'As soon as things are settled here I shall leave, otherwise it will be the end of me'; he believed that 'only Gneisenau's loyal assistance and my iron will' had made victory complete. 'The lamentations and pleas to give the troops some rest have almost made me go out of my mind.' Next day, 22nd June, he reached Châtillon-sur-Sambre. He told his wife that he felt better and added: 'It is said that Napoleon wants to reconcentrate near Laon. It will not trouble me much. If the Parisians do not kill the tyrant before I get to Paris, I will kill the Parisians. They certainly are a treacherous lot.'(17) Blücher demanded in public that Napoleon must be captured dead or alive: this, he declared, remained his condition for ending hostilities. On the 26th he reached Guivry, only about sixty kilometres from Paris. 'I am marching on Paris today,' he wrote to Katharina. 'I shall hammer the steel while it is hot.' He repeated the words to Hardenberg: he intended to finish the war before the monarchs 'put bit and bridle on me. . . . The steel is hot. I shall hammer it.' Blücher continued: 'In three days we must be in Paris. It is possible and very probable that Napoleon will be handed over to me and Lord Wellington. I could not act more wisely than to have him shot.'(18)

Blücher stressed this ruthless policy towards Napoleon in directions sent to Müffling.

The Duke of Wellington might, for Parliamentary reasons, have scruples about carrying out the sentence. You will therefore direct the negotiations in this matter towards having Bonaparte surrendered to *us* so that he may be executed. Such is the requirement of everlasting justice.(19)

Gneisenau believed Napoleon should be executed on the spot where the Duke of Enghien had been executed in 1804, after having been dragged from Prussian territory by the French. 'Does not the death of the Duke of Enghien alone demand such vengeance?'(20) Wellington expressed horror at Blücher's apparent determination to put to death the fallen French Emperor. Yet Blücher may never have actually intended such a drastic punishment, and a difference existed between public statements, or statements which might become public, and his private attitude. To his closest colleagues he admitted that 'if you had brought Napoleon to me I could not have received him but with the greatest respect, in spite of the fact that he has often called me a drunken hussar. He is still a tremendously brave man.'(21) Blücher admired bravery above all. He might also have recalled the courteous fashion in which he himself had been received as a prisoner in 1807; he remembered the excellent treatment shown to his son Franz in Dresden.

Whatever his private feelings, Blücher's public policy achieved success. While Prussian troops battled forward, Napoleon found his personal support crumbling inside Paris. He fled to Malmaison, leaving a last bitter message: 'I counted on a united effort, a united will, and the help of all those in power. . . . Circumstances appear to me to be changed. I am sacrificing myself to the hatred of France's enemies.' On 29th June, with Prussian guns thudding in the distance, he bade farewell to his mother and fled towards the Biscay coast.(22) 'I stand before Paris,' wrote Blücher to his wife during this Thursday evening. 'Wellington dined with me and we took counsel as to how to end the whole matter.'(23)

Paris defences had been hastily organized by Marshal Davout: 60,000 French troops lay in the city or in the immediate area, plus some 30,000 National Guardsmen of doubtful value. The combined Prussian and Anglo-Dutch armies totalled about 120,000 and Russian and Austrian armies were crossing into France. Davout sought an armistice on 30th June, but both

Blücher and Wellington rejected the suggestion, believing the armistice was only intended to allow the arrival of the Austrians – who might offer the French better terms. But Wellington's resolve began to weaken during the next two days, after bitter fighting around the capital failed to shake Davout's determination. For his part, Blücher prepared to storm the city, asking the British to provide a rocket battery. Then, at seven o'clock in the morning, 3rd July, French artillery ceased firing. A French officer rode under a white flag to the Prussians and asked for peace negotiations to begin. Troops on both sides waited by their weapons throughout this warm, cloudless Monday, the nineteenth day since the beginning of the 1815 campaign. Tense talks continued at St Cloud; also on the 3rd, Napoleon fell into British hands at Rochefort.

'I sit here and await the French generals and the five Deputies of the French Chamber about settling the capitulation,' wrote Blücher. 'Yesterday and today I have lost about 3,000 men. I hope to God they will be the last ones in this war.' He told Katharina he would end the letter when the conference finished at St Cloud. And next morning he added three triumphant words: 'Paris is mine!'(24)

*　　*　　*

By the convention signed at St Cloud the French army was to evacuate Paris within three days and move south of the Loire. Blücher insisted his army should march in triumph into the French capital; he declared it a matter of honour 'to enjoy the same distinction that the French had enjoyed in Berlin, in Vienna, and in Moscow'. Wellington feared the consequences. Discussions led to a compromise: only Zieten's corps would make a ceremonial entry, and the Prussian army as a whole would not be quartered in French homes. Blücher's severity towards the French soon led to further disagreement. 'The character of the whole nation has sunk so low that they do not deserve any respect,' he declared, and he insisted that all works of art stolen by the French should be returned to their rightful countries.

Blücher also demanded that the Pont de Jena should be destroyed, thus removing a shameful monument of Prussia's humiliation in 1806. French officials saw the Prussian engineers preparing the charges at the bridge and protested vigorously, to which the engineers replied that the structure had been built with Prussian money and therefore the French should mind their own business. Wellington condemned the plan to blow the bridge as 'a barbaric deed', to which Gneisenau replied that Wellington might feel differently if a 'Saratoga' bridge existed in Paris, commemorating the British surrender to American rebels in 1777. Wellington made no reply, and thereafter treated Gneisenau with increased coldness.(25) By 6th July preparations for demolishing the Pont de Jena were almost completed, but strong opposition came from Talleyrand, now back in Paris. Blücher wrote on the 7th: 'The bridge shall be blown up, and I should be pleased if Herr Talleyrand would previously sit himself upon it.'(26)

But also on the 7th, Blücher's period of power in Paris ended with the arrival of the allied monarchs, accompanied by Louis XVIII of France. Attempts were still made to blow the offending bridge on the 10th, but insufficient charges were laid and the explosion merely cracked the stonework. Blücher had to be satisfied with the structure being renamed the Pont des Invalides. The whole incident augured ill. Talleyrand and Joseph Fouché headed a provisional Government and the diplomats arrived to discuss peace terms, and once again Blücher bickered and bellowed over the apparent betrayal of all his army's efforts. The atmosphere in Paris during this summer of 1815 became polluted by mutual recriminations and barely concealed hostility between the Prussian army and the French. Colonel von der Marwitz wrote:

Now Louis *dix huit* – whom the French called mockingly Louis *tout de suite* and Louis *biscuit* because he followed directly, and because he was baked over, as it were – came waddling into Paris behind the English army and met there the three monarchs of Prussia, Austria and Russia. Things at once assumed the appearance as though the whole war had been waged solely for his sake.(27)

Blücher stayed outside the capital at St Cloud, merely taking temporary lodgings in the city. He continued to bombard the authorities for maximum demands to be made on the defeated enemy. He insisted his troops should be thoroughly re-equipped at the city's expense, and demanded a payment from the French of 100 million francs for his army. Quarrels over this sum lasted throughout July and August, until Blücher was informed that as the French had insufficient money to pay, it would have to come from Prussia. Blücher then declared the army would rather 'tighten our belts to the last notch' than extinguish 'the flickering life of the Fatherland'. At the same time the Field-Marshal raged against the politicians who might allow a lenient peace treaty, and once again Hardenberg became a target for his wrath. 'If you masters of the pen could only once come under fire,' he stormed, 'then you would know what it means to have to rectify your mistakes.'

At the start of October he poured out his feelings to the Prince Regent of England. His letter also turned down an invitation to re-visit London on account of the lateness of the season.

The diplomatic gentlemen want to prolong this thing, as they did in Vienna, so winter would be here before everything could be arranged. [He continued:] Your Majesty, it is regrettable that such unity is never to be found among Ministers as has existed so beneficially in these last wars among companions in arms. . . . Although I had sacrificed 26,000 brave Prussians no regard was paid to that at all, and everything that I had ordered for the general good was reversed because, according to the opinion of the book-worms, it had not been done according to the rules. Herr Talleyrand and Fouché more readily obtained a hearing . . .(28)

Throughout these confused, unpleasant quarrels one theme remained constant, and this in itself accounted for much of Blücher's belligerent behaviour. The Field-Marshal was tired, ageing, sick of it all; he wanted an end to war and all to do with it; he wanted to go home and live in peace. Blücher had been fighting the French, or seeking to fight them, for twenty-three years, and now a crushing anti-climax set in. As early as 3rd July, when he told his wife that talks had begun for the capitulation of Paris, he declared: 'I'm sick of murder,' and he said to Knesebeck: 'Now, friend, my day's work is done!' Wellington suffered a similar reaction. 'I hope to God,' he told Lady Shelley, 'that I've fought my last battle. . . . Both mind and feelings are exhausted. I am wretched even at the moment of victory.'(29)

Blücher's health remained fragile during this summer of 1815, and his eyes became inflamed once more. He again suffered delusions, although he seemed to control them better. '*Je sens un éléphant là*', he confided to Wellington, rubbing his stomach. This latest phantom pregnancy seemed especially ironical: he believed the elephant had been fathered on him by a French soldier.(30) Suddenly, Blücher became an old, peevish and rather lonely man. He sought pleasure where he could, and especially at the gaming table, yet his gambling seemed to be conducted with a resignation, a fixity, which precluded enjoyment. 'I have everything I want,' he told his wife, 'so why should I gamble.' Yet he did, almost as if nothing else remained. His dreary hours at the tables contrasted sharply with the evenings gone by when he gathered officers around him at an upturned drum, throwing dice with a cheerfulness unaffected by losses or gains. An English visitor to Paris left this sad, even pathetic, description of the aged Field-Marshal.

> And look at that old and weather-beaten man with grey eyebrows and moustache who throws from the breast-pocket of his frockcoat over and anon a handful of gold pieces upon the table. He evidently neither knows nor cares for the amount, for the banker himself is obliged to count over the stakes for him – that is Blücher, the never-failing attendant at the Salon. He has been an immense loser but plays on with the same stern perseverance with which he would pour his bold cavalry through a ravine torn by artillery. He stands by the still waning chance with a courage that never falters. . . .(31)

Blücher wrote to Katharina on 30th August:

> Yesterday for luncheon I had sea-fish and crab. I thought of you and drank your health. My health is still tolerable, but my discontent gets greater hour by hour. I am afraid I have sacrificed 25,000 men for nothing. I am very worried about Franz . . . God will help him. [And again on 4th October:] The peace is as good as settled. . . . It is not very edifying and will probably be of short duration. But it will mean nothing to me. I shall not fight any more, I've had my fill, and we get nothing for our pains.(32)

October dragged slowly by. Finally his permission to return home arrived, and on the last day of the month he said goodbye to his army: 'You are worthy of the name Prussians, Germans. Accept my gratitude, comrades, for the courage, for the endurance, for the bravery which you have shown. . . .'(33) Blücher left Paris with his right arm in a sling. His shoulder, barely recovered from the savage jar suffered at Ligny, had been dislocated; Blücher, in his last days in Paris, had briefly returned to his old madcap self. Wellington had organized a horse race, and Blücher had insisted upon participating, despite his age and despite entreaties from Wellington and his staff. His horse crashed into the rope which cordoned off the course, throwing Blücher violently to the ground. His chief regret from the injury lay in the hindrance it imposed during the journey home.

A further delay was encountered at Namur, where Blücher waited while the peace proposals were published. These were formulated in the Second Treaty of Paris on 20th November, and seemed harsh enough, but Blücher remained dissatisfied. The Treaty pushed back the frontiers of France from those of 1792, as agreed in the First Treaty of Paris in 1814, to those of 1790, resulting in a loss of strategically important territory on France's north-eastern frontier; France had to submit to allied occupation until 1818 and had to pay an indemnity of 700 million francs. Blücher continued his journey, spending his 73rd birthday at Coblenz. Early in the New Year, 1816, he returned at last to Breslau.

*   *   *

For the next three years Blücher spent his time in Berlin or near Breslau at Krieblowitz. He also took the waters at Carlsbad and visited Pyrmont. He wanted no more war. In answer to a toast at a dinner in Carlsbad in spring 1816, held to celebrate the Waterloo anniversary, he declared: 'The monarchs witnessed for themselves in two fateful years what horror and devastation war inevitably causes. Woe betide the sovereign, woe betide the nation, which begins an unjustified war out of pure ambition.'(34) Blücher gradually turned his back on the army and took to farming again. He had one major source of unhappiness: Franz suffered further mental deterioration. In the summer of 1816 the Mayor of Potsdam called to see Blücher with disturbing reports of his son's behaviour; on one occasion Franz had run through the streets of Potsdam, shooting wildly. Blücher tried to take the news calmly, but one of those present described how the tears rolled down his lined cheeks. Franz entered another asylum; he died in October 1829.

Despite his sadness over Franz, peace brought back Blücher's boisterous energy. He persisted with his gambling, and on one occasion had to ask the King for money to pay his debts. Frederick William sent a strict reply: 'The money given you was for your household and to enable you to maintain a suitable establishment, not for gambling purposes.'

'You have been gambling with my bones all these years,' retorted Blücher, 'so now I have a right to gamble with your money.'(35) He continued to hunt and rode as hard as ever. Nostitz stayed with him, and Gneisenau remained a close friend. Blücher also recovered his sense of humour; in 1819 the King visited him at Krieblowitz, bringing a large and distinguished entourage. A servant whispered to Blücher that there would be insufficient seats for these dignitaries.

'Well you blockhead,' exclaimed Blücher, 'tell them to fetch milking-stools.'

Throughout Prussia he was known as old *Vorwärts* or *Pater der Patria* – Father of the Fatherland, abbreviated by friends in letters to him as PP. One Breslau official attempted a similar familiarity in correspondence to him, addressing the Field-Marshal as 'dear PP Blücher'. The old warrior, who could never stand officials or being taken advantage of, immediately replied: 'PP stands for Pair of Pistols', and he challenged the unfortunate offender to a duel.

Blücher savoured his peaceful time at Krieblowitz.

When I came into the parlour I thought I saw paradise [he wrote to Katharina whilst she was visiting Berlin in June 1819]. Meadows, woods and wheat laughed at me. . . . I have engaged a gardener and already he has begun to put the place in order and to make some paths in the woods behind the *Tiergarten*. My beautiful stable will be quite finished on 1st July, and in front of the house the fence will be finished. . . .(36)

He wrote to Bonin:

If in previous years I have eaten up my money or gambled it away, now I build with it, and I dig and plant it. Breeding horses gives me great pleasure: during this year I've got 15 most beautiful foals and 46 mares have been covered. Also I have 152 cows and 1,600 sheep.(37)

During the summer of 1819 he planned a visit to Schwarzenberg, his old Austrian ally, and he wrote:

I am looking forward to 1st September, because then the hunting season will start again.(38) [He visited Carlsbad in mid-1819, but returned to Krieblowitz feeling ill. He felt strong enough to send instructions to his estate manager on 15th August.] Bring three good greyhounds. I shall stay here to the 6th or 8th September, then shall go to Zauche and I shall take my wife with me. There are enough partridges here, also hares. My winter corn has been put in already with God's blessing. . . .(39)

But by the opening of the hunting season on 1st September 1819, the seventy-six-year-old Field-Marshal lay in bed again. During the first days of sickness he chatted with Nostitz and made plans for his farms. He was worried because the weather had broken and the summer crop lay unharvested. Then came a diversion. Silesian troops were exercising nearby, engaged in mock battle. His servants thought the noise might be too much for him.

'Why on earth should it be?' he exclaimed. 'I have heard plenty cannon-fire in my lifetime – surely I can stand some more now.' The windows stayed open, and he listened once more to the cannon, the musket volleys, the bugles and drums. But day by day he grew weaker and quieter.

'They have learnt a great deal from me,' he said to Nostitz. 'Now they must learn from me also how to die peacefully.' Nostitz noticed how he stared for hours at a portrait of his son Franz, placed near his bed. On 6th September the King visited him. The manoeuvres continued outside his window and the smoke of the guns drifted across the garden; bugles blew the calls for Advance and Charge, and some say Blücher asked them to sound one call rare to his ears, but at last the most fitting – Retreat. During the evening of 12th September he pressed Katharina's hand, and he died soon after ten o'clock.

'What is it that you praise?' asked 'Field-Marshal Forwards' amidst the frenzied hero-worship after the Battle of Waterloo. He answered himself, and summed up his career: 'It was my resolution, Gneisenau's wisdom, and the compassion of Almighty God.'(40)

SOURCES

Chapter One: *Salad Days*

1. Seeley, III, 22
2. Förster, I, 219
3. Fisher, 833, 834
4. Marston, 4
5. ib., 8
6. Paret, 27
7. ib., 9
8. ib., 27
9. Stanhope, 119
10. Unger, I, 57
11. Demeter, 120–123
12. Unger, I, 60–62
13. ib., 64
14. Parkinson, 324
15. Unger, I, 67
16. Marston, 9
17. Blücher, 11

Chapter Two: *Return to Revolution*

1. Unger, I, 110
2. Gooch, 399
3. Anon, *Cursory View*, 20
4. Unger, I, 113
5. Förster, I, 220
6. Unger, I, 115
7. ib., 117
8. Paget, 47
9. Seeley, II, 129
10. Unger, I, 127
11. Unger, I, 137
12. Seeley, I, 108
13. Unger, I, 143
14. ib., 144
15. ib., 146
16. ib., 149
17. ib., 150
18. ib., 151
19. ib.
20. ib.
21. Henderson, 7
22. Unger, I, 161, 165
23. ib., 167

Chapter Three: *Approaching Catastrophe*

1. Unger, I, 173
2. ib., 176
3. ib., 178
4. ib., 181
5. ib., 193
6. ib., 198
7. ib., 201
8. ib., 212–216
9. ib., 217
10. Paget, 47, 48
11. Stanhope, 182
12. Unger, I, 221
13. Seeley, I, 114
14. Anon, *Cursory View*, 18
15. Unger, I, 237
16. Seeley, I, 231
17. ib., 277
18. Unger, I, 247
19. ib., 251
20. ib., 258
21. ib., 259
22. ib., 261

Chapter Four: *Auerstedt Agony*

1. Unger, I, 259
2. Henderson, 11
3. Unger, I, 263
4. ib., 264

5. Seeley, I, 113
6. ib., 368
7. Maude, *Jena*, 62
8. Lettow-Vorbeck, 163
9. Anon, *Cursory View*, 63
10. Unger, I, 274
11. ib., 275
12. Steffens, 47, 51
13. Henderson, 13
14. Parkinson, 34
15. Unger, I, 291
16. ib., 292
17. Henderson, 16
18. Henderson, 14
19. Unger, I, 300
20. Marston, 46, 47; Unger, I, 308

21. Brett-James, *Leipzig*, 45
22. Linnebach, I, 296
23. Seeley, I, 369
24. ib., 263
25. Anon, *Cursory View*, 119
26. Seeley, I, 305
27. Anon, *Cursory View*, 123
28. Unger, I, 309–314
29. ib., 319
30. ib.
31. Cronin, 275
32. Unger, I, 321
33. ib., 329
34. ib., 330
35. ib., 231
36. ib., 332

Chapter Five: *Despair*

1. Unger, I, 333
2. Henderson, 20
3. Parkinson, 84
4. Schulze, 22, 23
5. Henderson, 47, 48; Unger, I, 338
6. Roques, 41
7. Seeley, II, 34, 47
8. ib., 50–53
9. ib., 139
10. Colomb, 10
11. Unger, I, 342, 343
12. ib., 344
13. ib.
14. Henderson, 56, 57
15. Colomb, 11–13
16. Seeley, II, 131
17. Henderson, 57
18. Unger, I, 353
19. Henderson, 63
20. Cronin, 309
21. Pertz, II, 191

22. Unger, I, 362
23. ib., 363
24. Seeley, II, 390
25. Droysen, 323
26. Unger, I, 364
27. Parkinson, 130, 131
28. Boyen, II, 104
29. Henderson, 72
30. ib., 76
31. Vossler, intro.
32. Steffens, 76
33. Arndt, 118
34. Steffens, 73
35. Parkinson, 203–207
36. Seeley, III, 30; Paret, 194
37. Parkinson, 208
38. Seeley, III, 48–49
39. Unger, II, 4
40. Seeley, III, 47
41. Unger, II, 5
42. Seeley, III, 78
43. Henderson, 85–86

Chapter Six: *For Freedom and Fatherland*

1. Unger, II, 6–7
2. Langeron, 209
3. Förster, I, 220
4. Clausewitz, *Scharnhorst*, 197
5. Henderson, 116; Ense, 270
6. Henderson, 79
7. Schönfeldt, 191–192
8. Steffens, 79–80
9. Schubert, 315, 316
10. Brett-James, *Leipzig*, 99
11. Colomb, 16
12. Henderson, 93
13. Colomb, 20
14. ib., 21
15. ib., 23
16. Henderson, 96
17. Caulaincourt, II, 404
18. Brett-James, *Leipzig*, 23
19. Unger, II, 25
20. Steffens, 77
21. ib., 96, 97

22. Henderson, 102
23. Parkinson, 219–222
24. Henderson, 103
25. Steffens, 97, 98
26. Unger, II, 30
27. Steffens, 99
28. Unger, II, 30
29. Parkinson, 221
30. Linnebach, I, 480
31. Steffens, 73, 74
32. Seeley, II, 305
33. Henderson, 105
34. Colomb, 21
35. Seeley, III, 145
36. Steffens, 102
37. ib., 104–105
38. Henderson, 110
39. Parkinson, 226–227
40. Unger, II, 51, 52
41. Seeley, III, 147
42. Unger, II, 54

Chapter Seven: *Carnage at the Katzbach*

1. Brett-James, *Leipzig*, 121–122
2. Colomb, 31
3. Unger, II, 65
4. Steffens, 114
5. Henderson, 122
6. Colomb, 36
7. Unger, II, 72
8. ib., 73
9. ib., 75; Pertz, iv, 335
10. Blücher, 20–21
11. Marston, 164–165
12. Henderson, 130
13. Colomb, 39–40
14. Unger, II, 80
15. ib., 81
16. Parkinson, 232
17. Henderson, 132–133
18. Blücher, 21

19. Colomb, 44–45
20. Brett-James, *Leipzig*, 21–22
21. ib., 30, 31
22. Klein, 281
23. Unger, II, 95
24. Unger, II, 96; Brett-James, *Leipzig*, 48
25. Colomb, 48
26. Steffens, 114
27. Parkinson, 238
28. Colomb, 49–50
29. Henderson, 145
30. Clausewitz, *On War*, Bk. vi, ch. v
31. Brett-James, *Leipzig*, 47–48
32. Henderson, 148
33. ib., 149
34. Steffens, 166

35. Blücher, 23
36. Henderson, 160
37. ib., 161–163
38. Boyen, II, 377–378

39. Brett-James, *Leipzig*, 102–103
40. ib., 107
41. ib., 139

Chapter Eight: *The Battle of Nations*

1. Gerlach, 118–119
2. Brett-James, *Leipzig*, 140–141
3. Henderson, 171
4. Brett-James, *Leipzig*, 146, 147
5. Steffens, 118, 119
6. Pflugk-Harttung, *1813–1815*, 261
7. Unger, II, 114
8. Steffens, 120
9. Unger, II, 114
10. Nostitz, V, 66–69
11. Brett-James, *Leipzig*, 159
12. Steffens, 121–122
13. Marston, 229–231 n
14. Steffens, 121, 122
15. Brett-James, *Leipzig*, 190
16. Steffens, 123
17. Brett-James, *Leipzig*, 179

18. Steffens, 123, 124
19. Brett-James, *Leipzig*, 191
20. ib., 215–217; Nostitz, V, 70
21. Brett-James, *Leipzig*, 227
22. Seeley, III, 197
23. Colomb, 59
24. Steffens, 125
25. ib., 126
26. Henderson, 191
27. ib., 192
28. Colomb, 61
29. Förster, II, 489–490
30. ib., 388–389
31. Steffens, 128
32. Unger, II, 126
33. Colomb, 63
34. Brett-James, *Leipzig*, 292

Chapter Nine: *Invasion*

1. Unger, II, 128–129
2. ib., 129
3. ib., 128
4. Seeley, III, 198–199
5. Colomb, 70
6. ib., 72, 82
7. ib., 71
8. Unger, II, 139
9. Cronin, 351
10. Brett-James, *Leipzig*, 295
11. Pertz, I, 364
12. Clausewitz, *On War*, Bk. v, ch. xvii
13. Parkinson, 245
14. Müffling, 33
15. Colomb, 74, 75
16. Brett-James, *Leipzig*, 296

17. Henderson, 201
18. ib., 202
19. Capelle, 57
20. Henderson, 203
21. Marston, 310
22. Cronin, 353
23. Colomb, 87
24. Unger, II, 153, 154
25. ib., 154
26. Henderson, 204
27. ib.
28. Colomb, 90
29. Henderson, 205
30. ib., 206
31. Cronin, 354
32. Henderson, 207
33. Blücher, 30

34. Unger, II, 363
35. ib., 170–175; Henderson, 214; Blücher, 30
36. Blücher, 30–31
37. Henderson, 216
38. Unger, II, 171
39. Seeley, III, 223
40. Steffens, 135
41. Cronin, 355–356
42. Pertz, IV, 76
43. Colomb, 37
44. Steffens, 140
45. Unger, II, 188–189
46. Henderson, 224
47. ib., 224, 225
48. ib., 231
49. ib., 232
50. Unger, II, 203
51. ib., 202; Brett-James, *Leipzig*, 48

52. Henderson, 236–237
53. Unger, II, 208
54. Colomb, 118
55. Steffens, 152–153; Blücher, 31
56. Henderson, 238
57. Unger, II, 214
58. Blücher, 31
59. Henderson, 242
60. ib.; Unger, II, 225
61. Unger, II, 226
62. Henderson, 245
63. Unger, II, 227
64. Henderson, 242
65. ib.; Pertz, IV, 111
66. Cronin, 358
67. Brett-James, *Leipzig*, 302
68. Henderson, 248
69. Cronin, 316, 362

Chapter Ten: *Interlude*

1. Henderson, 255
2. ib., 254
3. Cronin, 369–370
4. Henderson, 256–257
5. Colomb, 122
6. ib., 124
7. ib., 125
8. Steffens, 165–166
9. Colomb, 125–126
10. ib., 127
11. Marston, 16–17
12. Henderson, 263
13. Colomb, 128–129
14. ib., 171
15. ib.
16. Blücher, 35
17. ib., 36
18. Henderson, 262

19. Colomb, 132
20. Unger, II, 247
21. Henderson, 263
22. Unger, II, 249
23. Henderson, 264–265
24. ib., 268
25. Pertz, IV, 547
26. ib., 321
27. Cronin, 394–395
28. Blücher, 37
29. Pertz, IV, 483
30. Henderson, 273
31. Pertz, IV, 497
32. ib., 511
33. Blücher, 38–39
34. Henderson, 278–279; Unger, II, 216–262
35. Henderson, 273–274

Chapter Eleven: *Ligny*

1. Brett-James, *Hundred Days,* 31–32
2. Longford, 402
3. Müffling, 212–214
4. Colomb, 143
5. Henderson, 280
6. Unger, II, 271
7. ib.
8. Unger, II, 272
9. Henderson, 281–282
10. Pertz, IV, 521
11. Henderson, 286–287
12. Blücher, 39
13. Henderson, 287, 288
14. Müffling, 230
15. Longford, 421
16. Maxwell, II, 19–20
17. Brett-James, *Hundred Days,* 69–70
18. ib., 75
19. Gardner, 97–98
20. ib., 112
21. ib., 107
22. Parkinson, 260
23. Pertz, IV, 522
24. Henderson, 290
25. Brett-James, *Hundred Days,* 79–80
26. Stanhope, 110
27. ib., 111
28. Longford, 435–436
29. Brett-James, *Hundred Days,* 86
30. ib., 85
31. Colomb, 146–147
32. Houssaye, 163
33. Unger, II, 296

Chapter Twelve: *Waterloo – The Last Battle*

1. Brett-James, *Hundred Days,* 148
2. Unger, II, 298
3. Brett-James, *Hundred Days,* 130
4. ib., 139
5. ib., 158–159
6. Unger, II, 302
7. Henderson, 308–309
8. Longford, 484–485
9. Blücher, 39
10. Creevey, 142
11. Gronow, I, 201
12. Parkinson, 286
13. Müffling, 251
14. Colomb, 150–151
15. Unger, II, 307
16. ib., 308
17. Colomb, 153
18. Unger, II, 313
19. Henderson, 314
20. ib., 316
21. Unger, II, 315
22. Cronin, 404–405
23. Henderson, 316
24. Blücher, 44
25. Pertz, IV, 456
26. Henderson, 318
27. ib., 318–319
28. ib., 320–321
29. ib., 317; Blücher, 215
30. Stanhope, 119
31. Blücher, 54
32. ib., 46–47
33. Unger, II, 342
34. Colomb, 178
35. Blücher, 54
36. ib., 52
37. Schulze, 75
38. ib., 74
39. ib., 77
40. Colomb, 175

BIBLIOGRAPHY

Only two biographies of Blücher have previously been published in English. The first, *The Life and Campaigns of Field-Marshal Prince Blücher* (London 1815), must have been written immediately after Waterloo, and the biography is therefore obviously incomplete. The book contains numerous inaccuracies, but nevertheless has the value of spontaneity, and the author interviewed eye-witnesses. The second English work on Blücher, Ernest F. Henderson's *Blücher and the Uprising against Napoleon* (New York 1911), is dated and, as the title suggests, also incomplete. Amongst the many German biographies, the most comprehensive is Major-General W. von Unger's *Blücher*, 2 vols. (Berlin 1907), upon which I have relied extensively. Blücher's letters have been reprinted in a number of German books; I have chiefly used Lieutenant-General E. von Colomb's *Blücher in Briefen aus den Feldzügen 1813–1815* (Stuttgart 1876).

OTHER GERMAN BIOGRAPHIES

Bieske, Carl Ludwig, *Der Feldmarschall Fürst Gebhard Leberecht Blücher von Wahlstatt* (Berlin 1862)
Blasendorf, Karl, *Gebhard Leberecht von Blücher* (Berlin 1887)
Bleck, Otto, *Marschall Blücher* (Berlin 1939)
Blücher, G. L. von, *Memoirs* (London 1932). The author was the great-great-grandson of the Field-Marshal
Burckhardt, Wilhelm, *Gebhard Leberecht v. Blücher* (Stuttgart 1835)
Capelle, Wilhelm von, *Blücher – Briefe* (Leipzig 1920)
Ense, Varnhagen, *Blücher* (Berlin 1933)
Görlitz, Walter, *Fürst Blücher von Wahlstatt* (Rostock 1940)
Luntowski, *Fürst Blücher* (Berlin 1912)
Miethke, Helmuth, *Marschall Vorwärts* (Berlin 1956)
Scherr, J., *Blücher* (Leipzig 1887)
Schulze, Frederick, *Ausgewahlte Briefe des Feldmarschalls Leberecht von Blücher* (Leipzig 1912)
Wigger, Frederick, *Feldmarschall Fürst Blücher von Wahlstatt* (Schwerin 1878)

OTHER BIOGRAPHIES AND AUTOBIOGRAPHIES

Anglesey, Marquess of, *One-Leg: The Life and Letters of Henry William Paget, 1768–1854* (London 1961)
Arndt, Ernst, *Erinnerungen aus dem äusseren Leben* (Leipzig 1840)
Boyen, Field-Marshal Hermann von, *Denkwürdigkenten und Erinnerungen, 1771–1813*, 2 vols. (Stuttgart 1899)
Caulaincourt, Armand de, *Mémoires*, 3 vols. (Paris 1933)
Conrady, E. von, *Leben und Wirken des Generals Carl von Grolman* (Berlin 1894–96)
Cronin, Vincent, *Napoleon* (London 1971)
Droysen, J. G., *Das Leben des Feldmarschalls Grafen Yorck*, 3 vols. (Berlin 1851–52)
Gronow, Captain, *Reminiscences and Recollections* (London 1900)
Langeron, L. A.-A. Comte de, *Mémoires* (Paris 1902)
Lehmann, Max, *Scharnhorst* (Berlin 1886–87)
Linnebach, Karl, *Von Scharnhorst's Briefe* (Munich-Leipzig 1914)
Longford, Elizabeth, *Wellington: the Years of the Sword* (London 1969)

Maxwell, Sir Herbert, *The Life of Wellington* 2 vols. (London 1899)
Müffling, F. C., *Aus Meinem Leben* (Berlin 1851)
Nostitz, Captain August von, *Tagebuch des Generals der Kavellerie Grafen von Nostitz* (Berlin 1884–85)
Paret, Peter, *Yorck and the Era of Prussian Reform 1807–1815* (Princeton 1966)
Parkinson, Roger, *Clausewitz* (London 1970)
Pertz, G. H., *Das Leben des Feldmarschalls Grafen Neithardt v. Gneisenau* (Berlin 1864–65). Continuation of work by Hans Delbrück
Roques, P., *Le Général de Clausewitz* (Paris 1912)
Schönfeldt, Sybil Gräfin, *Kulturgeschichte des Herrn* (Hamburg 1965)
Schwartz, Karl, *Leben des Generals Carl von Clausewitz* 2 vols. (Berlin 1878)
Seeley, J. R., *Life and Times of Stein* 3 vols. (Cambridge 1878)
Stanhope, Philip Henry, *Notes of Conversations with the Duke of Wellington, 1831–1851* (London 1888)
Steffens, Henry, *Adventures on the Road to Paris, 1813–1814* (London 1861)
Stein, Frieherr von, *Briefwechsel, Denschriften und Aufzeichnungen* 7 vols. (Berlin 1931)
Vossler, H., *With Napoleon in Russia, 1812* (London 1969)

OTHER WORKS

Anon., *A Cursory View of Prussia from the Death of Frederick II to the Peace of Tilsit* (London 1809)
Brett-James, Antony, *Europe against Napoleon: The Leipzig Campaign 1813* (London 1970)
Brett-James, Antony, *The Hundred Days* (London 1964)
Clausewitz, Carl von, *On War* (London 1918). British translation by Colonel Graham
Clausewitz, Carl von, *Über das Leben und den Charackter von Scharnhorst* (Berlin 1832)
Craig, G. A., *Problems of Coalition Warfare: The Military Alliance against Napoleon, 1813–1814* (U.S.A.F. Academy 1965)
Demeter, Karl, *The German Officer Corps in Society and State, 1650–1945* (London 1965)
Fisher, H. A. L., *A History of Europe*, vol. III (London, Fontana 1968)
Förster, Frederick, *Geschichte der Befreiungskriege 1813, 1814, 1815,* 3 vols. (Berlin 1890)
Gardner, D., *Quatre Bras, Ligny and Waterloo* (London 1882)
Gerlach, *Aus den Jahren preussischer Not und Erneurung* (Berlin 1966)
Gooch, G. P., *Germany and the French Revolution* (London 1920)
Görlitz, W., *History of the German General Staff* (New York 1953)
Houssaye, Henry, *1815* (London 1900)
Howarth, David, *A Near Run Thing* (London 1968)
Hyde, Kelly W., *The Battle of Wavre and Grouchy's Retreat* (London 1905)
Klein, *Die Befreiung 1813, 1814, 1815* (Munich 1913)
Lettow-Vorbeck, O. von, *Der Krieg von 1806–1807* (Berlin 1899)
Maude, F. N., *The Jena Campaign, 1806* (London 1909)
Maude, F. N., *The Leipzig Campaign, 1813* (London 1908)
Pfister, Albert, *Aus dem Lager der Verbündeten, 1814, 1815* (Stuttgart and Leipzig 1897)
Pflugk, Harttung J. von, *1813–1815* (Berlin 1913)
Schubert, Frederick von, *Unter dem Doppeladler* (Stuttgart 1962)
Tasle, E., *Napoleon's Invasion of Russia, 1812* (London 1922)

INDEX